DEMOCRACY AGAINST CAPITALISM

DEMOCRACY AGAINST CAPITALISM

Renewing Historical Materialism

ELLEN MEIKSINS WOOD

VERSO

London • New York

This edition first published by Verso 2016
First published by Cambridge University Press 1995
© Ellen Meiksins Wood 1995, 1996, 1999, 2000, 2016

5 7 9 10 8 6 4

Verso
UK: 6 Meard Street, London W1F 0EG
US: 20 Jay Street, Suite 1010, Brooklyn, NY 11201
versobooks.com

Verso is the imprint of New Left Books

ISBN-13: 978-1-78478-244-3 (PB)

British Library Cataloguing in Publication Data
A catalogue record for this book is available from the British Library

Library of Congress Cataloging-in-Publication Data
A catalog record for this book is available from the Library of Congress

Printed and bound by CPI Group (UK) Ltd, Croydon, CR0 4YY

For Peter, Joyce and Robin

Contents

Acknowledgements

This volume is, and is not, a collection of essays. It is a collection in the sense that the volume is in large part based on articles already published or in press, but I hope it is more than 'merely' a collection. This is so both because I have not simply included these essays just as they were but have revised and integrated them, or in some cases only parts of them, and also because I regard them as from the start a coherent body of work. The unifying themes and the ways in which one essay builds upon another will, I think, be more or less self-evident, though in the Introduction there are some general reflections on the dominant themes and their historical context, as well as some comments on what I have done to the essays for the purposes of this volume. Here, I simply wish to thank all the original publishers and the many people who have, in one way or another and at one time or another, helped me with one or more of the chapters.

Chapter 1 is a modified version of 'The Separation of the Economic and the Political in Capitalism', originally published in *New Left Review* 127 (1981); chapter 2 is an edited version of 'Falling Through the Cracks: E.P. Thompson and the Debate on Base and Superstructure' from Harvey J. Kaye and Keith McLelland eds., *E.P. Thompson: Critical Perspectives* (Oxford: Polity Press, 1990); chapter 3 is a revision, with some new material, of 'The Politics of Theory and the Concept of Class: E.P. Thompson and His Critics', first published in *Studies in Political Economy* 9 (1982). Chapter 4 contains new material, together with several combined and integrated essays, or parts of them, from the *New Left Review*: 'Marxism and the Course of History', *NLR* 147 (1984); some small sections from 'Rational Choice Marxism: Is the Game Worth the Candle?', *NLR* 177 (1989), and 'Explaining Everything or Nothing?', *NLR* (1990). Chapter 5 is a new essay, intended for a volume on Marxist historiography, edited by John Saville and Marcel van der Linden, the fate of which is, as I write, still unknown. Chapter 6 has not yet been published but is a more or less unchanged essay written for volume I (*I Greci e Noi*) of a multi-volume work on the ancient Greeks, to be published in Italian by Einaudi. I am very grateful to the publishers for allowing me to include the essay in this volume before the publication of *I Greci*, contrary to their usual contractual conditions, and am very happy to say that it appears here with the kind permission of Giulio Einaudi editore s.p.a. Chapter 7 is, again, a combination and integration of several articles, or parts of them, together with new material: 'A Tale of Two Democracies', published in *History Today*, June 1994, and two articles: 'Democracy: An Idea of Ambiguous Ancestry', in J. Peter Euben, Josiah Ober and John Wallach eds., *Educating Democracy* (Cornell University Press, 1994); and 'Freedom and Democracy, Ancient and Modern', based on a talk given in Washington DC in April 1993, at a conference on Democracy Ancient and Modern, sponsored by the National Endowment for the Humanities, the (edited and enlarged) proceedings of which should be published soon, under the editorship of Josiah Ober and Charles Hedrick. Chapter 8 is a revised and, I hope, improved, version, again with some new material, of 'The Uses and Abuses of "Civil Society"', *Socialist Register* 1990; and chapter 9 is based, with some modifications, on my Deutscher Memorial Lecture, originally published as 'Captialism and Human Emancipation' in *New Left Review* 167 (1988).

Needless to say, these essays owe much to many people. Some have read several essays, some only one, though the extent of my debt to them does not always correspond simply to the number of essays on which they have commented. It hardly needs saying how much I owe to Neal Wood's help and support. I am grateful to George Comninel, my former student, now friend and colleague, and to Karen Orren, whose friendship extends back to our early (and long-distant) teens, my brother Peter Meiksins and my father Gregory Meiksins, not only for comments but for many years of discussion, argument and encouragement, not to mention their own exciting work. Frances Abele, David McNally and Colin Mooers, whose critical intelligence as students was an inspiration when I first started writing these essays, have continued to be a great help, now as friends, both in discussion and in their own writings. Other friends who have helped with their critical insights on one or another of the essays are John Saville, Harvey Kaye, Norman Geras and Patrick Camiller. Perry Anderson and Robert Brenner each read three or four of the original essays on which this volume is based, and for several years during which I was thinking and writing on the relevant themes were invaluable resources and interlocutors. Ralph Miliband, whose death as this volume was being copy-edited was a very great loss not only to those who knew him but to the whole of the socialist left, commented on two or three of these essays; but my debt to him goes beyond any specific contribution to my work, since, like many others, I owe a great deal to the example of his firm and lucid socialist commitment.

I also owe thanks to various other people who made useful comments on one or more of the essays: Chris Bertram, Alan Carling, Paul Cartledge, Diane Elson, Peter Euben, Leo Panitch, Bryan Palmer, Nicholas Rogers, and an anonymous reader for Cambridge University Press. My thanks, finally, to John Haslam at CUP for his friendly and efficient guidance through the publication process, and to the copy-editor, Anne Rix, especially for her patience with my last-minute changes.

Introduction

There is something odd about the assumption that the collapse of Communism represents a terminal crisis for Marxism. One might think, among other things, that in a period of capitalist triumphalism there is more scope than ever for the pursuit of Marxism's principal project, the critique of capitalism.

Yet the critique of capitalism is out of fashion. Capitalist triumphalism on the right is mirrored on the left by a sharp contraction of socialist aspirations. Left intellectuals, if not embracing capitalism as the best of all possible worlds, hope for little more than a space in its interstices and look forward to only the most local and particular resistances. At the very moment when a critical understanding of the capitalist system is most urgently needed, large sections of the intellectual left, instead of developing, enriching and refining the required conceptual instruments, show every sign of discarding them altogether. 'Post-Marxism' has given way to the cult of postmodernism, with its principles of contingency, fragmentation and heterogeneity, its hostility to any notion of totality, system, structure, process and 'grand narratives'. But if this hostility extends to the very idea of capitalism as a social system, this does not prevent these intellectual currents from treating 'the market' as if it were a universal and inevitable law of nature while paradoxically closing off critical access to this totalizing power by denying its systemic unity and insisting on the impossibility of 'totalizing' knowledges. Post-modern fragmentation and contingency here join a strange alliance with the ultimate 'grand narrative' the 'end of History'.

Intellectuals of the left, then, have been trying to define new ways, other than contestation, of relating to capitalism. The typical mode, at best, is to seek out the interstices of capitalism, to make space within it for alternative 'discourses', activities and identities. Much is made of the *fragmentary* character of advanced capitalism –

whether that fragmentation is characterized by the culture of post-modernism or by the political economy of post-Fordism; and this is supposed to multiply the spaces in which a culture of the left can operate. But underlying all of these seems to be a conviction that capitalism is here to stay, at least in any foreseeable historical perspective.

The reformulation of the left's relation to capitalism as a making of space within it, rather than a direct challenge to and contestation of it, helps, among other things, to explain the major shifts from traditional discourses of the left, such as political economy and history, to the more currently fashionable ones: the study of discourses, texts, and what might be called the culture of 'identity'. If Marxist political economy and history are intended to challenge capitalism as a totality head-on from the vantage point of its anti-thesis, socialism, 'cultural studies' (conceived in the 'post-modern' way) and other favoured post-left enterprises are defined by the notion that the terrain of politics is within and between the fragments of capitalism, especially in the academy, where discourses and identities can be deconstructed and proliferated without material constraints.

In a fragmented world composed of 'de-centred subjects', where totalizing knowledges are impossible and undesirable, what other kind of politics is there than a sort of de-centred and intellectualized radicalization of liberal pluralism? What better escape, in theory, from a confrontation with capitalism, the most totalizing system the world has ever known, than a rejection of totalizing knowledge? What greater obstacle, in practice, to anything more than the most local and particularistic resistances to the global, totalizing power of capitalism than the de-centred and fragmented subject? What better excuse for submitting to the *force majeure* of capitalism than the conviction that its power, while pervasive, has no systemic origin, no unified logic, no identifiable social roots?

In opposition to this dominant trend, I propose to start from the premise that the critique of capitalism is urgently needed, that historical materialism still provides the best foundation on which to construct it, and that the *critical* element in Marxism lies above all in its insistence on the historical specificity of capitalism – with the emphasis on both the specificity of its systemic logic and on its historicity. In other words, historical materialism approaches capitalism in a way exactly antithetical to the current fashions: the systemic unity of capitalism instead of just post-modern fragments, but also historicity – and hence the possibility of supersession – instead of capitalist inevitability and the end of History.

It is fair enough to say that a body of work produced to deal with capitalism in the nineteenth century cannot be adequate to the conditions of the late twentieth. But it is a great deal less self-evident that anything else has emerged in the interim which provides a better foundation – or even one remotely as good – for a critical analysis of capitalism. The very least that can be said about Marxism is that it has one inestimable advantage over all other systems of economic and social theory that have claimed to super-sede it, namely that it subjects to critical scrutiny not only capitalism itself but also the analytic categories associated with it. Other theories have remained enclosed within, and limited by, conceptual categories derived from the specific historical experience of capital-ism, together with capitalist assumptions about human nature, rationality, systemic 'laws of motion', historical processes.

Classical political economy, however much it may have illumi-nated the workings of capitalism, could never, in Marx's view, penetrate beneath the surface, beneath (at best) the 'real appear-ances' of capitalism, because its own conceptual framework took for granted the logic of the capitalist system. Even at its best, it was permeated by uncritical assumptions specific to capitalism. This is the sense in which it was 'ideological' even when it was not a 'crude apology'. Hence the need for a critique of capitalism through the medium of a 'critique of political economy' which acknowledged the historical and systemic specificity of capitalism and the need to explain what political economy took as given.

An effective critique of capitalism at the end of the twentieth century would have to be conducted along the same lines – and this time, it would have to take into account not only the massive changes that the capitalist economy has undergone but also the new theoretical systems that have evolved to comprehend them. Neo-classical economics, for example, is more rather than less 'ideo-logical' than was classical political economy, more rather than less circumscribed by a conceptual framework that takes the logic of capitalism for granted. But what complicates the matter even more is that varieties of Marxism have developed, and even become dominant within the Marxist tradition, that in their own ways also universalize the logic of capitalism – typically by adhering to some

Introduction

kind of technological determinism (which universalisizes the specific drive of capitalism to improve the forces of production) and/or taking over the procedures of conventional economics. The critique of political economy has been set aside, together with the insights of historical materialism – especially its first premise that every mode of production has a specific systemic logic of its own – by treating capitalist 'laws of motion' as if they were the universal laws of history.

So the critique of capitalism requires not only adaptations to every transformation of the system but a constantly renewed critique of the analytic instruments designed to understand it. There can never have been a time since Marx's day when such a task needed doing more urgently, as more and more branches of knowledge, both in cultural studies and in the social sciences, are absorbed into the self-validating assumptions of capitalism or at least into a defeatist conviction that nothing else is possible.

II

Almost from the beginning, there have been two major theories of history in Marxism. Alongside the critical historical materialism which has its roots in the critique of political economy and has reached its peak in the best of Marxist historiography, there has always existed a contrary tendency to draw out of Marxist theory those aspects that are most compatible with capitalist ideology and to suppress what is most innovative and critical. In particular, there have always been Marxists (not, of course, without encouragement from Marx himself and especially from Engels' 'dialectics of nature') who prefer to forget the critique of political economy and everything it entails in favour of a technological determinism and a mechanical, unilinear succession of modes of production, in which less productive modes are inexorably followed by more productive ones according to some universal law of nature. This version of Marxism has little to distinguish it from conventional theories of social evolution and progress, or the 'stagist' view of history as a succession of 'modes of subsistence' associated with classical political economy.

In this classical conception of progress, the historical evolution of 'modes of subsistence' had culminated in the current, highest stage of 'commercial society'; but this did not mean that commercial society was, like earlier stages, merely another historical phenomenon, specific and transitory like its predecessors. It had a universal, transhistorical status not only in the sense that it represented the final destination of progress but also in the more fundamental sense that the movement of history itself had from the beginning been governed by what amounted to the natural laws of commercial society, the laws of competition, the division of labour and increasing productivity rooted in the natural inclination of human beings to 'truck, barter and exchange'.

There is no doubt that Marx went a long way toward accepting the view of classical political economy and conventional conceptions of progress that history had been on the side of 'commercial society'. But the kernel of historical materialism was an insistence on the historicity and specificity of capitalism, and a denial that its laws were the universal laws of history. The critique of political economy was intended to discover why and how capitalism's specific laws of motion operated as laws at all – for example, to find the key to technological determination and the laws of the market as specific imperatives of capitalism instead of taking them for granted as inherent in human nature or in the laws of universal history. This focus on the specificity of capitalism, as a moment with historical origins as well as an end, with a systemic logic specific to it, encouraged a truly historical sense lacking in classical political economy and conventional ideas of progress, and this had potentially fruitful implications for the historical study of other modes of production too.

The other, uncritical Marxism effectively repudiated everything Marx had to say against the metaphysical and ahistorical materialism of his predecessors, his insistence on the specificity of capitalism with its drive to improve the forces of production, and his attacks on classical political economy for its tendency to treat the laws of motion of capitalism not as the historical product of specific social relations but as transhistorical natural laws. This other Marxism had several notable features: first, a conception of the economic 'base' in non-social, technicist terms, incompatible with anything but the most mechanical application of the 'base/superstructure' metaphor; second, a conception of history as a mechanical, pre-ordained and unilinear succession of modes of production, which had a great deal in common with classical political economy and its 'stages' of civilization; and third, an ahistorical conception of historical transitions – in particular, the transition from feudalism to capitalism – which assumes precisely what needs to be explained, by reading capitalist principles and laws of motion back into all history. According to this view, for example, capitalism existed within the interstices of feudalism, indeed must always have existed; and somehow it became dominant as it broke through the integument of feudalism, according to some transhistorical necessity, in fulfilment of its natural destiny.

This ahistorical version certainly appears in Marx's own work, particularly in those occasional and polemical texts written in a kind of aphoristic short hand. But alongside it, and much more distinctively Marxist, is a historical materialism that allows no pre-ordained and unilinear sequence, in which the origin of capitalism – or any other mode of production – is something that needs to be explained, not presupposed, and which looks for explanations not in some transhistorical natural law but in historically specific social relations, contradictions and struggles.

Marxism as an extension of capitalist ideology has then always existed alongside historical materialism as a critical theory; but it was only with the advent of Stalinist orthodoxies that the critical version was threatened with eclipse. For reasons specific to the circumstances of the Soviet Union and the imperatives of rapid economic development, the development of productive forces on the model of industrial capitalism, and in response to the pressures of the international capitalist economy (not to mention geo-political and military pressures), technological determinism took precedence over historical materialism, and *history* gave way to universal laws. At the same time, this determinist view tended to lapse into contradictory moments of extreme voluntarism, as the drive to leap over stages of development produced an inclination toward detachment from material constraints.

Although the critical tradition had continued to flourish in the shadow of Stalinism – notably among the British Marxist historians – the end of Stalinism did not restore the theoretical fortunes of historical materialism. For one thing, the philosophical and cultural preoccupations of 'Western Marxism' since the 1920s had by default abandoned too much of the material and historical terrain to Stalinism. Stalinist Marxism had come, for many, to represent Marxist materialism as such; and the alternative appeared to be a distancing of Marxist theory from its materialist self-definition and, in some cases, a wholesale refusal of its materialist preoccupations, in particular its focus on political economy. This tendency was often reinforced by a conviction that the 'masses' in advanced capitalist societies, and specifically the working class, had fallen under the more or less permanent hegemonic spell of 'consumer capitalism'. At any rate, in the following decades, and especially in the wake of the rupture with Stalinism represented by the Twentieth Party Congress, there emerged a variety of Marxisms in the West, which – often very fruitfully – shifted Marxism onto new 'humanist' or cultural terrains, while leaving unresolved the ambiguities in their relations with the *materialism* in historical materialism. For that matter, the *historical* term in the equation was left largely ambiguous too. Although a great deal of first-rate Marxist history was written, the technological determinism of uncritical Marxism, while subject to humanist critique, was never decisively displaced by a comprehensive theoretical alternative – so that for some the only available option appeared to be an escape into pure historical contingency.

This is the context in which the last influential current of Western Marxism entered the fray, the Marxism of Louis Althusser. Althusser had described himself as responding to what he considered to be the 'inflation' of 'humanist' tendencies in Marxist theory in the wake of the liberation experienced by Marxists after the Twentieth Party Congress. He claimed to be defending the scientific rigour of Marxist materialism against a reversion to pre-Marxist idealism entailed by the then fashionable Hegelian readings of Marx, and the empiricism and voluntarism which had invaded socialist theory as structural determinations were supplanted by a preoccupation with human agency.

He was not, however, prepared to relinquish all the gains of the post-Stalinist liberation and sought other ways of preserving the non-reductivist, non-deterministic, non-economistic impulses of that ideological emancipation. His most notable contribution in that regard was the concept of 'overdetermination', which stressed the complexity and multiplicity of social causation, while reserving economic determination to a distant 'last instance'. But more fundamentally, the non-reductionist effect was achieved by establishing a rigid dualism between theory and history (about which more in chapter 2); and, here, there was a paradox, for in his insistence on the autonomy of theory and scientific knowledge – against empiricism, voluntarism, humanism and the 'historicism' which, he maintained, relativized theoretical and scientific knowledge – Althusser ended by displacing structural determinations from history altogether. Structural determinations might be the proper object of an autonomous theory, but the real historical world, it appeared, remained irreducibly contingent. This Althusserian dualism allowed its adherents both to abandon 'crude economism' and to retain, on the theoretical plane, a fairly crude determinism; and, where the Stalinist mechanical determinism had been interrupted by moments of extreme voluntarism, Althusserians could unite these two contradictory moments in one uneasy synthesis – or rather, juxtaposition.

This theoretical juxtaposition was to be short lived. Although not all Althusserians took the same route, there emerged a significant current that seized upon such concepts as overdetermination, 'relative autonomy' and 'social formation' (to which I shall return in chapter 2) as an excuse for effectively repudiating causation altogether, even castigating Althusser for clinging to the last remnant of 'economism' by refusing to relinquish determination 'in the last instance'. In the end, while the 'new social movements' were for some people the main political motivation for abandoning Marxism, Althusserianism became the main theoretical channel through which Western Marxism travelled in its passage to post-Marxism and beyond.

And then came the collapse of Communism. The condition of the left today may appear to differ as sharply from its state in 1981, when I published the first of the essays on which this volume is based, as the 'new world order' contrasts with the world before the collapse. Few but the most hardline right-wing critics would venture to deny that this historic rupture has brought about a transformation in the intellectual culture of the left, as people have entered a phase of 'rethinking' and soul searching of a kind unprecedented in the history of socialism.

Yet, without wishing to question the impact of these world-historic events on the thinking of Western socialists, I have been no less struck by the fundamental continuities between the dominant intellectual culture of the left on the eve of the collapse and the state of that culture today. I do not mean by this the kind of thing that critics of the right are likely to say – namely that, in the face of all the evidence, there are still too many people on the left who refuse to face reality and who cling to discredited old ideas. On the contrary,

I have in mind the political and theoretical trends which, well before the collapse of Communism and the 'triumph of capitalism' were even a gleam in the neo-conservative eye, were already moving rapidly away from the critique of capitalism and toward its conceptual dissolution in post-modern fragments and contingencies. The 'new world order', together with the restructuration of the capitalist economy, has certainly had profound effects, but current fashions on the intellectual left are in many ways simply exhausting the theoretical and political currents of the sixties and seventies rather than beginning to confront the problems of the late 1980s and 1990s.

In this post-modern moment, the ahistorical, metaphysical materialist tradition of Marxism has won a kind of victory. The most recent fashion in academic Marxism, the 'Rational Choice' variety, is deeply indebted to the old technological determinism (while embracing the procedures and many of the premises of conventional economics); and post-Marxist theories with their various successors, having defined themselves in relation to the old brand of uncritical Marxism, have made a simple choice between economistic determinism and post-modern contingency, without ever engaging the more difficult option of historical materialism.

It is not so surprising that, for many people, there has been a more or less direct route, with or without a stopover at Althusserianism, from determinist Marxism to what seems the opposite extreme. Determinism is always bound to be disappointed by history. In particular, technological-determinist Marxists, imbued with a teleological conviction that the automatic development of productive forces would mechanically produce a revolutionary working class, were bound to feel betrayed by the real working class responding not to the prophecies of a metaphysical materialism but to the exigencies of history. The intellectual history of the (stunningly rapid) transition from the structuralist Marxism of the sixties and seventies, through the brief moment of 'post-Marxism', to the current fashions of 'post-modernism' has in large part been the story of a disappointed determinism.

It is by now a commonplace that Western Marxism has been deeply influenced by the default of revolutionary consciousness within the working class and by the resulting dissociation of intellectual practice from any political movement. This seems to have encouraged people not only to seek political programmes less reliant on the working class but also to look for theories of social transformation freed from the constraints and disappointments of history. So there has been a wide range of ahistorical theories, from the abstractions of various philosophical and cultural Marxisms to Western adaptations of Maoism. Western Maoists, for example, were particularly attracted to its voluntarism and the suggestion that revolutions can be made by sheer political will, in defiance of material, historical conditions. As Althusser himself illustrated, such an attraction was not incompatible with a theoretical determinism. No doubt, too, the autonomy apparently accorded to ideology, politics and 'cultural revolution' held very particular attractions for intellectuals, situating revolution on their very own terrain. Now, with the decline of even these ahistorical revolutionary aspirations, there has remained an affinity with any theoretical tendency that stresses the autonomy of culture and, finally, *discourse*.

This suggests that the particular flavour of Western Marxism and its successors comes not just from the negative fact of their separation from working-class politics but from a tendency to fill the vacuum by putting intellectual activity in place of class struggle. There has been a kind of self-promotion of intellectuals as world-historic forces; and though this self-glorification has gone through various phases since the 1960s, it has in all its manifestations reinforced the detachment from history. Now, discursive construction has replaced material production as the constitutive practice of social life. There may never be a revolutionary reconstruction of society, but there can always be a ruthless deconstruction of texts. We have gone a long way beyond the healthy and fruitful attention to the ideological and cultural dimensions of human experience exemplified in the best of Marxist historiography or by a theorist like Gramsci. Here is vanguardism with a vengeance.

III

This volume is an attempt to shift debate on the left, as well as between socialism and its critics, away from the barren Hobson's choices that have occupied the theoretical terrain for too long, and toward an engagement with historical materialism and the critique of capitalism. This is not a work of technical economics. It is not a critique of neo-classical economics, nor is it an intervention in the long-standing debates on value theory or the falling rate of profit. Instead, its purpose is to define the specificity of capitalism as a system of social relations and as a political terrain, while reconsidering the theoretical foundations of historical materialism in general. It is a 'critique' in the sense that it seeks to break those conceptual and theoretical habits that tend to obscure the specificity of capitalism.

The issues here are both historical and theoretical. The main historical issue is the widespread tendency, almost universal in non-Marxist accounts of capitalist development and shared by some varieties of Marxism, to read capitalist principles and laws of motion back into all history and to explain the emergence of modern capitalism by assuming the very thing that needs to be explained. The remedy for this essentially teleological procedure is to put *history* in place of teleology. Theoretically, the principal issues have to do, first, as I suggest in chapter 3, with the difference between two conceptions of theory: 'on the one hand, a view that theoretical knowledge – the knowledge of structures – is a matter of "static conceptual representation", while motion and flux (together with history) belong to a different, empirical sphere of cognition; and on the other hand, a view of knowledge that does not oppose structure to history, in which theory can accommodate *historical* categories, "concepts appropriate to the investigation of process"'.

More specifically, there is a range of questions having to do with the historicity of certain theoretical categories. In particular, our current conceptions of the 'political' and the 'economic' are here subjected to critical scrutiny in order not to take for granted the delineation and separation of these categories specific to – and only to – capitalism. This conceptual separation, while it reflects a reality specific to capitalism, not only fails to comprehend the very different realities of pre- or non-capitalist societies but also disguises the new forms of power and domination created by capitalism.

The critical project I am outlining here requires treating capitalism as a system of social relations; and this means rethinking some of the ways in which the principal concepts of historical materialism – forces and relations of production, class, base and superstructure, etc. – have been conceived. These are the main themes of part i. But the original critique of capitalism could not have been conducted without the conviction that alternatives were possible, and it was carried out from the vantage point of capitalism's antithesis, socialism. This demanded a critique not only of capitalism or of political economy but also of the then available *oppositions* to capitalism, which meant subjecting the socialist tradition itself to critical scrutiny. The principal object of this critique was to transform the socialist idea from an ahistorical aspiration into a political programme grounded in the historical conditions of capitalism. My own point of orientation is still socialism, but today's oppositions and resistances are of a different kind and require a 'critique' of their own. If there is now any single unifying theme among the various fragmented oppositions, it is the aspiration to *democracy*. Part II, then, explores the concept of democracy as a challenge to capitalism, and it does so critically, that is, above all, historically.

The volume proceeds as follows. The chapter on 'The separation of the "economic" and the "political" in capitalism' sets the agenda for the whole volume. It is an attempt both to identify what is distinctive about capitalism and the historical process that produced it, and to scrutinize the conceptual categories associated with this distinctive historical pattern. In the process, the fundamental categories of historical materialism – forces and relations of production, base and superstructure, and so on – are also redefined. If I were to start this essay from scratch today, I would stress even more than I did then the specificity of capitalism and its historical development. Since I first wrote it, I have become increasingly preoccupied with the ways in which the retrospective imposition of capitalist principles upon all previous history has affected our understanding of both history in general and capitalism in particular. One product of this preoccupation was my book, *The Pristine Culture of Capitalism: A Historical Essay on Old Regimes and Modern States* (London, 1991) which distinguishes the historical development of English capitalism from other historical paths out of European feudalism, especially in France, where the outcome was not capitalism but absolutism. Rethinking the history of capitalism in this way involved disentangling the conventional ensemble of 'capitalism' and 'bourgeois society', and raising some questions about our understanding of progress and 'modernity'. Behind all this lay further questions about the connection between markets, trade and towns, on the one hand, and capitalism, on the other – questions that also arise in connection with my discussion of Max Weber in chapter 5.

The other essays in part I develop themes introduced in the first essay, elaborating on the forces and relations of production, the question of base and superstructure, the concept of class, the problem of technological determinism, the antithesis of *history* and *teleology*. I should perhaps explain the special role I assign here to E.P. Thompson. In chapters 2 and 3, I use his work as a point of departure for reconstructing some of the fundamental categories of historical materialism – notably the metaphor of 'base and super-structure' and the concept of class. I have been told repeatedly that I read too much of my own theoretical predispositions into his historical writings; but while I would certainly like to take credit for some of the insights I ascribe to him, it still seems to me that, however allusive (and illusive) his own theoretical pronouncements may have been, he remains the closest thing we have to a theorist of historical materialism as I understand it.

In chapter 3, I talk about Thompson's conception of class as *process* and *relationship*, as opposed to class as a structural location; and I contrast his *historical* conception to what I call the *geological* model in conventional theories of 'stratification'. It occurs to me that this distinction – together with the underlying epistemological difference between Thompson's conception of theoretical know-ledge as having to do with 'concepts appropriate to the investigation of process' and other conceptions of theory as 'static conceptual representation' – is a very nice way of identifying what I take to be the defining characteristics of historical materialism.

Thompson also exemplifies for me the critical role of historical materialism as a way of learning – or relearning – how to *think* in non-capitalist terms, challenging the universality of its constitutive categories – conceptions of property, labour, the market, and so on. His work has been unequalled in its capacity to undermine capitalist assumptions by a kind of historical–anthropological deconstruction, tracking the *transformations*, against resistances, which produced this unique social form – the market against the resistance of the 'moral economy'; capitalist definitions of property as against other, earlier and/or alternative definitions, reflecting customs, codes, practices and expectations resistant to the logic of capitalist property rela-tions. His subversive genealogy of capitalist principles, tracing capitalist practices, values and categories to their systemic roots in specific relations of production and exploitation, restores not only the historicity of capitalism but also its contestability.

At any rate, my discussion of the fundamental categories of historical materialism leads into the Marxist conception of history and a reconsideration of technological determinism in chapter 4. One issue, again, dominates this discussion of history: the antithesis between historical materialism on the one hand, and on the other the teleological tendency to see capitalism in all its historical predecessors, to assume its pre-existence in order to explain its coming into being, and to translate its specific laws of motion into a general law of history. This tendency, I argue in chapter 5, is exemplified even by Max Weber and more than anything else distinguishes him from Marx.

The first chapter of the book also lays the foundation for the chapters in part II, which explore the political implications that follow from the specificities of capitalism. If the defining characteristic of capitalism as a political terrain is the formal 'separation of the economic and the political', or the transfer of certain 'political' powers to the 'economy' and 'civil society', what consequences does this have for the nature and scope of the state and citizenship? Since capitalism entails, among other things, new forms of domination and coercion which are outside the reach of instruments designed to check traditional forms of political power, it also reduces the salience of citizenship and the scope of democratic accountability. Capitalism, to put it simply, can afford a universal distribution of political goods without endangering its constitutive relations, its coercions and inequities. This, needless to say, has wide-ranging implications for our understanding of democracy and the possibilities of its expansion.

Throughout this section, democracy is examined in historical perspective. The object is to situate it in specific historical contexts instead of treating it as a socially indeterminate abstraction. Capitalist democracy is scrutinized in contrast to other forms, in the context of different social relations (in particular, the ancient Greek form which gave rise to the concept of democracy itself). In chapter 6, I compare the implications of democracy for the status of labour in ancient Athenian and modern capitalist democracy; and, in chapter 7, I trace the changes in the meaning of democracy and citizenship from classical antiquity, through the redefinition carried out by the founders of the US Constitution, to the modern conception of liberal democracy. I also explore the particular ways in which capitalism both advances and inhibits democracy, raising questions about the possible direction of further advances.

'Formal' democracy and the identification of democracy with *liberalism* would have been impossible in practice and literally unthinkable in theory in any other context but the very specific social relations of capitalism. These social relations have both advanced and strictly limited democracy, and the greatest challenge to capitalism would be an extension of democracy beyond its narrowly circumscribed limits. It is at this point that 'democracy' arguably becomes synonymous with socialism. The question then is what socialist emancipation means beyond the abolition of class exploitation. In chapter 8, I extend the discussion of democracy to current preoccupations with 'civil society' and the 'politics of identity'; and chapter 9 reflects on the prospects and limits of human emancipation in capitalist society and the effects of capitalism on 'extra-economic' goods, not only democracy but racial and especially gender equality. The Conclusion makes some tentative suggestions about the kinds of questions socialist thought should now address.

A few final words about the connection between the chapters in this book and the essays on which they are based. Although the essays, published between 1981 and 1994, were written at different times and for various purposes, they seem to me to comprise a coherent set of ideas. I have emphasized that coherence by arranging the essays more thematically than chronologically, by integrating overlapping texts, and by introducing some bridging arguments. Some essays have been more extensively altered than others. Chapters 4 and 7 represent the revision and integration of several essays or sections extracted from them. Elsewhere, I have cut some things and elaborated or clarified others, modifying some particularly leaden prose, incoherence or opacity, or amplifying some point that seemed to me unclear or in need of explication.

Although I have sometimes interjected a current observation into an older text, I have tried not to alter the text in such a way as to make myself seem more perspicacious than I was. This, of course, raises questions about whether and how the massive transformations that have occurred in the world between the first and the last of these essays have obliged me to 'rethink', and why I am not ashamed to persist in such unfashionable views. I want to make a few remarks in the conclusion about the 'current conjuncture' and the continuing timeliness of socialist aspirations; but for now, I shall simply repeat that, since historical materialism still represents the most fruitful critique of capitalism, it seems to me that the 'triumph of capitalism' has made it more relevant today than ever before.

PART I

Historical materialism and the specificity of capitalism

The separation of the 'economic' and the 'political' in capitalism

The original intention of historical materialism was to provide a theoretical foundation for interpreting the world in order to change it. This was not an empty slogan. It had a very precise meaning. It meant that Marxism sought a particular kind of knowledge, uniquely capable of illuminating the principles of historical movement and, at least implicitly, the points at which political action could most effectively intervene. This is not to say that the object of Marxist theory was to discover a 'scientific' programme or technique of political action. Instead, the purpose was to provide a mode of analysis especially well equipped to explore the terrain on which political action must take place.

Marxism since Marx has often lost sight of his theoretical project and its quintessentially political character. In particular, there has been a tendency to perpetuate the rigid conceptual separation of the 'economic' and the 'political' which has served capitalist ideology so well ever since the classical economists discovered the 'economy' in the abstract and began emptying capitalism of its social and political content.

These conceptual devices do reflect, if only in a distorting mirror, a historical reality specific to capitalism, a real differentiation of the 'economy'; and it may be possible to reformulate them so that they illuminate more than they obscure, by reexamining the historical conditions that made such conceptions possible and plausible. The purpose of this reexamination would not be to explain away the 'fragmentation' of social life in capitalism, but to understand exactly what it is in the historical nature of capitalism that appears as a differentiation of 'spheres', especially the 'economic' and the 'political'.

This differentiation is, of course, not simply a theoretical but a practical problem. It has had a very immediate practical expression in the separation of economic and political struggles which has typified modern working-class movements. For many revolutionary socialists, this has represented nothing more than the product of a misguided, 'underdeveloped', or 'false' consciousness. If there were nothing more to it than that, it might be easier to overcome; but what has made working-class 'economism' so tenacious is that it does correspond to the realities of capitalism, to the ways in which capitalist appropriation and exploitation actually do divide the arenas of economic and political action, and actually do transform certain essential political issues – struggles over domination and exploitation which have in the past been inextricably bound up with political power – into distinctively 'economic' issues. This 'structural' separation may, indeed, be the most effective defence mechanism available to capital.

The point, then, is to explain how and in what sense capitalism has driven a wedge between the economic and the political – how and in what sense essentially political issues like the disposition of power to control production and appropriation, or the allocation of social labour and resources, have been cut off from the political arena and displaced to a separate sphere.

ECONOMIC AND POLITICAL 'FACTORS'

Marx presented the world in its political aspect, not only in his explicitly political works but even in his most technical economic writings. His critique of political economy was, among other things, intended to reveal the political face of the economy which had been obscured by classical political economists. The fundamental secret of capitalist production disclosed by Marx – the secret that political economy systematically concealed, making it finally incapable of accounting for capitalist accumulation – concerns the social relation and the disposition of power that obtains between workers and the capitalist to whom they sell their labour power. This secret has a corollary: that the disposition of power between the individual capitalist and worker has as its condition the political configuration of society as a whole – the balance of class forces and the powers of the state which permit the expropriation of the direct producer, the maintenance of absolute private property for the capitalist, and his control over production and appropriation.

In volume I of *Capital* Marx works his way from the commodity form through surplus value to the 'secret of primitive accumulation', disclosing at last that the 'starting point' of capitalist production' is nothing else than the historical process of divorcing the producer from the means of production',[1] a process of class struggle and coercive intervention by the state on behalf of the expropriating class. The very structure of the argument suggests that, for Marx, the ultimate secret of capitalist production is a *political* one. What distinguishes his analysis so radically from classical political economy is that it creates no sharp discontinuities between economic and political spheres; and he is able to trace the continuities because he treats the economy itself not as a network of disembodied forces but, like the political sphere, as a set of social relations.

This has not been equally true of Marxism since Marx. In one form or another and in varying degrees, Marxists have generally adopted modes of analysis which, explicitly or implicitly, treat the economic 'base' and the legal, political, and ideological 'super-structures' that 'reflect' or 'correspond' to it as qualitatively different, more or less enclosed and 'regionally' separated spheres. This is most obviously true of orthodox base-superstructure theories. It is also true of their variants which speak of economic, political and ideological 'factors,' 'levels' or 'instances', no matter how insistent they may be about the *interaction* of factors or instances, or about the remoteness of the 'last instance' in which the economic sphere finally determines the rest. If anything, these formulations merely reinforce the spatial separation of spheres.

Other schools of Marxism have maintained the abstraction and enclosure of spheres in other ways – for example, by abstracting the *economy* or the *circuit* of capital in order to construct a technically sophisticated alternative to bourgeois economics, meeting it on its own ground (and going significantly further than Marx himself in this respect, without grounding the economic abstractions in historical and sociological analysis as he did). The social relations in which this economic mechanism is embedded – which indeed consti-tute it – are treated as somehow external. At best, a spatially separate political power may *intervene* in the economy, but the economy itself is evacuated of social content and depoliticized. In these respects, Marxist theory has perpetuated the very ideological practices that Marx was attacking, those practices that confirmed to

---

[1] Karl Marx, *Capital* I, (Moscow, 1971), p. 668.

the bourgeoisie the naturalness and eternity of capitalist production relations.

Bourgeois political economy, according to Marx, universalizes capitalist relations of production by analysing production in abstraction from its specific social determinations. Marx's approach differs from theirs in his insistence that a productive system is made up of its specific social determinations – specific social relations, modes of property and domination, legal and political forms. This does not mean simply that the economic 'base' is reflected in and maintained by certain 'superstructural' institutions, but that the productive base itself exists in the shape of social, juridical and political forms – in particular, forms of property and domination.

Bourgeois political economists are able to demonstrate 'the eternity and harmoniousness of the existing social relations' by divorcing the system of production from its specific social attributes. For Marx, production is 'not only a particular production . . . it is always a certain social body, a social subject, which is active in a greater or sparser totality of branches of production'.[2] Bourgeois political economy, in contrast, achieves its ideological purpose by dealing with *society in the abstract*, treating production as 'encased in eternal natural laws independent of history, at which opportunity *bourgeois* relations are then quietly smuggled in as the inviolable natural laws on which society in the abstract is founded. This is the more or less conscious purpose of the whole proceeding.'[3] While bourgeois economists may recognize that certain legal and political forms facilitate production, they do not treat them as organic constituents of a productive system. Thus they bring things that are organically related 'into an accidental relation, into a merely reflective connection'.[4]

The distinction between 'organic' and 'merely reflective' connections is especially significant. It suggests that any application of the base/superstructure metaphor that stresses the separation and enclosure of spheres – however much it may insist on the connection of one to the other, even the reflection of one by the other – reproduces the mystifications of bourgeois ideology because it fails to treat the productive sphere itself as defined by its social determinations and in effect deals with society 'in the abstract'. The basic

[2] Marx, *Grundrisse* tr. M. Nicolaus (Harmondsworth, 1973), p. 86.   [3] *Ibid.*, p. 87.
[4] *Ibid.*, p. 88.

principle about the primacy of production, the very foundation of historical materialism, loses its critical edge and is assimilated to bourgeois ideology.

This is, of course, not to say that Marx saw no value in the approach of bourgeois political economy. On the contrary, he adopted its categories as his point of departure because they expressed, not a universal truth, but a historical reality in capitalist society, at least a 'real appearance'. What he undertook was neither the reproduction nor the repudiation of bourgeois categories but their critical elaboration and transcendence.

TOWARD A THEORETICAL ALTERNATIVE: 'BASE' AND 'SUPERSTRUCTURE' RECONSIDERED

It should be possible to sustain a historical materialism that takes seriously Marx's own insistence, in opposition to the ideological abstractions of bourgeois political economy, that (for example) 'capital is a social relation of production', that *economic* categories express certain determinate *social* relations. There ought to be a theoretical alternative to 'vulgar economism' that attempts to preserve the integrity of the 'mode of production', while working out the implications of the fact that the productive 'base' exists in the shape of specific social processes and relations and particular juridical and political forms. There has been no explicit and systematic account of such a theoretical position (at least not since Marx's own), although something like it is implicit in the work of certain Marxist historians.

The theoretical standpoint being proposed here is perhaps what has been called – pejoratively – 'political Marxism'. This brand of Marxism, according to one Marxist critic, is a

reaction to the wave of economist[ic] tendencies in contemporary historiography. As the role of class struggle is widely underestimated, so [political Marxism] injects strong doses of it into historical explanation. ... It amounts to a voluntarist vision of history in which the class struggle is divorced from all other objective contingencies and, in the first instance, from such laws of development as may be peculiar to a specific mode of production. Could one imagine accounting for the development of capitalism in the nineteenth and twentieth centuries solely by reference to social factors, and without bringing into the picture the law of capitalist accumulation and its mainspring, that is to say the mechanism of surplus value? In fact, the result ... is to deprive the basic concept of historical materialism,

that is the mode of production, of all real substance. . . . The error of such
'political Marxism' lies not only in its neglect of the most operative concept
of historical materialism (the mode of production). It also consists in its
abandonment of the field of economic realities. . . .[5]

The purpose of my argument here is to overcome the false dichotomy on which this characterization of 'political Marxism' is
based, a dichotomy that permits some Marxists to accuse others of
abandoning the 'field of economic realities' when they concern
themselves with the political and social factors that constitute relations of production and exploitation. The premise here is that there
is no such thing as a mode of production *in opposition* to 'social
factors', and that Marx's radical innovation on bourgeois political
economy was precisely to define the mode of production and
economic laws themselves in terms of 'social factors'.

What does it mean to talk about a mode of production or an
economy as if they were distinct from, even opposed to, 'social
factors'? What, for example, are 'objective contingencies' like the
law of capitalist accumulation and its 'mainspring', the 'mechanism'
of surplus value? The mechanism of surplus value is a particular
social relation between appropriator and producer. It operates
through a particular organization of production, distribution and
exchange; and it is based on a particular class relation maintained
by a particular configuration of power. What is the subjection of
labour to capital, which is the essence of capitalist production, if not
a social relation and the product of a class struggle? What, after all,
did Marx mean when he insisted that capital is a social relation of
production; that the category 'capital' had no meaning apart from
its social determinations; that money or capital goods are not in
themselves capital but become so only in the context of a particular
social relation between appropriator and producer; that the so-
called primitive accumulation of capital which is the pre-condition
for capitalist production is nothing more than the process – i.e. the
class struggle – whereby the direct producer is expropriated?, and so
on. For that matter, why did the grand old man of bourgeois social
science, Max Weber, insist on a 'purely economic' definition of
capitalism without reference to extraneous *social factors* (like, for

[5] Guy Bois, 'Against the Neo-Malthusian Orthodoxy', in T.H. Aston and C.H.E. Philpin eds.
The Brenner Debate: Agrarian Class Structure and Economic Development in Pre-Industrial Europe
(Cambridge, 1985), pp. 115–16. The author is referring specifically to the article by Robert
Brenner cited below in note 9.

example, the exploitation of labour), evacuating the social meaning of capitalism in deliberate opposition to Marx?[6]

To raise these questions and to insist on the social constitution of the economy is not at all to say that there *is* no economy, that there *are* no economic 'laws', no mode of production, no 'laws of development' in a mode of production, no law of capitalist accumulation; nor is it to deny that the mode of production is the 'most operative concept of historical materialism'. 'Political Marxism', as understood here, is no less convinced of the primacy of production than are the 'economistic tendencies' of Marxism. It does not define production out of existence or extend its boundaries to embrace indiscriminately all social activities. It simply takes seriously the principle that a mode of production is a *social* phenomenon.

Equally important – and this is the point of the whole exercise – relations of production are, from this theoretical standpoint, presented in their *political* aspect, that aspect in which they are actually *contested*, as relations of domination, as rights of property, as the power to organize and govern production and appropriation. In other words, the object of this theoretical stance is a *practical* one, to illuminate the terrain of struggle by viewing modes of production not as abstract structures but as they actually confront people who must *act* in relation to them.

'Political Marxism' recognizes the specificity of material production and production relations; but it insists that 'base' and 'superstructure', or the 'levels' of a social formation, cannot be viewed as compartments or 'regionally' separated spheres. However much we may stress the interaction among 'factors', these theoretical practices mislead because they obscure not only the historical processes by which modes of production are constituted but also the structural definition of productive systems as living social phenomena.

'Political Marxism', then, does not present the relation between base and superstructure as an opposition, a 'regional' separation, between a basic 'objective' economic structure, on the one hand, and social, juridical and political forms, on the other, but rather as a continuous structure of social relations and forms with varying degrees of distance from the immediate processes of production and

---

[6] See, for example, Weber's *Economy and Society* (New York, 1968), pp. 91 and 94, and *The Agrarian Sociology of Ancient Civilizations* (London, 1976), pp. 50–1.

appropriation, beginning with those relations and forms that constitute the system of production itself. The connections between 'base'
and 'superstructure' can then be traced without great conceptual
leaps because they do not represent two essentially different and
discontinuous orders of reality.

The argument begins with one of the first principles of Marx's
materialism: that while human beings work within definite material
limits not of their own making, including purely physical and
ecological factors, the material world as it exists for them is not
simply a natural given; it is a mode of productive *activity*, a system of
social relations, a historical product. Even nature, 'the nature that
preceded human history ... is nature which no longer exists anywhere ... ';[7] 'the sensuous world ... is, not a thing given direct from
all eternity, remaining ever the same, but the product of industry
and the state of society – and, indeed, in the sense that it is an
historical product, the result of the activity of a whole succession of
generations, each standing on the shoulders of the preceding one,
developing its industry and its intercourse, modifying its social
system according to the changing needs'.[8]

A materialist understanding of the world, then, is an understanding of the social activity and the social relations through which
human beings interact with nature in producing the conditions of
life; and it is a historical understanding which acknowledges that the
products of social activity, the forms of social interaction produced
by human beings, themselves become material forces, no less than
are natural givens.

This account of materialism, with its insistence on the role played
by social forms and historical legacies as material forces, inevitably
raises the vexed question of 'base' and 'superstructure'. If forms of
social interaction, and not just natural or technological forces, are to
be treated as integral parts of the material base, where is the line to
be drawn between social forms that belong to the base and those
that can be relegated to superstructure? Or, in fact, does the base/
superstructure dichotomy obscure as much as it reveals about the
productive 'base' itself?

Some legal and political institutions are external to the relations
of production even while helping to sustain and reproduce them;

Marx, *German Ideology*, in *Collected Works*, vol. v (New York, 1976), p. 39.
Ibid., p. 40.

and perhaps the term 'superstructure' should be reserved for these. But relations of production themselves take the form of particular juridical and political relations – modes of domination and coercion, forms of property and social organization – which are not mere secondary reflexes, nor even just external supports, but *constituents* of these production relations. The 'sphere' of production is dominant not in the sense that it stands apart from or precedes these juridical-political forms, but rather in the sense that these forms are precisely forms of production, the *attributes* of a particular productive system.

A mode of production is not simply a technology but a social organization of productive activity; and a mode of exploitation is a relationship of power. Furthermore, the power relationship that conditions the nature and extent of exploitation is a matter of political organization within and between the contending classes. In the final analysis the relation between appropriators and producers rests on the relative strength of classes, and this is largely determined by the internal organization and the political forces with which each enters into the class struggle.

For example, as Robert Brenner has argued, the varying patterns of development in different parts of late medieval Europe can be accounted for in large part by the differences in class organization which characterized struggles between lords and peasants in various places according to their specific historical experiences. In some cases, the struggle issued in a breakdown of the old order and old forms of surplus extraction; in others, a retrenchment of the old forms took place. These different outcomes of agrarian class conflict, argues Brenner,

> tended to be bound up with certain *historically specific* patterns of development of the contending agrarian classes and their relative strength in the different European societies: their relative levels of internal solidarity, their self-consciousness and organization, and their general political resources – especially their relationships to the non-agricultural classes (in particular, potential urban class allies) and to the state (in particular, whether or not the state developed as a 'class-like' competitor of the lords for the peasants' surplus).[9]

Brenner illustrates how the particular form as well as the strength of political organization in the contending classes shaped relations of

---

[9] Robert Brenner, 'Agrarian Class Structure and Economic Development in Pre-Industrial Europe', in Aston and Philpin, *The Brenner Debate*, p. 55.

production: for example, how *village* institutions acted as a form of peasant class organization and how the development of 'independent political institutions in the village'[10] – or the lack of such institutions – affected the exploitative relations between lord and peasant. In cases like this, political organization plays a significant part in *constructing* relations of production.

There are, then, at least two senses in which the juridical-political 'sphere' is implicated in the productive 'base'. First, a system of production always exists in the shape of specific social determinations, the particular modes of organization and domination and the forms of property in which relations of production are embodied – what might be called the 'basic' as distinct from 'superstructural' juridical-political attributes of the productive system. Second, from a *historical* point of view even political institutions like village and state enter directly into the constitution of production relations and are in a sense prior to them (even where these institutions are not the direct instruments of surplus appropriation), because relations of production are historically constituted by the configuration of power that determines the outcome of class conflict.

THE 'ECONOMIC' AND THE 'POLITICAL' IN CAPITALISM

What, then, does it mean to say that capitalism is marked by a unique differentiation of the 'economic' sphere? It means several things: that production and distribution assume a completely 'economic' form, no longer (as Karl Polanyi put it) 'embedded' in extra-economic social relations,[11] in a system where production is generally production for exchange; that the allocation of social labour and the distribution of resources are achieved through the 'economic' mechanism of commodity exchange; that the 'economic' forces of the commodity and labour markets acquire a life of their own; that, to quote Marx, property 'receives its purely economic form by discarding all its former political and social embellishments and associations'.[12]

Above all, it means that the appropriation of surplus labour takes place in the 'economic' sphere by 'economic' means. In other words, surplus appropriation is achieved in ways determined by the com-

[10] *Ibid.*, p. 42.   [11] Karl Polanyi, *The Great Transformation* (Boston, 1957), pp. 57, 69–71.
[12] Marx, *Capital* III, p. 618.

plete separation of the producer from the conditions of labour and by the appropriator's absolute private property in the means of production. Direct 'extra-economic' pressure or overt coercion are, in principle, unnecessary to compel the expropriated labourer to give up surplus labour. Although the coercive force of the 'political' sphere is ultimately necessary to sustain private property and the power of appropriation, economic need supplies the immediate compulsion forcing the worker to transfer surplus labour to the capitalist in order to gain access to the means of production.

The labourer is 'free', not in a relationship of dependence or servitude; the transfer of surplus labour and its appropriation by someone else are not conditioned by such an extra-economic relationship. The forfeit of surplus labour is an immediate condition of production itself. Capitalism in these respects differs from pre-capitalist forms because the latter are characterized by extra-economic modes of surplus extraction, political, legal, or military coercion, traditional bonds or duties, etc., which demand the transfer of surplus labour to a private lord or to the state by means of labour services, rent, tax, and so on.

The differentiation of the economic sphere in capitalism, then, can be summed up like this: the social functions of production and distribution, surplus extraction and appropriation, and the allocation of social labour are, so to speak, privatized and they are achieved by non-authoritative, non-political means. In other words, the social allocation of resources and labour does not, on the whole, take place by means of political direction, communal deliberation, hereditary duty, custom, or religious obligation, but rather through the mechanisms of commodity exchange. The powers of surplus appropriation and exploitation do not rest directly on relations of juridical or political dependence but are based on a contractual relation between 'free' producers – juridically free and free from the means of production – and an appropriator who has absolute private property in the means of production.

To speak of the differentiation of the economic sphere in these senses is not, of course, to suggest that the political dimension is somehow extraneous to capitalist relations of production. The political sphere in capitalism has a special character because the coercive power supporting capitalist exploitation is not wielded directly by the appropriator and is not based on the producer's political or juridical subordination to an appropriating master. But a coercive power and a structure of domination remain essential, even if the ostensible freedom and equality of the exchange between capital and labour mean that the 'moment' of coercion is separate from the 'moment' of appropriation. Absolute private property, the contractual relation that binds producer to appropriator, the process of commodity exchange – all these require the legal forms, the coercive apparatus, the policing functions of the state. Historically, too the state has been essential to the process of expropriation that is the basis of capitalism. In all these senses, despite their differentiation, the economic sphere rests firmly on the political.

Furthermore, the economic sphere itself has a juridical and political dimension. In one sense, the differentiation of the economic sphere means simply that the economy has its own juridical and political forms whose purpose is purely 'economic'. Absolute property, contractual relations and the legal apparatus that sustains them are the juridical conditions of capitalist production relations; and they constitute the basis of a new relation of authority, domination and subjection between appropriator and producer.

The correlative of these private, economic juridical-political forms is a separate specialized public political sphere. The 'autonomy' of the capitalist state is inextricably bound up with the juridical freedom and equality of the free, purely economic exchange between free expropriated producers and the private appropriators who have absolute property in the means of production and therefore a new form of authority over the producers. This is the significance of the division of labour in which the two moments of capitalist exploitation – appropriation and coercion – are allocated separately to a private appropriating class and a specialized public coercive institution, the state: on the one hand, the 'relatively autonomous' state has a monopoly of coercive force; on the other hand, that force sustains a private 'economic' power which invests capitalist property with an authority to organize production itself – an authority probably unprecedented in its degree of control over productive activity and the human beings who engage in it.

The direct political powers that capitalist proprietors have lost to the state they have gained in the direct control of production. While the 'economic' power of appropriation possessed by the capitalist is separated from the coercive political instruments that ultimately enforce it, that appropriative power is integrated more closely and directly than ever before with the authority to organize production.

Not only is the forfeit of surplus labour an immediate condition of production, but capitalist property unites to a degree probably not enjoyed by any previous appropriating class the power of surplus extraction and the capacity to organize and intensify production directly for the purposes of the appropriator. However exploitive earlier modes of production have been, however effective the means of surplus extraction available to exploiting classes, in no other system has social production answered so immediately and universally to the demands of the exploiter.

At the same time, the powers of the appropriator no longer carry with them the obligation to perform social, public functions. In capitalism, there is a complete separation of private appropriation from public duties; and this means the development of a new sphere of power devoted completely to private rather than social purposes. In this respect, capitalism differs from pre-capitalist forms in which the fusion of economic and political powers meant not only that surplus extraction was an 'extra-economic' transaction separate from the production process itself, but also that the power to appropriate surplus labour – whether it belonged to the state or to a private lord – was bound up with the performance of military, juridical and administrative functions.

In a sense, then, the differentiation of the economic and the political in capitalism is, more precisely, a differentiation of political functions themselves and their separate allocation to the private economic sphere and the public sphere of the state. This allocation separates political functions immediately concerned with the extraction and appropriation of surplus labour from those with a more general, communal purpose. This formulation, suggesting that the differentiation of the economic is in fact a differentiation within the political sphere, is in certain respects better suited to explain the unique process of Western development and the special character of capitalism. It may, then, be useful to sketch this historical process of differentiation before looking more closely at capitalism.

THE HISTORICAL PROCESS OF DIFFERENTIATION: CLASS POWER AND STATE POWER

If the evolution of capitalism is viewed as a process in which an 'economic' sphere is differentiated from the 'political', an explanation of that evolution entails a theory of the *state* and its development. For the purposes of this discussion, the state will be defined in very broad terms as 'the complex of institutions by means of which the power of the society is organized on a basis superior to kinship'[13] – an organization of power which means a claim 'to paramountcy in the application of naked force to social problems' and consists of 'formal, specialized instruments of coercion'.[14] These instruments of coercion may or may not be intended from the outset as a means for one section of the population to oppress and exploit the rest. In either case, the state requires the performance of certain common social functions which other less comprehensive institutions – households, clans, kinship groups, etc. – cannot carry out.

Whether or not the essential object of the state is to maintain exploitation, its performance of social functions implies a social division of labour and the appropriation by some social groups of surplus produced by others. It seems reasonable to suppose, then, that however this 'complex of institutions' came into being, the state emerged as a means of appropriating surplus product – perhaps even as a means of intensifying production in order to increase surplus – and as a mode of distributing that surplus in one way or another. In fact, it may be that the state – at least some form of communal or public power – was the first systematic means of surplus appropriation and perhaps even the first systematic organizer of surplus production.[15]

While this conception of the state implies that the evolution of a specialized, coercive public authority necessarily entails a division between producers and appropriators, it does not mean that private appropriation is a necessary pre-condition to the emergence of such an authority. The two may develop together, and a long historical process may intervene before private appropriation clearly disso- ciates itself from public power. Propositions about the relation between *class* and state must, therefore, be cautiously formulated. It may be misleading to suggest, as Marxist arguments often seem to do, that there is a universal sequence of development in which class precedes state.

What *can* perhaps be said is that, whichever came first, the

---

[13] Morton Fried, *The Evolution of Political Society* (New York, 1968), p. 229.
[14] *Ibid.*, p. 230.
[15] See Marshall Sahlins, *Stone Age Economics* (London, 1974), chaps. 2 and 3, for some illuminating suggestions about how a public authority might emerge as a means of intensifying production.

existence of a state has always implied the existence of classes – although this proposition requires a definition of class capable of encompassing all divisions between direct producers and the appropriators of their surplus labour, even cases in which economic power is scarcely distinguishable from political power, where private property remains undeveloped, and where class and state are in effect one.[16] The essential point is the recognition that some of the major divergences among various historical patterns have to do with the nature and sequence of relations between public power and private appropriation.

This point is especially important in identifying the distinctive characteristics of the historical path leading to capitalism, with its unprecedented degree of differentiation between the economic and the political. The long historical process that ultimately issued in capitalism could be seen as an increasing – and uniquely well-developed – differentiation of *class* power as something distinct from *state* power, a power of surplus extraction not directly grounded in the coercive apparatus of the state. This would also be a process in which private appropriation is increasingly divorced from the performance of communal functions. If we are to understand the unique development of capitalism, then, we must understand how property and class relations, as well as the functions of surplus appropriation and distribution, so to speak liberate themselves from – and yet are served by – the coercive institutions that constitute the state, and develop autonomously.

The foundations of this argument are to be found in Marx's discussion of pre-capitalist formations and the distinctive character of capitalism in the *Grundrisse* and *Capital*, especially volume III. In the *Grundrisse* Marx discusses the nature of capitalism in contrast to, and as a development from, pre-capitalist forms in terms of the gradual separation of the direct producer from the natural conditions of labour. It is characteristic of pre-capitalist forms that producers remain, in one way or another, directly related to the conditions of labour, at least as possessors if not owners of the means of production. The principal case in which the direct producer is completely expropriated – the case of chattel slavery – is itself determined by the typically direct relation of the producer to the

[16] Problems may emerge out of such an inclusive definition of class, not the least of which are their implications for the analysis of Soviet-type states, which have been analysed, alternatively, as autonomous from class or as a particular form of class organization.

natural conditions of labour, since the slave is seized as an accessory to captured land, rendered propertyless by military means and thus transformed into a mere condition of production.

Where a division between appropriators and producers has evolved, surplus appropriation takes 'extra-economic' forms – whether it be the outright coercion of master against slave, or, where the labourer remains in possession of the conditions of labour, a relationship of lordship and servitude in other forms. In one of the major pre-capitalist cases, which Marx calls the 'Asiatic', the state itself is the direct appropriator of surplus labour from producers who remain in possession of the land that they work. It is the special characteristic of capitalism that surplus appropriation and the relationship between direct producers and the appropriators of their surplus labour do not take the form of direct political domination or legal servitude; and the authority confronting the mass of direct producers appears 'only as the personification of the conditions of labour in contrast to labour, and not as political or theocratic rulers as under earlier modes of production'.[17]

It is in this discussion of pre-capitalist forms and their 'political' modes of surplus extraction, in both the *Grundrisse* and *Capital*, that Marx's ill-fated conception of Asiatic societies makes its appearance. This is not the place for a full debate on this contentious issue. For the moment, what is important is that in his discussion of 'Asiatic' forms Marx considers social types in which the state is the direct and dominant means of surplus appropriation. In this sense, the 'Asiatic' type represents the polar opposite of the capitalist case, in that economic and extra-economic, class power and state power, property relations and political relations, are least differentiated:

Should the direct producers not be confronted by a private landowner, but rather, as in Asia, under direct subordination to a state which stands over them as their landlord and simultaneously as sovereign, then rent and taxes coincide, or rather, there exists no tax which differs from this form of ground-rent. Under such circumstances there need exist no stronger political or economic pressure than that common to all subjection to that state. The state is then the supreme lord. Sovereignty here consists in the ownership of land concentrated on a national scale. But, on the other hand, no private ownership of land exists, although there is both private and common possession and use of land.[18]

[17] Marx, *Capital* III, p. 881.   [18] *Ibid.*, p. 791.

Even if there has never been a perfect representative of this social type – for example, if there has never been a well-developed appropriating and redistributive state in the complete absence of private ownership of land – the concept must still be taken seriously. The state as the major and direct appropriator of surplus labour has certainly existed; and there is considerable evidence that this mode of surplus appropriation has been a dominant, if not universal, pattern of social development – for example, in Bronze Age Greece, as well as in the larger palace-dominated 'redistributive' economies of the ancient Near East and Asia. Whatever other characteristics Marx may have attributed to the 'Asiatic' form, this one, which has sparked the most controversy, needs to be explored for what it may reveal about the process of differentiation that concerns us here.

The implication of Marx's argument is that the division between appropriators and producers – a division implied by any form of state – can take different forms, forms to which the notion of 'class' can be applied only with great caution when there is no clearly differentiated 'economic' power. It is, of course, true that only in capitalist society is the economic power of class completely differentiated from extra-economic powers; and there is no intention here of arguing that there is class only in capitalist social formations. But it does at least seem important to recognize the polar extremes: the capitalist mode, in which the differentiation has taken place, and one in which – as in certain bureaucratic, palace-dominated 're-distributive' states of the ancient world – the state itself, as the major direct appropriator of surplus product, is both class and state at once.

Marx sometimes appears to suggest that, in the latter case, the dynamic of history has been inhibited, if property and class do not break free and develop autonomously from the 'hypertrophied' state. But to speak here of an 'inhibited' historical process may be misleading, if it implies that the course of development leading to capitalism – which Marx traces from ancient Graeco-Roman civilization through Western feudalism to capitalism – has been the rule rather than the exception in world history and that all other historical experiences have been aberrations. Since Marx's primary object is to explain the unique development of capitalism in the West, and not its 'failure' to evolve 'spontaneously' elsewhere, his project itself implies that – despite some apparently ethnocentric assumptions – for him it is the achievement not the 'failure' that must be accounted for.

At any rate, the particular dynamic of the 'Asiatic' form, as Marx's argument implies, may be more common than the movement set in train by the ancient, Graeco-Roman form. If the primitive state was the controller of economic resources and the major appropriator and distributor of surplus product, the advanced 'Asiatic' state may represent a more or less natural development out of that primitive form – the appropriating redistributive public power at its highest stage of development. Seen in this light, it is not so much the 'hypertrophy' of the 'Asiatic' state that needs to be explained. What requires explanation is the aberrant, uniquely 'autonomous' development of the economic sphere that eventually issued in capitalism.[19]

FEUDALISM AND PRIVATE PROPERTY

The capitalist organization of production can be viewed as the outcome of a long process in which certain *political* powers were gradually transformed into *economic* powers and transferred to a separate sphere.[20] The organization of production under the authority of capital presupposes the organization of production and the assembling of a labour force under the authority of earlier forms of

---

[19] Ernest Mandel has criticized writers like Maurice Godelier for extending the meaning of the 'Asiatic mode of production' to include both social formations in the process of transition from classless society to class state and advanced bureaucratic empires with 'hypertrophied' states (Mandel, *The Formation of the Economic Thought of Karl Marx* [London, 1971], pp. 124 ff.). While Mandel is correct to warn against obscuring the differences between, say, simple African kingdoms and complex states like that of ancient Egypt, Godelier's formulation is intended to emphasize the continuities between early forms of appropriative and redistributive public authorities and the advanced 'hypertrophied' state in order to stress that it is the *Western* case, with its 'autonomous' development of private property and class, which needs to be explained. Mandel often talks about the development of capitalism as if it were natural while other historical trajectories have been stunted or obstructed.

[20] I would now emphasize the specificity of capitalist development much more than I did when I first wrote this essay. Although I would still say that the particular characteristics of Western feudalism I am outlining here were a necessary condition of capitalism, I would now also stress their *insufficiency*. Capitalism seems to me only one of several paths out of Western feudalism (quite apart from the variations within feudalism), which occurred in the first instance in England, in contrast, for example, to the Italian city-republics or French absolutism. These are themes I hope to take up in the future, but for a discussion of the contrast between English capitalism and French absolutism, see my *The Pristine Culture of Capitalism: A Historical Essay on Old Regime and Modern States* (London, 1991).

private property. The process by which this authority of private property asserted itself, uniting the power of appropriation with the authority to organize production in the hands of a private proprietor for his own benefit, can be viewed as the privatization of political power. The supremacy of absolute private property appears to have established itself in large part by means of political *devolution*, the assumption by private proprietors of functions originally invested in a public or communal authority.

Again, the opposition of the 'Asiatic' mode of production at one extreme and the capitalist mode at the other helps to place this devolutionary process in perspective. From this point of view, the crucial issue is not the presence or absence of private property in land as such. China, for example, had well-established private landed property from a very early stage; and, in any case, some form of property in land was often a perquisite of office in the 'Asiatic' state. The important point is the relation between private property and political power, and its consequences for the organization of production and the relation between appropriator and producer. The unique characteristic of Western development in this respect is that it is marked by the earliest and most complete transfer of political power to private property, and therefore also the most thorough, generalized, and direct subservience of production to the demands of an appropriating *class*.

The peculiarities of Western feudalism shed light on the whole process. Feudalism is often described as a fragmentation or 'parcellization' of state power; but while this description certainly identifies an essential characteristic, it is not specific enough. Forms of state power vary, and different forms of state power are likely to be differently fragmented. Western feudalism resulted from the fragmentation of a very particular form of political power. It is not here simply a matter of fragmentation or parcellization but also of *privatization*. The state power whose fragmentation produced Western feudalism had already been substantially privatized, located in private property. The form of imperial administration that preceded feudalism in the West, built upon the foundations of a state already grounded in private property and class rule, was unique in that imperial power was exercised not so much through a hierarchy of bureaucratic officials in the manner of the 'Asiatic' state, but through what has been described as a confederation of local aristocracies, a municipal system dominated by local private proprietors whose property endowed them with political authority as well as the power of surplus appropriation.

This mode of administration was associated with a particular kind of relationship between appropriators and producers, especially in the Western Empire where there were no remnants of an older redistributive-bureaucratic state organization. The relationship between appropriators and producers was in principle a relationship between individuals, the owners of private property and the individuals whose labour they appropriated, the latter directly subject to the former. Even taxation by the central state was mediated by the municipal system; and the imperial aristocracy was notable for the degree to which it relied more on private property than on office for the accumulation of great wealth. If in practice the landlord's control over production was indirect and tenuous, this still represents a significant contrast to early bureaucratic forms in which typically producers were more directly subject to an appropriating state acting through the medium of its officials.

With the dissolution of the Roman Empire (and the repeated failures of successor states), the imperial state was in effect broken into fragments in which political and economic powers were united in the hands of private lords whose political, juridical and military functions were at the same time instruments of private appropriation and the organization of production. The decentralization of the Imperial state was accompanied by the decline of chattel slavery and its replacement by new forms of dependent labour. Slaves and formerly independent peasants began to converge toward conditions of dependence, in which the economic relationship between individual private appropriator and individual producer was at the same time a political relationship between a 'fragment' of the state and its subject. In other words, each basic 'fragment' of the state was at the same time a productive unit in which production was organized under the authority and for the benefit of a private proprietor. Although in comparison to the later developments of capitalism the power of the feudal lord to direct production remained far from complete, a considerable step had been taken toward the integration of surplus extraction and the organization of production.[21]

[21] Cf. Rodney Hilton's discussion of the limited control exercised in practice by feudal lords over the productive process, in 'A Crisis of Feudalism', *Past and Present*, no. 80 (August 1978), pp. 9–10. It should be noted, however, that in stressing the limited nature of feudal

The fact that the property of the feudal lord was not 'absolute' but 'conditional' does not alter the fact that feudalism represents a great advance in the authority of private property. In fact, the conditional nature of feudal property was in a sense a hallmark of its strength, not a sign of weakness, since the condition on which the lord held his land was that he must become a fragment of the state invested with the very functions that gave him the power of surplus extraction. The coincidence of the political unit with the unit of property meant also a greater coincidence between the unit of appropriation and the unit of production, so that production could be organized more directly in the interests of the private appropriator.

The fragmentation of the state, the fact that feudal relations were at once a method of governing and a mode of exploitation, also meant that many *free* farmers now became subject with their properties to private masters, forfeiting surplus labour in exchange for personal protection, in a relationship of dependence that was both political and economic. As many more independent producers were brought into dependence, more production fell within the scope of direct, personal exploitation and class relations. The particular nature of the exploitive relation in feudalism and the fragmentation of the state also, of course, affected the configuration of class power, eventually making it both more desirable – in some respects, even necessary – and more possible for private appropriators to expropriate direct producers.

The essential characteristic of feudalism, then, was a privatization of political power which meant a growing integration of private appropriation with the authoritative organization of production. The eventual development of capitalism out of the feudal system perfected this privatization and integration – by the complete expropriation of the direct producer and the establishment of absolute private property. At the same time, these developments had as their necessary condition a new and stronger form of centralized public power. The state divested the appropriating class of direct political powers and duties not immediately concerned with production and appropriation, leaving them with private exploitative powers purified of public, social functions.

lordship, Hilton is not comparing feudalism to other pre-capitalist formations, but, at least implicitly, to capitalism, where the appropriator's direct control of production is more complete because of the expropriation of the direct producer, and the collective, concentrated nature of capitalist production.

CAPITALISM AS THE PRIVATIZATION OF POLITICAL POWER

It may seem perverse to suggest that capitalism represents the
ultimate privatization of political power. This proposition on the
face of it runs directly counter to the description of capitalism as
uniquely characterized by a differentiation of the economic and the
political. The intention of this description is, among other things,
precisely to contrast capitalism to the 'parcellization' of state power
which unites private political and economic power in the hands of
the feudal lord. It is, after all, capitalism that is marked not only by
a specialized economic sphere and economic modes of surplus
extraction but also by a central state with an unprecedented *public*
character.

Capitalism is uniquely capable of maintaining private property
and the power of surplus extraction without the proprietor wielding
direct political power in the conventional sense. The state – which
stands apart from the economy even though it *intervenes* in it – can
ostensibly (notably, by means of universal suffrage) belong to everyone, producer and appropriator, without usurping the exploitive
power of the appropriator. The expropriation of the direct producer
simply makes certain direct political powers less immediately necessary to surplus extraction. This is exactly what it means to say that
the capitalist has economic rather than extra-economic powers of
exploitation.

Overcoming the 'privatization' of political power may even be an
essential condition for the transformation of the labour process and
the forces of production which is the distinguishing characteristic of
capitalism. For example, as Robert Brenner has argued

where the direct application of force is the condition for ruling-class
surplus-extraction, the very difficulties of increasing productive potential
through the improvement of the productive forces may encourage the
expenditure of surplus to enhance precisely the capacity for the application
of force. In this way, the ruling class can increase its capacity to exploit the
direct producers, or acquire increased means of production (land, labour,
tools) through military methods. Rather than being accumulated, the
economic surplus is here systematically diverted from reproduction to
unproductive labour.[22]

[22] Robert Brenner, 'The Origins of Capitalism', *New Left Review*, 104 (1977), p. 37.

On the other hand, there is another sense in which private 'political' power is an essential condition of capitalist production and, in fact, the form assumed by the 'autonomy' of the economic sphere. The capitalist is, of course, subject to the imperatives of accumulation and competition which oblige him to expand surplus value; and the labourer is bound to the capitalist not simply by the latter's personal authority but by the laws of the market which dictate the sale of labour power. In these senses, it is the 'autonomous' laws of the economy and capital 'in the abstract' that exercise power, not the capitalist wilfully imposing his personal authority upon labour.

But what the 'abstract' laws of capitalist accumulation compel the capitalist to do – and what the impersonal laws of the labour market enable him to do – is precisely to exercise an unprecedented degree of control over production. 'The law of capitalist accumulation, metamorphosed by economists into pretended [sic] law of nature, in reality merely states that the very nature of accumulation excludes every diminution in the degree of exploitation';[23] and this means firm command of the labour process, even an internal legal code, to ensure the reduction of necessary labour time and the production of maximum surplus value within a fixed period of work. The need for a 'directing authority', as Marx explains, is intensified in capitalist production both by the highly socialized, cooperative nature of production – a condition of its high productivity – and by the antagonistic nature of an exploitive relationship based on the demand for maximum extraction of surplus value.

Capitalist *production* truly begins, argues Marx,

when each individual capital employs simultaneously a comparatively large number of labourers; when consequently the labour-process is carried on on an extensive scale and yields, relatively, large quantities of products. A greater number of labourers working together at the same time, in one place (or, if you will, in the same field of labour), in order to produce the same sort of commodity under the mastership of one capitalist, constitutes, both historically and logically, the starting point of capitalist production.[24]

A fundamental condition of this transformation is capital's control of the labour process. In other words, a specifically capitalist form of production begins when direct 'political' power is introduced into the production process itself, as a basic condition of production: 'By

---

[23] Marx, *Capital* I, p. 582.
[24] *Ibid.*, p. 305. Capitalist *production*, however, presupposes capitalist *social relations*. See below, p. 136 n. 35.

the cooperation of numerous wage-labourers, the sway of capital develops into a requisite for carrying on the labour process itself, into a real requisite of production. That a capitalist should command on the field of production is now as indispensable as that a general should command on the field of battle.'[25]

In pre-capitalist societies, cooperative production was simple and sporadic, though sometimes it had, as Marx puts it, 'colossal effects', for example, under the command of Asiatic and Egyptian kings or Etruscan theocrats. The special characteristic of capitalism is its systematic and continuous cooperative production. The political significance of this development in production is expressed by Marx himself: '*This power of Asiatic and Egyptian kings, Etruscan theocrats, etc., has in modern society been transferred to the capitalist*, whether he be an isolated, or as in joint-stock companies, a collective capitalist.'[26]

The issue here is not whether capitalist control is more 'despotic' than the harsh personal authoritarianism of the slave driver with whip in hand; nor whether capitalist exploitation is more oppressive than the demands of a rent-hungry feudal lord. The degree of control exercised by capital over production is not necessarily dependent upon its degree of 'despotism'. To some extent, control is imposed not by personal authority but by the impersonal exigencies of machine production and the technical integration of the labour process (though this can be exaggerated and, in any case, the need for technical integration is itself to a great extent imposed by the compulsions of capitalist accumulation and the demands of the appropriator).

While capital, with its absolute property in the means of production, has at its disposal new forms of purely 'economic' coercion – such as the power to dismiss workers or close plants – the nature of its control of the labour process is in part conditioned by its *lack* of direct coercive force. The intricate and hierarchical organization and supervision of the labour process as a means of increasing surplus in *production* is a substitute for a coercive power of surplus *extraction*. The nature of the free working class is also such that new forms of workers' organization and resistance are built into the production process.

In any case, capitalist control, in different circumstances, can be exercised in ways ranging from the most 'despotic' organization

---

[25] *Ibid.*, p. 313.   [26] *Ibid.*, p. 316. Emphasis added.

(e.g., 'Taylorism') to varying degrees of 'workers' control' (though the pressures against the latter inherent in the structure of capitalist accumulation should not be underestimated). But whatever specific forms capitalist control may take its essential conditions remain: in no other system of production is work so thoroughly disciplined and *organized*, and no other organization of production is so directly responsive to the demands of appropriation.

There are, then, two critical points about the capitalist organization of production which help to account for the peculiar character of the 'political' in capitalist society and to situate the *economy* in the political arena: first, the unprecedented degree to which the organization of production is integrated with the organization of appropriation; and second, the scope and generality of that integration, the virtually universal extent to which production in society as a whole comes under the control of the capitalist appropriator.[27] The corollary of these developments in production is that the appropriator relinquishes direct political power in the conventional, public sense, and loses many of the traditional forms of personal control over the lives of labourers outside the immediate production process which were available to pre-capitalist appropriators. New forms of indirect class control pass into the 'impersonal' hands of the state.

At the same time, if capitalism – with its juridically free working class and its impersonal economic powers – removes many spheres of personal and social activity from direct class control, human life generally is drawn more firmly than ever into the orbit of the production process. Directly or indirectly, the demands and

---

[27] Chattel slavery is the pre-capitalist form of class exploitation about which it might most convincingly be argued that the exploiter exercises a continuous and direct control over production; but leaving aside the many questions surrounding the nature and degree of the slave-owner's control of the labour process, one thing is clear: that even among the very few societies in which slavery has been widespread in production, it has never come close to the generality of wage labour in advanced capitalist societies but has always been accompanied, and possibly exceeded, by other forms of production. For example, in the Roman Empire, where ancient slavery reached its culmination in the slave latifundia, peasant producers still outnumbered slaves. Even if independent producers were subject to various forms of surplus *extraction*, large sections of *production* remained outside the scope of direct control by an exploiting class. It can be argued, too, that this was not accidental; that the nature of slave production made its generalization impossible; that not the least obstacle to its further expansion was its dependence on direct coercion and military power; and that, conversely, the uniquely universal character of capitalist production and its capacity to subordinate virtually all production to the demands of exploitation is inextricably bound up with the differentiation of the economic and the political.

discipline of capitalist production, imposed by the exigencies of capitalist appropriation, competition and accumulation, bring within their sphere of influence – and thus under the sway of capital – an enormous range of activity and exercise an unprecedented control over the organization of *time*, within and without the production process.

These developments betoken the existence of a differentiated economic sphere and economic laws, but their full significance may be obscured by viewing them only in this light. It is at least as important to regard them as a transformation of the *political* sphere. In one sense, the integration of production and appropriation represents the ultimate 'privatization' of politics, since functions formerly associated with a coercive political power – centralized or 'parcellized' – are now firmly lodged in the private sphere, as functions of a private appropriating class relieved of obligations to fulfil larger social purposes. In another sense, it represents the *expulsion* of politics from spheres in which it has always been directly involved.

Direct political coercion is excluded from the process of surplus extraction and removed to a state that generally intervenes only indirectly in the relations of production, and surplus extraction ceases to be an immediately political issue. This means that the focus of class struggle necessarily changes. As always, the disposition of surplus labour remains the central issue of class conflict; but now, that issue is no longer distinguishable from the organization of production. The struggle over appropriation appears not as a political struggle but as a battle over the terms and conditions of work.

THE LOCALIZATION OF CLASS STRUGGLE

Throughout most of history, the central issues in class struggle have been surplus extraction and appropriation, not production. Capitalism is unique in its concentration of class struggle 'at the point of production', because it is only in capitalism that the organization of production and of appropriation so completely coincide. It is also unique in its transformation of struggles over appropriation into apparently non-political contests. For example, while the wage struggle in capitalism may be perceived as merely 'economic' ('economism'), the same is not true of the rent struggle waged by medieval peasants, even though the issue in both cases is the disposition of surplus labour and its relative distribution between direct producers and exploiting appropriators. However fierce the struggle over wages may be, the wage relationship itself, as Marx points out, remains intact: the basis of the appropriator's extractive powers – the status of his property and the propertylessness of the labourer – are not immediately at stake. Struggles over rent, wherever appropriation rests on 'extra-economic' powers, tend more immediately to implicate property rights, political powers and jurisdictions.

Class conflict in capitalism tends to be encapsulated within the individual unit of production, and this gives class struggle a special character. Each individual plant, a highly organized and integrated unity with its own hierarchy and structure of authority, contains within it the main sources of class conflict. At the same time class struggle enters directly into the organization of production: that is, the management of antagonistic relations of production is inseparable from the management of the production process itself. While class conflict remains an integral part of the production process which it must not disrupt, class struggle must be *domesticated*.

Class conflict generally breaks into open war only when it goes outdoors, particularly since the coercive arm of capital is outside the wall of the productive unit. This means that when there are violent confrontations, they are usually not directly between capital and labour. It is not capital itself but the state that conducts class conflict when it intermittently breaks outside the walls and takes a more violent form. The armed power of capital usually remains in the background; and when class domination makes itself felt as a direct and personal coercive force, it appears in the guise of an 'autonomous' and 'neutral' state.

The transformation of political into economic conflicts and the location of struggles at the point of production also tend to make class struggle in capitalism *local* and *particularistic*. In this respect, the organization of capitalist production itself resists the working-class unity which capitalism is supposed to encourage. On the one hand, the nature of the capitalist economy – its national, even supra-national, character, the interdependence of its constituent parts, the homogenization of work produced by the capitalist labour process – make both necessary and possible a working-class consciousness and class organization on a mass scale. This is the aspect of capitalism's effects on class consciousness that Marxist theory has so often emphasized. On the other hand, the development of this consciousness and this organization must take place against the centrifugal force of capitalist production and its privatization of political issues.

The consequences of this centrifugal effect, if not adequately accounted for by theories of class consciousness, have often been remarked upon by observers of industrial relations who have noted the growing rather than declining importance of 'domestic' struggles in contemporary capitalism. While the concentration of working-class battles on the domestic front may detract from the political and universal character of these struggles, it does not necessarily imply a declining militancy. The paradoxical effect of capitalism's differentiation of the economic and the political is that militancy and political consciousness have become separate issues.

It is worth considering, by contrast, that modern revolutions have tended to occur where the capitalist mode of production has been less developed; where it has coexisted with older forms of production, notably peasant production; where 'extra-economic' compulsion has played a greater role in the organization of production and the extraction of surplus labour; and where the state has acted not only as a support for appropriating classes but as something like a pre-capitalist appropriator in its own right – in short, where economic struggle has been inseparable from political conflict and where the state, as a more visibly centralized and universal class enemy, has served as a focus for mass struggle. Even in more developed capitalist societies, mass militancy tends to emerge in response to 'extra-economic' compulsion, particularly in the form of oppressive action by the state, and also varies in proportion to the state's involvement in conflicts over the terms and conditions of work.

These considerations again raise questions about the sense in which it is appropriate to regard working-class 'economism' in advanced capitalist societies as reflecting an undeveloped state of class consciousness, as many socialists do. Seen from the perspective of historical process, it can be said to represent a more, rather than a less, advanced stage of development. If this stage is to be surpassed in turn, it is important to recognize that the so-called 'economism' of working-class attitudes does not so much reflect a lack of political consciousness as an objective shift in the location of politics, a change in the arena and the objects of political struggle inherent in the very structure of capitalist production.

These are some of the ways in which capitalist production tends to transform 'political' into 'economic' struggles. There are, it is true, certain trends in contemporary capitalism that may work to counteract these tendencies. The national and international integration of the advanced capitalist economy increasingly shifts the problems of capitalist accumulation from the individual enterprise to the 'macro-economic' sphere. It is possible that capital's powers of appropriation, which the state has so far left intact, indeed reproduced and reinforced, will be subverted by capital's own growing need for the state – not only to facilitate capitalist planning, to assume liabilities or to conduct and contain class conflict, but also to perform the social functions abandoned by the appropriating class, indeed to counteract its anti-social effects. At the same time, if capital in its mounting crises demands, and obtains, the state's complicity in its anti-social purposes, that state may increasingly become a prime target of resistance in advanced capitalist countries, as it has been in every successful modern revolution. The effect of this may be to overcome the particularism and the 'economism' imposed on the class struggle by the capitalist system of production, with its differentiation of the economic and the political.

In any case, the strategic lesson to be learned from the transfer of 'political' issues to the 'economy' is not that class struggles ought to be primarily concentrated in the economic sphere or 'at the point of production'. Nor does the division of 'political' functions between class and state mean that power in capitalism is so diffused throughout civil society that the state ceases to have any specific and privileged role as a locus of power and a target of political action, nor, alternatively, that everything *is* the 'state'. Indeed, the opposite is true. The division of labour between class and state means not so much that power is diffuse, but, on the contrary, that the state, which represents the coercive 'moment' of capitalist class domination, embodied in the most highly specialized, exclusive, and centralized monopoly of social force, is ultimately the decisive point of concentration for all power in society.

Struggles at the point of production, then, even in their economic aspects as struggles over the terms of sale of labour power or over the conditions of work, remain incomplete as long as they do not extend to the locus of power on which capitalist property, with its control of production and appropriation, ultimately rests. At the same time, purely 'political' battles, over the power to govern and rule, remain unfinished until they implicate not only the institutions of the state but the political powers that have been privatized and transferred to the economic sphere. In this sense, the very differentiation of the economic and the political in capitalism – the symbiotic division of labour between class and state – is precisely what makes the unity of economic and political struggles essential, and what ought to make socialism and democracy synonymous.

CHAPTER 2

Rethinking base and superstructure

The base/superstructure metaphor has always been more trouble than it is worth. Although Marx himself used it very rarely and only in the most aphoristic and allusive formulations, it has been made to bear a theoretical weight far beyond its limited capacities. To some extent, the problems already inherent in its original short-hand usage were aggravated by Engels' tendency to use language suggesting the compartmentalization of self-enclosed spheres or 'levels' – economic, political, ideological – whose relations with one another were external. But the real problems began with the establishment of Stalinist orthodoxies which elevated – or reduced – the metaphor to the first principle of Marxist–Leninist dogma, asserting the supremacy of a self-contained economic sphere over other passively reflexive subordinate spheres. More particularly, the economic sphere tended to be conceived as more or less synonymous with the technical forces of production, operating according to intrinsic natural laws of technological progress, so that history became a more or less mechanical process of technological development.

These deformations of Marx's original historical–materialist insights have fixed the terms of Marxist debate ever since. Both sides of the various disputes that have raged among Marxists in the past several decades have been effectively locked into this theoretical grid. Sometimes there has been a tendency to treat the deformations as the Marxist gospel, and to accept or reject Marxism accordingly. Anyone (like E.P. Thompson) working somewhere in the fissures between the alternatives presented by this theoretical framework is likely to be badly misunderstood by supporters and critics alike, or to be dismissed as an anomaly, a theoretical impossibility.

Objections to the base/superstructure metaphor have generally concerned its 'reductionism', both its denial of human agency and its failure to accord a proper place to 'superstructural' factors, to consciousness as embodied in ideology, culture or politics. Corrections to this reductionism have most commonly taken the form of a so-called Marxist 'humanism', or else an emphasis on the 'relative autonomy' of the 'levels' of society, their mutual interaction, and a deferral of determination by the 'economic' to 'the last instance'. One of the most important developments in contemporary Western Marxist theory, the structuralist Marxism of Althusser, rejected the humanist option and elaborated the other in a number of peculiar and theoretically sophisticated ways.

Faced with a choice between a simplistic and mechanical base/superstructure model, on the one hand, and apparently unstructured 'human agency', on the other, Althusser and his adherents found an ingenious solution. They redefined the relations between base and superstructure in such a way that the vagaries of human agency could be 'rigorously' excluded from the science of society, insisting on completely 'structural' determinations, while at the same time allowing for the unpredictable specificity of historical reality. This they achieved by a certain amount of conceptual trickery; for while a rigid determinism prevailed in the realm of social structure, it turned out that this realm belonged for all practical purposes to the sphere of pure theory, while the real, empirical world – albeit of little interest to most Althusserian theoreticists – remained (all explicit denunciations of contingency notwithstanding) effectively contingent and irreducibly particular.

The critical Althusserian distinction between 'mode of production' and 'social formation' illustrates the point. The structurally determined mode of production simply does not exist empirically, while the actually existing social formation is particular, 'conjunctural', and capable of combining the various modes of production, and even various 'relatively (absolutely?) autonomous' structural levels, in an infinite number of indeterminate ways. The consequences of this simple dualism between the determinism of structuralist theory and the contingency to which it relegated history were disguised by the fact that Althusserians wrote very little history, but also by the deceptive rigour of their ventures into the empirical world, where simple description was dressed up as theoretically rigorous causal explanation through the medium of infinitely expandable taxonomic categories derived from the theory of structure.

Althusserian Marxism, then, did little to shift the terms of Marxist theoretical debate decisively away from the terrain established by Stalinist orthodoxy. The base/superstructure model retained its mechanical character and its conceptualization of social structure in terms of discrete, discontinuous, externally related 'factors', 'levels' or 'instances', even if the mechanically deterministic relation between the base and its superstructural reflections was rendered effectively inoperative in the real world by the rigid separation between structure and history and by the indefinite postponement of economic determination to an unforeseeable 'last instance'. The structuralist conceptual apparatus also tended to encourage the kind of separation of the 'economic' from the 'social' and 'historical' which often entails the identification of the 'economic' with technology; and it is not surprising to find Marxists of structuralist persuasion looking to technological determinism to supply the historical dynamism missing from their view of the world as a series of discontinuous, self-enclosed and static structures.

For the time being, then, without abandoning the false alternatives of the debates surrounding Stalinism, Marxists could have their cake and eat it too. They could eschew 'crude economism' or 'vulgar reductionism' without abandoning the crudely mechanical model of base and superstructure. All that was required was that they adopt the sharp Althusserian dualism between structure and history, absolute determinism and irreducible contingency. And despite the Althusserian contempt for 'empiricism' – or precisely because of it (at least, precisely because of the conceptual dualism on which it was based) – it was in principle even possible to engage in the purest theory and the most unalloyed empiricism at once.

Yet it was only a matter of time before this uneasy synthesis fell apart. It soon turned out that Althusserianism had simply replaced – or supplemented – the old false alternatives with new ones. Marxists had been offered a choice between structure and history, absolute determinism and irreducible contingency, pure theory and unalloyed empiricism. It is not surprising, then, that the purest theoreticists of the Althusserian school became the most unalloyed empiricists of the post-Althusserian generation, at least in theory. In the work of writers like Hindess and Hirst, formerly the most rabid of anti-'historicists' and anti-'empiricists', the absolute and unconditional determinations of structure gave way to the absolute and irreducible contingency of the particular 'conjuncture'.[1] The 'post-Marxist' assertion of the 'non-correspondence' between the economic and the political – as well as the abandonment of class politics which this implies – the rejection not only of the crude base/superstructure model but also of the complex historical materialist insights for which that unfortunate metaphor was intended to stand is thus simply the other side of the Althusserian coin.

The result has been a completely distorted framework of debate which threatens to exclude Marx himself from the range of theoretical possibility. According to the 'post-Marxist' frame of reference, it is simply not possible, for example, to reject 'crude economism' – generally conceived as technological determinism – and still to believe in class politics, the centrality of class conflict in history or the primacy of the working class in the struggle for socialism. If a united, revolutionary working class does not emerge full grown from the natural development of productive forces in capitalism, there is no organic or 'privileged' connection between the working class and socialism, or indeed between economic conditions and political forces. In other words, again, where there is no simple, absolute and mechanical determination, there is absolute contingency. So much for Marx and historical materialism.

And so much, too, for Edward Thompson; for perhaps more than anyone else, he has fallen through the cracks of Marxist debate in recent years because he fails to match any of the recognized alternatives. This is, of course, not to say that he has been ignored, discounted or undervalued, but rather that both his critics and his admirers have often misrepresented him by forcing him into one of the available categories. In the opposition between 'crude economism' and 'Marxist humanism', he must be a humanist for whom economic laws give way to an arbitrary human will and agency. In the debate between Althusserians and culturalists, he is a – even the original – culturalist, for whom structural determinations are dissolved in 'experience'. And in current debates, he is perhaps equally likely to be misappropriated by the philosophers of 'discourse', relegated to the camp of 'class reductionists', or else dismissed as a theoretical anomaly who, while showing a healthy disdain for 'crude economism' and an appreciation of ideology and culture, still retains

---

[1] These bald assertions about Hindess, Hirst *et al.* are developed at greater length in my book, *The Retreat from Class* (London, 1986).

an irrational belief in the centrality of class. To some extent he invited these distorting classifications by allowing himself to be trapped in the prevailing terms of debate; but in his explicit pronouncements on theoretical matters, and even more in his historiographical practice, can be found the lost threads of a Marxist tradition which these false choices have systematically hidden from view.

MODES OF PRODUCTION AND SOCIAL FORMATIONS

Let us approach the question as it were from behind, with Thompson's controversial criticisms of Althusser and in particular his remarks on the Althusserian conceptions of mode of production and social formation. In *The Poverty of Theory*, Thompson accused Althusser of identifying the mode of production with the social formation – for example, the capitalist mode of production with capitalism – so that an abstract though not crudely economistic account of the laws of capital comes to stand for 'a social formation in the totality of its relations'.[2] In other words, Althusser, like Marx in his 'Grundrisse face', was accused by Thompson of treating capital virtually as a Hegelian Idea unfolding itself in history and embodying within itself the whole of capitalist society, 'capital in the totality of its relations'.

This criticism, as it stands, was rather ill-judged; for as Perry Anderson pointed out, Althusser and Balibar took up the concept of social formation, deliberately distinguishing it from 'mode of production', precisely in order to correct the 'constant confusion in Marxist literature between the social formation and its economic infrastructure'.[3] The concept 'social formation' was adopted by the Althusserians in preference to 'society' – a concept that 'suggested a deceptive simplicity and unity ... the Hegelian notion of a circular, expressive totality' –

as a forcible reminder that the diversity of human practices in any society is irreducible to economic practice alone. The issue it addressed was precisely that which gives rise to Thompson's anxieties about base and superstructure: the difference between the bare economic structures of 'capital' and the intricate fabric of social, political, cultural and moral life of (French or English or American) capitalism.[4]

[2] E.P. Thompson, *The Poverty of Theory* (London, 1978), p. 346.
[3] Perry Anderson, *Arguments Within English Marxism* (London, 1980), p. 67.
[4] *Ibid.*, p. 68 .

In other words, argued Anderson, Thompson had 'contrived to convict his opponents of an error which they were the first to name'.

And yet, there remains an important sense in which Thompson was right, because the very form in which the distinction between mode of production and social formation was drawn by Althusser and Balibar reinforced rather than corrected the confusion. In part, their correction simply reproduced the very mistakes in the base/superstructure metaphor which it was intended to correct; in part, they deprived the metaphor of precisely those valuable insights which it was intended to convey.

The 'mode of production' as conceived by Althusserians has theoretically inscribed within it an entire social structure, containing various 'levels', economic, political, ideological. In the case of Althusser and Balibar themselves, it may not be so clear that the concept 'mode of production' is actually synonymous with that totality, but it certainly constitutes the basis from which a social totality – 'capitalism' in the totality of its economic, political and ideological relations – can be theoretically generated. In other prominent theorists of Althusserian provenance – notably Nicos Poulantzas – the 'mode of production' itself explicitly stands for the totality:

By *mode of production* we shall designate not what is generally marked out as the economic (i.e. relations of production in the strict sense), but a specific combination of various structures and practices which, in combination, appear as so many instances or levels, i.e. as so many regional structures of this mode. A mode of production, as Engels stated schematically, is composed of different levels or instances, the economic, political, ideological and theoretical.[5]

The concept of 'social formation' as used by these theoreticians is not intended to deny this relation between the mode of production and the social totality embodied in it – it is not, for example, intended to deny that the capitalist mode of production (CMP) equals capitalism in the totality of its relations. Instead, the concept of social formation simply implies that no historically existing indi-

[5] Nicos Poulantzas, *Political Power and Social Classes* (London, 1973), p. 15. There is, incidentally, little justification for Poulantzas' appeal to Engels' authority for this conception of the mode of production. Engels' reference to 'factors' or 'elements' – however much it may have contributed to the treatment of the 'economic', the 'political', etc., as spatially separate and self-enclosed spheres or 'levels' – applies to the various forces which together determine the history of any social whole; but it does not appear in the definition of the 'mode of production' itself.

vidual social entity is 'pure'; for example, no existing society represents the CMP pure and simple. Or, to put it another way, 'The mode of production constitutes an abstract-formal object which does not exist in the strong sense in reality.'[6] Only impure 'social formations' actually exist, and these will contain several coexisting modes of production with all their constitutent 'levels', or even several 'relatively autonomous' fragments of modes of production. The various elements comprising a social formation may even be out of phase with one another.

So rigidly determined and monolithic structural relations between self-enclosed economic and superstructural levels continue to exist in the theoretically constructed mode of production; but in the historical world, this structural bloc can be fragmented and recombined in an infinite number of ways. It is as if 'real, concrete' historical social formations are composed of elements whose inner structural logic is theoretically determined, while historical processes simply break up and recombine these elements in various (arbitrary and contingent?) ways. Historical analysis can, then, do little more than describe and classify the combinations of modes of production and fragments of modes of production that constitute any given social formation.

The practical consequences of this theoretical framework are vividly illustrated by Poulantzas's approach to the problem of politics in capitalist society. Having established the principle that an entire social structure – with economic, political, ideological and theoretical levels – is embodied in the 'abstract-formal' mode of production, he proceeds theoretically to construct the 'political instance' of the CMP and to produce a 'type' of state structurally befitting this mode of production. This involves the theoretical construction of connections between the state and different levels of the mode of production, as well as an elaboration of characteristics specific to the capitalist 'type' of state.

The effect of this argument is paradoxical. The implication seems to be that the connection among 'levels' of a mode of production, and specifically the correspondence between the CMP and the capitalist 'type' of state, is 'abstract-formal' rather than 'real-concrete', that the components of a mode of production may be related 'structurally' but not necessarily historically. On the one

[6] *Ibid.*

hand, then, structural logic overwhelms historical fact. On the other
hand, it appears that the relations that actually do prevail between
the state and the mode of production in historically existing social
formations may have little to do with this structural logic and
appear almost accidental. The parts of a mode of production, which
may be related by an ineluctable structural logic in the 'abstract-
formal' realm, can be easily detached from one another in historical
reality.

A state is capitalist, then, not by virtue of its connection to
capitalist relations of production but by virtue of certain structural
characteristics derived by autonomous theoretical construction from
an abstract formal CMP. Thus, it is possible to say that a social
formation in which capitalist relations of production do not yet
prevail may nevertheless be characterized by a 'capitalist' state.

This is, in fact, how Poulantzas describes European absolutism.[7]
The absolutist state is designated as a capitalist type of state not
because of any actual relation it bears to underlying capitalist
relations of production (Poulantzas is at pains to stress that capitalist
relations are very rudimentary at this stage) but because it displays
certain formal structural characteristics which he has, more or less
arbitrarily, established as corresponding in theory to the CMP.[8]

There is in these theoretical principles both too much rigid
determinism and too much arbitrariness and contingency – that is,
too much abstract, almost idealist, theoretical determination and
not enough historical causality. On the one hand, the mechanical
simplifications of the base/superstructure model have been left
intact; on the other hand, the critical questions indicated by that

[7] *Ibid.*, pp. 157–67.
[8] Treating absolutism as somehow a foretaste of capitalism, or as a reflection of a temporary
balance between a declining feudal class and a rising bourgeoisie, has been a common
practice among Marxists which reflects a tendency to beg the question of the transition from
feudalism to capitalism by assuming the existence of capitalism somewhere in the interstices
of feudalism, just waiting to be released. This procedure of assuming precisely what needs to
be explained is especially pronounced in structuralist Marxism, where bits of any or all
modes of production can, as required, be assumed to be present, without explanation and
without process, in any social formation, simply waiting to become 'dominant'. The rise of
capitalism can be 'explained' simply by asserting, tautologically, that the CMP, or some
significant piece of it (like a capitalist 'type' of state?) was already present in the combination of modes of production that constituted the relevant social formations. For a forceful
criticism of this aspect of Althusserianism, and of the Marxist tradition from which it arises,
together with a powerful argument demonstrating the origins of this view of history in
'bourgeois' historiography and ideology, see George Comninel's *Rethinking the French Revolution* (London, 1987).

metaphor about the effects of material conditions and production relations on historical processes have simply been evaded. In fact, a priori theoretical correspondences have been allowed to conceal real historical relations.

All this is in sharp contrast to Marx's own account of the connection between production relations and political forms:

The specific economic form, in which unpaid surplus labour is pumped out of direct producers, determines the relationship between rulers and ruled, as it grows directly out of production itself and, in turn, reacts upon it as a determined element. . . . It is always the direct relationship of the owners of the conditions of production to the direct producers . . . which reveals the innermost secret, the hidden basis of the entire social structure, and with it the political form of the relations of sovereignty and dependence, the corresponding specific form of the state. This does not prevent the same economic base – the same from the standpoint of its main conditions – due to innumerable different empirical conditions . . . from showing infinite variations and gradations in appearance, which can be ascertained only by analysis of the empirically given circumstances.[9]

Although parts of this passage are much quoted by Poulantzas *et al.*, it reveals a conceptual framework rather different from the Althusserian distinction between 'mode of production' and 'social formation'. It conveys neither the mechanical determinism of the Althusserian 'mode of production' nor the arbitrary contingency of the 'social formation'. Instead, it suggests both the complex variability of empirical reality and the operation within it of a logic derived from production relations.

The difference is further illustrated by Marx's own use of the concept rendered by the Althusserians as 'social formation', a usage that differs substantially from that of Althusser, Balibar or Poulantzas (quite apart from whether the concept was ever intended to carry the theoretical burden it has recently acquired). In a passage that figures centrally in Althusserian theory, Marx writes:

In all forms of society [which is in the context a less misleading translation of *Gesellschaftsformen* than is 'social formation'] there is a specific kind of production which predominates over the rest, whose relations thus assign rank and influence to the others. It is a general illumination which bathes all the other colours and modifies their particularity. It is a particular ether which determines the specific gravity of every being which has materialized within it.[10]

[9] Karl Marx, *Capital* III (Moscow, 1971), pp. 791–3.
[10] Karl Marx, *Grundrisse*, tr. M. Nicolaus (Harmondsworth, 1973), pp. 106–7.

It is instructive to note what he means by 'forms of society'. They include 'pastoral peoples', 'antiquity', 'the feudal order', 'modern bourgeois society'. Whatever else this passage may mean – and whatever problems may arise from Marx's formulations – it implies that:

1. 'form of society' refers to something like feudalism (the feudal order) or capitalism (bourgeois society), not simply an individual and unique 'concrete' phenomenon like 'England during the Industrial Revolution' (one of Poulantzas' examples of a 'social formation'), but a class of concrete phenomena which have some kind of common socio-historical logic; and

2. the point of the passage is, if anything, to stress the unity, not the 'heterogeneity', of a 'social formation'.

It is not a question of several modes of production dominated by one, but, for example, different branches of production assimilated to the specific character of the branch that predominates in that social form: the particular nature of agriculture in feudal society – characterized by peasant production and feudal appropriation – affects the nature of industry; the particular nature of industry in 'bourgeois society' – industry dominated by capital – affects the nature of agriculture. Marx's use of the concept here has a rather limited and narrow application, but one which is not inconsistent with his later, more developed insights as outlined in volume III of *Capital*.

Taken together, then, these passages from *Capital* and the *Grundrisse* convey that there is a unifying logic in the relations of production which imposes itself throughout a society, in the complex variety of its empirical reality, in a way that entitles us to speak of a 'feudal order' or 'capitalist society' but without depriving individual feudal or capitalist societies of their 'intricate fabric of social, political, cultural, and moral life'.

Thompson himself, despite his reservations about Marx's 'Grundrisse face', makes a distinction that nicely sums up Marx's approach. The 'profound intuition' of historical materialism as conceived by Marx, argues Thompson, is not that capitalist societies are simply 'capital in the totality of its relations', but rather 'that the logic of capitalist process has found expression within all the activities of a society, and exerted a determining pressure upon its development and form: hence entitling us to speak of capitalism, or of capitalist societies'.[11] There is a critical difference, he continues, between a

---

[11] Thompson, *Poverty of Theory*, p. 254.

structuralism which suggests an 'Idea of capital unfolding itself', and historical materialism, which has to do with 'a real historical process'.

Thompson was, then, at least half right in his criticism of Althusser, not because Althusser dissolved history into structure, but, on the contrary, because, while indeed adhering to a kind of structuralism, which identified the CMP with capitalism, he reserved its operations for the sphere of pure theory while leaving history more or less to itself. In fact, Thompson himself formulated his criticism of Althusser in almost exactly these terms in an essay far less well known than *The Poverty of Theory*, but dating from about the same time: in Althusserian theory, he writes, 'with its emphasis upon "relative autonomy" and "in the last instance determination", the problems of historical and cultural materialism are not so much solved as shuffled away or evaded; since the lonely hour of the last instance never strikes, we may at one and the same time pay pious lip-service to the theory and take out a licence to ignore it in our practice'.[12]

If there is some truth in the suggestion that the Althusserian distinction between mode of production and social formation was intended to make Marxists, brought up in the shadow of a crudely economistic and reductionist base/superstructure model, more sensitive to historical specificity and the complexity of social life, this too is only a half truth; for the distinction achieved its end simply by driving a wedge between structure and history and creating a rigid dualism between determination and contingency which left structural determinations more or less impotent in the sphere of historical explanation and in effect disabled historical materialism as a way of explaining historical processes. This was simply an evasion of the challenge posed by Marx himself: how to encompass historical specificity, as well as human agency, while recognizing within it the logic of modes of production.

HISTORICAL MATERIALISM VERSUS ECONOMIC DETERMINISM

It is precisely this challenge that Edward Thompson tried to meet in his historical writings. His theoretical pronouncements are not

[12] Thompson, 'Folklore, Anthropology, and Social History', *Studies in Labour History Pamphlet* (1979), p. 19 (originally published in *Indian Historical Review*, 3 (2) (1978), pp. 247–66).

always helpful in illuminating his historical practice – partly
because he occasionally allows himself to be trapped in the false
alternatives offered by the prevailing terms of Marxist debate.[13]
Even here, however, there is much wealth that could be mined to
emancipate Marxist theory from these Hobson's choices and put it
back on the fruitful track marked out by Marx himself. One or two
things are particularly worth noting in Thompson's explicit remarks
on the base/superstructure metaphor over the years. It is well known
that he was always concerned to rescue human agency and
consciousness from the dead hand of crudely reductionist econo-
misms, and there is no need to rehearse that point here. His preoccupation with 'experience' has received more than enough attention,
even if the effects of that attention have often been misleading.[14]
What has tended to get lost in this emphasis on Thompson's
'humanism' is that its corollary is often an appreciation of structural
determinations in historical processes which is rather more illuminating than that of his structuralist critics.

The mechanical base/superstructure model, with its 'levels' conceived as self-enclosed, spatially separate and discontinuous boxes,
allows only two unacceptable choices: either we adhere to the
'orthodox' simplistic reductionism according to which the basic
'economic' box is simply 'reflected' in superstructural boxes; or we
can avoid 'crude economism' only by postponing determination by
the 'economic' to some infinitely distant 'last instance', an effect
achieved by rendering the rigid determinations of structure inoperative in history. Between these two extremes, there is little room for
'economic' determinations which, while allowing the full range of

[13] Nowhere is this more vividly illustrated than in Thompson's distaste for Marx's 'Grundrisse face' and his analysis of Marx's political economy. It is difficult to explain Thompson's
failure to see that it is precisely in Marx's critique of political economy that he spells out the
fully developed principles of historical materialism. Indeed, it can be argued that this is
where Marx laid down the very principles that Thompson has found most valuable in his
own historical work. In contrast, the *German Ideology*, for all its vital contributions to
historical materialism, still bears the traces of a relatively uncritical adherence to bourgeois
historiography. (This argument concerning the difference between Marx's uncritical
historiography, and the critique of political economy in which his own distinctive views
receive their fullest elaboration, appears in Comninel, *Rethinking the French Revolution.*) One
possible explanation of Thompson's blind spot is that he has been too ready to accept the
dichotomies arising from Stalinist theory, which seem to compel us to choose between a
crudely reductionist economism and a complete abandonment of Marx's political economy
'face'.

[14] See Harvey J. Kaye, *The British Marxist Historians* (Oxford, 1984) for an excellent general
discussion of Thompson and specifically his relationship to the Anglo-Marxist historiographical tradition of Dobb, Hilton, Hill *et al.*

historical complexity and specificity, are nevertheless (to quote Thompson) 'there all the time' – not just 'in the last instance', not 'thrust back to an area of ultimate causation ... [which] can be forgotten in its empyrean', not 'operative only in an epochal sense', but all the time.[15]

This is the difficult dialectic between historical specificity and the always present logic of historical process that historical materialism asks us to comprehend. It requires, as Thompson has always understood, a conception of the 'economic', not as a 'regionally' separate sphere which is somehow 'material' as opposed to 'social', but rather as itself irreducibly social – indeed, a conception of the 'material' as constituted by social relations and practices. Furthermore, the 'base' – the process and relations of production – is not just 'economic' but also entails, and is embodied in, juridical-political and ideological forms and relations that cannot be relegated to a spatially separate superstructure.

If the base/superstructure metaphor can be made to encompass these insights, all well and good; but it is, according to Thompson, a bad metaphor because it obscures the nature of the very relations it is meant to indicate. 'We must say', Thompson suggests about this unfortunate metaphor, 'that the sign-post was pointing in the wrong direction, while, at the same time, we must accept the existence of the place towards which it was mispointing. . . .'[16] That place is the 'kernel of human relationships' embodied in the mode of production, a kernel of relationships that imposes its logic at every 'level' of society. In a comment on Raymond Williams's *The Long Revolution*, Thompson writes:

when we speak of the capitalist mode of production for profit we are indicating at the same time a 'kernel' of characteristic human relationships – of exploitation, domination, and acquisitiveness which are inseparable from this mode, and which find simultaneous expression in all of Mr Williams' 'systems'. Within the limits of the epoch there are characteristic tensions and contradictions, which cannot be transcended unless we transcend the epoch itself: there is an economic logic *and* a moral logic and it is futile to argue as to which we give priority since they are different expressions of the same 'kernel of human relationship'. We may then rehabilitate the notion of capitalist or bourgeois culture. . . .[17]

---

[15] Thompson, 'The Peculiarities of the English', in *The Poverty of Theory*, pp. 81–2.

[16] 'An Open Letter to Leszek Kolakowski', in Thompson, *Poverty of Theory*, p. 120.

[17] E.P. Thompson, 'The Long Revolution, II', *New Left Review* 10 (1961), pp. 28–9.

There are undoubtedly pitfalls in the formula that production relations 'find simultaneous expression' at all 'levels' of society, not in an ascending sequence proceeding from a determinative economic 'base' to an epiphenomenal superstructure. 'Simultaneous' determination could be construed as no determination, even no causality, at all. But Thompson's conception of 'simultaneity' is rather more subtle than that.[18] His argument is directed, as we have seen, against both reductionist conceptions of causality that dissolve historical specificity *and* conceptions of economic determination in which determination is indefinitely postponed. The first conflates cause and effect, the second opens up an unbridgeable distance between them. Neither requires investigation of the *relation* between cause and effect or the *process* of determination. What interests Thompson is the relations and processes in which production relations – relations of exploitation, domination and appropriation – shape or exert pressure upon all aspects of social life at once and all the time.

The process and relations of production which constitute a mode of production are expressed in a 'moral' as well as an 'economic' logic, in characteristic values and modes of thought as well as in characteristic patterns of accumulation and exchange. It is only in the capitalist mode of production that it is even possible to distinguish institutions and practices that are purely and distinctly 'economic' (in the narrow sense of the word, which is itself derived from the experience of capitalism); and even here, the mode of production is expressed simultaneously in those 'economic' institutions and practices and in certain attendant norms and values that sustain the processes and relations of production and the system of power and domination around which they are organized. These values, norms and cultural forms, argues Thompson, are no less 'real' than the specifically 'economic' forms in which the mode of production is expressed.

There are two inseparable and equally important sides to Thompson's argument about the simultaneity of 'economic' and 'cultural' expressions in any mode of production. The first, which is the one most commonly stressed by his critics and admirers alike, insists that ideology and culture have a 'logic' of their own which constitutes an 'authentic' element in social and historical processes.

[18] The notion of 'simultaneity' is also discussed in Thompson, 'Folklore', pp. 17–18.

'We may legitimately analyse ideology not only as product but also as process,' he observes in his critical appreciation of Christopher Caudwell, in which he both approves Caudwell's understanding of the 'authenticity' of culture and castigates him for attributing to the logic of ideology an autonomy that suggests 'an idea imposing itself on history'.[19] He continues:

it has its own logic which is, in part, self-determined, in that given categories tend to reproduce themselves in consecutive ways. While we cannot substitute the ideological logic for the real history – capitalist evolution is not the acting out of a basic bourgeois idea – nevertheless this logic is an authentic component of that history, a history inconceivable and indescribable independent of the 'idea'.

The other side of the argument is that, if the determinative effects of the mode of production are simultaneously operative in both the 'economy' and in 'non-economic' spheres, they are also ubiquitous. The intent of the argument is not to deny or play down the determinative effects of the mode of production, but on the contrary, to reinforce the proposition that they are 'operative all the time' and everywhere. In other words, Thompson is perhaps at his most materialist at the very moment when he refuses to privilege the 'economy' over 'culture'. Indeed, the insistence on 'simultaneity' appears not as a departure from, or correction of, classical Marxist materialism but as a gloss on Marx's own words. Commenting on the above-cited 'general illumination' passage of the *Grundrisse*, for example, Thompson writes:

What this emphasizes is the simultaneity of expression of characteristic productive relations in *all* systems and areas of social life rather than any notion of primacy (more 'real') of the 'economic', with the norms and culture seen as some secondary 'reflection' of the primary. What I am calling in question is not the centrality of the mode of production (and attendant relations of power and ownership) to any materialist under-standing of history. I am calling in question . . . the notion that it is possible to describe a mode of production in 'economic' terms, leaving aside as secondary (less 'real') the norms, the culture, the critical concepts around which this mode of production is organized.[20]

We might wish for more precise indications of the boundaries between the 'mode of production' and that which is determined by

[19] E.P. Thompson, 'Caudwell', *Socialist Register* (1977), pp. 265–6.
[20] Thompson, 'Folklore', pp. 17–18.

it, and perhaps something less of a tendency to slide from the proposition that the mode of production is 'expressed' simultaneously in both economic and non-economic spheres, into the rather different suggestion that the mode of production *is* every social thing at once. But there can be little doubt that the intention of this argument is not only to stress the 'authenticity' of culture but also to rescue a materialist understanding of history from formulations which separate out the social 'levels' in a way that effectively detaches the 'superstructure' from the effects of the material 'base'.

It is also an effort to rescue the original Marxist conception of the 'mode of production' from its identification with the capitalist 'economy', as embodied in market relations and/or some abstractly autonomous 'technology'. This is an identification which Stalinist orthodoxy shared with bourgeois ideology; which Althusserian theory perpetuated in its delineation of 'levels' or 'instances', in the very process of seeking to detach itself from 'vulgar economism'; and which today's 'post-Marxist' critics of Marxism – so many of whom were formed in the Althusserian school – have repeated, somewhat irrelevantly repudiating their own straw Marxism while reproducing its distortions in their own conceptions of the 'economic' sphere.

It may be true that Thompson does not always sustain the clarity of his 'unitary' conception and sometimes appears to allow the 'mode of production' to expand into an indeterminate totality of human relations. But there is a significant difference between the claim that 'base' is also and at the same time 'superstructure', and Thompson's proposition that

Production, distribution and consumption are not only digging, carrying and eating, but are also planning, organizing and enjoying. Imaginative and intellectual faculties are not confined to a 'superstructure' and erected on a 'base' of things (including men-things); they are implicit in the creative act of labour which makes man man.[21]

Another illustration might be his argument that the law does not 'keep politely' to a superstructural 'level' but appears 'at *every* bloody level' and is 'imbricated within the mode of production and productive relations themselves (as property rights, definitions of agrarian practice . . .)'.[22] These propositions do not mean that the base includes all superstructure, or that production relations are

[21] E.P. Thompson, 'Socialist Humanism', *New Reasoner*, 1 (1957), pp. 130–1.
[22] Thompson, *Poverty of Theory*, p. 288.

synonymous with all social relations structured by class antagonisms. (Isn't this just another way of saying that mode of production
equals social formation, a conception to which Thompson strongly
objects?) They mean that some so-called 'superstructure' belongs to
the productive 'base' and is the form in which production relations
themselves are organized, lived and contested. In this formulation
the specificity, integrity and determinative force of production relations are preserved; and, in a sense, the requisite distance which
makes causality possible, between the sphere of production and
other social 'levels', is established, while at the same time the
principle of connection and continuity between these separate
spheres is indicated by treating the 'economy' itself as a *social*
phenomenon.

This brings us to another, especially subtle, reason for Thompson's rejection of the conventional base/superstructure metaphor;
and here again the object is not to weaken but to reinforce the
materialism in the Marxist theory of history. Thompson has suggested that the metaphor fails to take account of the different ways
in which different classes are related to the mode of production, the
different ways in which their respective institutions, ideologies and
cultures 'express' the mode of production.[23] While the base/
superstructure model may have a certain value as an account of
partisan ruling-class institutions and ideologies, the supportive
structures of domination and the 'common sense of power', it is
ill-suited to describe the culture of the ruled.

The customs, rituals and values of subordinate classes can, as
Thompson puts it, 'often be seen to be intrinsic to the mode of
production' in a way that the dominant culture is not, because they
are integral to the very processes of reproducing life and its material
conditions. They are, in short, often the very practices that constitute productive activity itself. At the same time, although the
culture of the ruled often remains 'congruent' with the prevailing
system of production and power, it is because production relations
are experienced by subordinate classes in their own particular ways
that they can come into contradiction with the 'common sense of
power'; and it is such contradictions that produce the struggles
which determine the reorganization and transformation of modes of
production.

---

[23] See especially Thompson, 'Folklore', pp. 20–2.

Historical transformations of this kind, argues Thompson, do not occur simply and spontaneously because (autonomous) changes in the base produce changes in the superstructure (as, for example, in technological determinism). They occur because changes in material life become the terrain of struggle. If anything, it could be said – although Thompson does not say it in so many words, preferring to avoid the language of base and superstructure – that if historical transformations are produced by contradictions between base and superstructure, it is in the sense that these contradictions represent oppositions between, on the one hand, the experience of production relations as they are lived by subordinate classes and, on the other, the institutions and 'common sense' of power. But to put it this way is already to acknowledge that the single model of the relations between material 'base' and ideological 'superstructure' suggested by the conventional metaphor is not enough. That model misleads because it universalizes the ruling culture, or, more precisely, the relation between the ruling culture and the mode of production, and conceptualizes away the different kind of relation that generates historical movement.

Perhaps Thompson's view can best be summed up as an attempt to reassert Marx's own account of historical materialism as against the mechanical materialism of 'bourgeois' philosophy. His emphasis, like that of Marx, is on 'human sensuous activity, practice' (as Marx formulates his materialism in the famous attack on previous materialisms in the 'Theses on Feuerbach'), instead of on some abstract 'matter' or 'matter in motion'. And like Marx, Thompson recognizes that mechanical materialism is nothing more than another idealism, or the other side of the idealist coin. He recognizes, too, that the framework of contemporary Marxist debate has in many ways reproduced the same false dichotomies of bourgeois thought from which historical materialism was intended to liberate us:

we may have been witnessing within the heart of the Marxist tradition itself a reproduction of that phenomenon which Caudwell diagnosed within bourgeois culture: the generation of those pseudo-antagonists, mechanical materialism and idealism. The same subject/object dualism, entering into Marxism, has left us with the twins of economic determinism and Althusserian idealism, each regenerating the other: the material basis determines the superstructure, independent of ideality, while the superstructure of ideality retires into the autonomy of a self-determining theoretical practice.[24]

[24] Thompson, 'Caudwell', p. 244.

This is not, it must be stressed, simply a demand for a question-begging 'interactionism', or what Thompson himself calls a 'barren oscillation' between determinants in a process of 'mutual determination'. As Thompson understands very well, 'mutual interaction is scarcely determination';[25] and it is no more his intention than it was Marx's to evade the issue of determination in this way. His formulation is simply a way of taking seriously the Marxist understanding of the 'material base' as embodied in human practical activity, which, however much it may violate the sensibilities of 'scientific' Marxists, requires us to come to grips with the fact that the activity of material production is *conscious* activity.

BASE AND SUPERSTRUCTURE IN HISTORY

The meaning of all this becomes fully apparent only in Thompson's historical practice, and the value of his disagreements with the language of base and superstructure can be tested only by examining what he can perceive through his conceptual prism which others cannot see as clearly through their own. Two aspects of his historical work in particular stand out: a profound sense of process, expressed in an unequalled capacity for tracing the intricate interplay between continuity and change; and an ability to reveal the logic of production relations not as an abstraction but as an operative historical principle visible in the daily transactions of social life, in concrete institutions and practices outside the sphere of production itself. Both these skills are at work in his characteristic 'decoding' of evidence indicating the presence of class forces and modes of consciousness structured by class in historical situations where no clear and explicit class consciousness is available as unambiguous proof of the presence of class.

The theme running through *The Making of the English Working Class*, for example, is how a continuous tradition of popular culture was transformed into a working-class culture as people resisted the logic of capitalist relations and the intensification of exploitation associated with capitalist modes of expropriation. Thompson's critics have tended to focus on the continuities in this process, suggesting that his insistence on the continuity of popular traditions betokens a preoccupation with cultural, 'superstructural' factors at

[25] *Ibid.*, pp. 246–7.

the expense of objective determinations, movements in the 'base' where capitalist accumulation takes place – a criticism I shall take up in the next chapter.

The point of Thompson's argument, however, is to demonstrate the *changes* within the continuities precisely in order to show the logic of capitalist production relations at work in the 'superstructure'. Where a structuralist Marxist, who tends to view history as a series of discontinuous chunks, might see nothing but an ideological 'level' out of phase with the economic, a superstructural fragment left over from another mode of production, a juxtaposition of structural boxes, Thompson sees – and can give an account of – a historical dynamic of change within continuity (which is, after all, the way history generally proceeds, even through revolutionary moments) structured by the logic of capitalist relations. The structuralist, for whom a priori theoretical correspondences would render the actual historical connections invisible (as in the case of Poulantzas and the absolutist state), would be disarmed in the face of non-Marxist historians who dismiss the concept of class as nothing but an abstract theoretical category imposed on the evidence from without, or those who would deny the existence of a working class in this 'pre-industrial' or 'one-class' society, citing as evidence the continuity of 'pre-industrial' patterns of thought. Thompson, in contrast, is able to trace the changing social meanings of popular traditions, tracking the operations of class in these changes within continuity. He can account for the emerging working-class formations, institutions and intellectual traditions which, despite their visible presence in the history of the period, are conceptualized out of existence by his adversaries.

It is worth adding that, for those who regard the 'base' as something 'material' as *opposed* to 'social' – which generally means that the base consists of the technical forces of production and history is a technological determinism – the existence of working-class formations joining together 'industrial' and 'pre-industrial' workers must remain inexplicable. The conceptual framework of technological determinism compels us to place a premium on the technical process of work as a determinant of class, rather than on the relations of production and exploitation which for Thompson (as for Marx) are the critical factors and which alone can explain the common experience imposed by the logic of capitalist accumulation upon workers engaged in different labour processes.

The principles underlying Thompson's 'decoding' procedures are made more explicit in 'Eighteenth-century English Society: Class Struggle without Class?'. Here his object is, among other things, to demonstrate that class struggle can operate as a historical force even when fully developed notions of class and class consciousness do not yet exist, that '[b]ecause in other places and periods we can observe "mature" (i.e., self-conscious and historically developed) class formations, with ideological and institutional expression, this does not mean that whatever happens less decisively is not class'.[26] This project requires a 'decoding' of evidence which to other historians bespeaks a 'traditional', 'paternalistic' or 'one-class' society, in which the labouring classes lack any class consciousness and social divisions are vertical rather than horizontal.

Significantly, here Thompson again invokes the 'general illumination' passage from the *Grundrisse*, which the Althusserians cite in support of their views on modes of production and social formations. And significantly, too, like Marx but unlike the Althusserians, he stresses the unity, not the heterogeneity, of social forms as they come within the 'field of force' of a particular mode of production:

it seems to me that the metaphor of a field-of-force can co-exist fruitfully with Marx's comment in the *Grundrisse*, that: 'In all forms of society. . . .'

What Marx describes in metaphors of 'rank and influence', 'general illumination' and 'tonalities' would today be offered in more systematic structuralist language: terms sometimes so hard and objective-seeming ... that they disguise the fact that they are still metaphors which offer to congeal a fluent social process. I prefer Marx's metaphor; and I prefer it, for many purposes, to his subsequent metaphors of 'base' and 'superstructure'. But my argument in this paper is (to the same degree as Marx's) a structural argument. I have been forced to see this when considering the force of the obvious objections to it. For every feature of eighteenth century society to which attention has been directed may be found, in more or less developed form, in other centuries. . . . What then is specific to the eighteenth century? What is the 'general illumination' which modifies the 'specific tonalities' of its social and cultural life?[27]

Thompson then sets out to answer these questions by examining '(1) the dialectic between what is and is *not* culture – the formative experiences in social being, and how these were handled in cultural

---

[26] E.P. Thompson, 'Eighteenth-century English Society: Class Struggle without Class?', *Social History* 3 (2) (1978), p. 150.

[27] *Ibid.*, pp. 151–2. Thompson is using a different translation from the one cited above. Thus, the word he renders as 'tonalities' appears as 'colours' in the translation cited earlier.

ways, and (2) the dialectical polarities – antagonisms and recon-
ciliations – between the polite and plebeian cultures of the time.'[28]
Though it would be helpful to have a clearer account of what is 'not
culture', the result is an intricate and subtle argument which reveals
how 'traditional' patterns of culture, which on the surface remain
apparently unchanged, acquire a new social meaning as they come
within the 'field of force' of 'capitalist process' and capitalist modes
of exploitation. Thompson demonstrates how customary behaviour
and plebeian culture are shaped by new class experiences, citing as a
particularly evocative example the riots for the possession of the
bodies of the hanged at Tyburn, 'decoded' by Peter Linebaugh in
Albion's Fatal Tree:

> we cannot present the rioter as an archaic figure, motivated by the 'debris'
> of older patterns of thought, and then pass the matter off with a reference to
> death-superstitions and *les rois thaumaturges*. . . . The code which informs
> these riots, whether at Tyburn in 1731 or Manchester in 1832, cannot be
> understood only in terms of beliefs about death and its proper treatment. It
> involves also class solidarities, and the hostility of the plebs to the psychic
> cruelty of the law and to the marketing of primary values. Nor is it, in the
> eighteenth century, just that a taboo is being threatened: in the case of the
> dissection of corpses or the hanging of corpses in chains, one class was
> deliberately and as an act of terror breaking or exploiting the taboos of
> another. It is, then, within this class field-of-force that the fragmented
> debris of older patterns are revivified and reintegrated.[29]

What makes the eighteenth century an especially complicated
case is that customary behaviour and ritual acquire a particular
significance because the logic of capitalism was experienced by the
plebs so often as an attack on customary use-rights and traditional
patterns of work and leisure – a process vividly described by Thompson in several of his works. Rebellion against the processes of capitalist accumulation, therefore, often took the form of a 'rebellion in
defence of custom', creating that characteristic paradox of the
eighteenth century, 'a rebellious traditional culture'.[30] Class conflict, then, tended to take the form of 'confrontations between an
innovative market economy and the customary moral economy of
the plebs'.[31]

If there is a danger in Thompson's formulations, it is perhaps that,
as some critics have suggested, he is too ready to see opposition and

---

[28] *Ibid.*, p. 152.   [29] *Ibid.*, p. 157.   [30] *Ibid.*, p. 154.   [31] *Ibid.*, p. 155.

rebellion in popular traditions and customs, and that there is too little room in his account for regressive impulses in popular consciousness or for its frequent penetration by ruling-class ideas. But excessive optimism is not required by his conceptual framework, and it has distinct advantages over theoretical systems which can recognize only 'backwardness' in popular traditions.

The argument, of course, belongs to his larger project of rescuing the agency of subordinate classes from analyses which effectively relegate them to permanent subordination, bondage to ruling-class hegemony, ancient superstition and irrationality. But his emphasis on the creative transformation of old traditions to meet new circumstances and resist new oppressions also represents a reaffirmation of materialist principles against theories of history that deny their efficacy in the explanation of historical process. His subtle analysis for example makes nonsense of historical treatments that see in these traditions and customs nothing but cultural remnants or 'debris', or regard their persistence as proof that class has no relevance for these 'traditional' 'pre-industrial' societies or even that culture is completely autonomous from material conditions.

It should be said, too, that in this respect Thompson accomplishes what the structuralists cannot with their version of the base/ superstructure metaphor. The latter can have little to say in response to the advocates of the 'debris' theory, which seems remarkably congruent with the Althusserian conception of 'social formation' – or, indeed, to those who deny the efficacy of class (or material conditions in general) in societies where ideological 'superstructures' apparently fail to correspond to the economic 'base'. Such arguments can be met only by acknowledging that history does not consist of discrete and discontinuous structural chunks, with separate and distinct superstructures to match every base; instead, it moves in *processes*, in which relations of production exert their pressures by transforming inherited realities.

It has long been one of Thompson's central projects to respond to historians who deny the existence, or at least the historical importance, of class in cases where clearly defined class institutions or self-conscious languages of class, on the model of industrial capitalism, are not immediately present in the evidence. Critics, and indeed often his admirers, have sometimes been confounded by formulations which appear to suggest that class does not exist for him in the absence of class consciousness. But this is directly contrary to his intention of demonstrating the determinative effects of class 'situations' even where 'mature' classes do not yet exist.

Perhaps he has adopted these ambiguous formulae because he has always seen himself as fighting on two fronts at once: against the anti-Marxist denial of class, and against those Marxisms that deny the working class its proper self-activity by postulating for it a predetermined ideal consciousness. In any case, his historiographical actions speak – or ought to speak – louder than his theoretical words; and it must be said that, in place of Thompson's very effective demonstrations of class forces operating in the absence of 'mature' class consciousness, his structuralist critics can offer little more than theoretical assertions according to which class may exist by definition but without implications for historical processes.

It is instructive to contrast Thompson's approach to that of Gareth Stedman Jones in his most recent study of Chartism.[32] Explicitly disavowing his earlier Marxist belief in the connection between politics and material conditions, Stedman Jones argues here that the politics of Chartism were 'autonomous' from the class situation of the Chartists. His principal evidence for this autonomy is the fact that there was a fundamental continuity between their ideology and an older radical tradition born in very different social conditions. He seems, among other things, to attach little significance to the changes which that radical tradition underwent as it came within the 'field of force' of capitalist relations. Changes there certainly were, as he acknowledges, but they evidently have no implications for the autonomy of Chartist politics or the non-correspondence of politics and class.

In other words, Stedman Jones's reading of evidence is exactly opposed to that of Thompson in similar circumstances: where one

---

[32] Gareth Stedman Jones, 'Rethinking Chartism', in *Languages of Class: Studies in English Working Class History, 1832–1982* (Cambridge, 1983). I examine this argument at length in *The Retreat From Class*. Stedman Jones distances himself from the tradition of historical materialism much more explicitly and emphatically in the introduction to *Languages of Class* than in the articles compiled in that volume. In the brief survey of his own development which he sketches in the introduction, he identifies 'Rethinking Chartism' as a turning-point marking a 'shift in [his] thinking', not only on the subject of Chartism 'but also about the social historical approach as such' (pp. 16–17). It is possible that when he wrote the article in 1981 and published it in a shorter version as 'The Language of Chartism', in J. Epstein and D. Thompson eds., *The Chartist Experience* (London, 1982), he did not intend to go quite as far in renouncing Marxism as he was later to claim, and a reading of 'Rethinking Chartism' without the benefit of his own later gloss on it might not be enough to reveal the full extent of his movement away from historical materialism; but in *Languages of Class*, he has certainly chosen to interpret his own intentions in that way.

sees the autonomy of ideology from class in the continuity of popular traditions, the other sees the magnetic force of class in the trans- formation of a continuous popular culture. It is as if Stedman Jones has given up historical materialism because he has discovered that history moves in continuous processes, disappointing his expectation that every new base at least in principle must have a pristinely new superstructure to match. This may have something to do with the fact that, by his own testimony, he was in his earlier (Marxist) days strongly influenced by Althusserian theory. Another flip of the Althusserian coin?

Thompson's attempts to refine the base/superstructure metaphor are not simply a matter of supplementing the old mechanical model with an acknowledgement that, even though superstructures are erected upon bases, 'bases need superstructures'.[33] This proposition does not adequately convey, for example, the insights that inform his study of law. Thompson contrasts his own 'older Marxist position' to a 'highly sophisticated, but (ultimately) highly schematic Marxism' for which the law is quintessentially and simply 'superstructural', 'adapting itself to the necessities of an infrastructure of productive forces and productive relations' and serving unambiguously as an instrument of the ruling class.[34] His answer to this 'schematic' Marxism, however, is not simply to assert that the law, like other superstructures, is 'relatively autonomous', that it 'interacts' with the base, or even that it acts as an indispensable condition of the base. His argument is more complex, both more historical and more materialist.

Accepting at the outset the 'class-bound and mystifying functions of the law', he continues:

First, analysis of the eighteenth century (and perhaps of other centuries) calls in question the validity of separating off the law as a whole and placing it in some typological superstructure. The law, when considered as institution (the courts, with their class theatre and class procedures) or as personnel (the judges, the lawyers, the Justices of the Peace) may very easily be assimilated to those of the ruling class. But all that is entailed in 'the law' is not subsumed in these institutions. . . .

Moreover, if we look closely into such an agrarian context, the distinction

---

[33] G.A. Cohen, *Karl Marx's Theory of History: A Defense* (Oxford, 1978). It is worth adding, incidentally, that if Cohen's technological determinism really did represent an accurate account of Marx's views on base and superstructure, then Thompson might not be so far wrong in his account of Marx's 'Grundrisse face'.

[34] E.P. Thompson, *Whigs and Hunters* (London, 1975), p. 259.

between law, on the one hand, conceived of as an element of 'super-structure', and the actualities of productive forces and relations, on the other hand, becomes more and more untenable. For law was often a definition of actual agrarian practice, as it had been pursued 'time out of mind'. . . .

Hence 'law' was deeply imbricated within the very basis of productive relations, which would have been inoperable without this law. And, in the second place, this law, as definition or as rules (imperfectly enforceable through institutional legal forms), was endorsed by norms, tenaciously transmitted through the community. There were alternative norms; that is a matter of course; this was a place, not of consensus, but of conflict.[35]

The notion of the 'imbrication' of the law 'within the very basis of productive relations' (which, incidentally, illustrates Thompson's point about the difference between those ideas, values and norms that are 'intrinsic' to the mode of production, and those that constitute the ruling apparatus and the 'common sense of power'), while not denying the 'superstructural' character of some parts of the law and its institutions, is something different from, and more than, the idea that 'bases need superstructures'. It is a different way of understanding the base itself, as it is embodied in actual social practices and relations. Nor is it simply a matter of analytically distinguishing the material base from the social forms in which it is inevitably embodied in the real world. Thompson's conception is, first, a refusal of any analytic distinction that conceals the social character of the 'material' itself (which is constituted not simply by a 'natural' substratum but by the social relations and practices entailed by human productive activity) – a refusal that is indispensable to historical materialism; but, beyond that, it is a way of discouraging analytic procedures that tend to obscure historical relations.

As Perry Anderson has pointed out, the principal objection levelled against the base/superstructure metaphor by Thompson and others is that the analytic distinction between various 'levels' or 'instances' may encourage the view that they 'exist substantively as separate objects, physically divisible from each other in the real world', creating a confusion between 'epistemological procedures' and 'ontological categories'.[36] He suggests that Althusser sought to avoid such confusions by insisting on a distinction between the

[35] *Ibid.*, pp. 260–1.
[36] Perry Anderson, *Arguments Within English Marxism* (London, 1980), p. 72.

'object of knowledge and the real object'. And yet, there is a sense in which the Althusserians have had the worst of both worlds; for while their 'instances' and 'levels' tend consistently to slip into 'ontological categories' physically separated from one another in the real world, the *relations* between these 'levels' have tended to remain in the realm of pure theory, as 'objects of knowledge' that have little connection with 'ontological categories'. For Thompson, it is the relations that count; and if he occasionally errs on the side of allowing 'ontological' relations to become analytic conflations, this mistake is far less damaging than the other to an understanding of history.

CHAPTER 3

Class as process and relationship

There are really only two ways of thinking theoretically about class: either as a structural *location* or as a social *relation*. The first and more common of these treats class as a form of 'stratification', a layer in a hierarchical structure, differentiated according to 'economic' criteria such as income, 'market chances' or occupation. In contrast to this geological model, there is a social-historical conception of class as a relation between appropriators and producers, determined by the specific form in which, to use Marx's phrase, 'surplus labour is pumped out of the direct producers'.

If the second of these conceptions is specifically Marxist, the first covers a broad spectrum from classical sociology up to and including some varieties of Marxism. So, for example, class defined as 'relation to the means of production' can take a form not so very different from the income differentiation of conventional stratification theory; and some of the most recent and influential theories of class elaborated under the rubric of 'Rational Choice Marxism' have deliberately shifted the focus of class away from the social relations of *surplus extraction* to the distribution of 'assets' or 'endowments'. Here, as in theories of stratification, the operative principle is relative advantage or *inequality*, not direct social relations between appropriators and producers but indirect relations of *comparison* among people differentially situated in a structural hierarchy.[1] By contrast, for 'classical' Marxism the focus is on the social relation itself, the

[1] I have discussed Rational Choice Marxism and its conception of class at great length in an article which I contemplated including in this volume: 'Rational Choice Marxism: Is the Game Worth the Candle?', *New Left Review*, 177 (1989), pp. 41–88. In the end, I decided to extract only a small section of it (in the next chapter), partly because it is already being included in a volume on rational choice Marxism edited by Paul Thomas and Terrell Carver, to be published by Macmillan, but also because debate with this school of theory tends to take discussion off on tangents which seem to me not very fruitful outside their own fairly self-enclosed game-theoretic universe.

dynamic of the relation between appropriators and producers, the contradictions and conflicts which account for social and historical processes; and *inequality*, as simply a comparative measure, has no theoretical purchase.

This distinctively Marxist conception of class has received remarkably little elaboration, either by Marx himself or by later theorists working in the historical materialist tradition. The most notable exception has been E.P. Thompson; but, while he self-consciously exemplified this conception in his historical work, he never actually spelled out a systematic theory of class in these terms. The few allusive and provocative remarks he did venture to make on the general definition of class have sparked a good deal of controversy, which has done little to clarify the issues between the dominant geological model and the historical-materialist theory of class.

What I sought to do when I wrote this essay was to tease out of Thompson's work a more elaborated theory of class than he ever explicitly outlined, knowing that I was taking the risk of attributing to him some of my own views on class but convinced – as I still am – that I was not traducing his. I proceeded by responding to Marxist critics who found Thompson's conception of class insufficiently 'structural'; and while this may seem an outmoded procedure in these post-Marxist days, when he is more likely to be criticized for being *too* economistic or *too* class reductionist, it still seems to me to capture the more general issues at stake in the theory of class.

There is also another reason for leaving this argument more or less as it was. There has been a curious convergence between Thompson's Marxist critics and current anti-Marxist fashions on the left. When I wrote this chapter originally, Thompson was also being criticized by people who were already moving in a 'post-Marxist' direction. Having conceded that there is no automatic equation of 'structural' class positions and conscious class formations, such critics suggested, he did not go far enough. Thompson was accused of failing to 'face up' to the consequences of his 'non-reductive' Marxism. Once he had opened the floodgates by renouncing 'reductionism', apparently nothing stood between him and post-Marxist contingency.

This criticism, as we shall see, paradoxically converged with the Marxist objection that he was guilty of dissolving 'objective' structures in subjective 'experience' and culture, of identifying class with class consciousness, of dissolving structural determinations into subjective experience – though where one castigated him for seeing *no* class where there is no class consciousness, the other accused him of seeing class everywhere, complete and 'at the ready', in all manifestations of popular culture. Both these apparently antithetical criticisms had as their starting point what I would regard as a fundamentally ahistorical view of the world, where there is nothing between structural necessity and empirical contingency, no room for *historical* determinations, structured processes with human agencies.

THE STRUCTURAL DEFINITION OF CLASS: E.P THOMPSON AND HIS CRITICS

Thompson has been accused of mistakenly believing that, because 'production relations do not mechanically determine class consciousness', 'class may not be defined purely in terms of production relations'.[2] In opposition to Thompson, Gerald Cohen argues that class may be defined 'structurally', 'with more or less (if not, perhaps, "mathematical") precision by reference to production relations'.[3] Thompson, he suggests, rejects the structural definition of class and defines class 'by reference to' class consciousness and culture instead of production relations. 'The result', argues Perry Anderson, concurring with Cohen and accusing Thompson of neglecting objective or structural determinations, 'is a definition of class that is far too voluntarist and subjectivist ...'.[4]

Neither Anderson nor Cohen means to suggest that production relations 'mechanically' determine class consciousness or the formation of class organizations. On the contrary, Cohen is here criticizing Thompson on the grounds that he is too ready to jettison the structural definition of class on the mistaken assumption that it necessarily implies this kind of mechanical determinism. Both critics insist that there is, for Thompson, no class in the absence of class consciousness. His conception of class, in other words, does not allow for Marx's distinction between a 'class-in-itself' and a 'class-for-itself', between a class that exists 'objectively' and a class that exists as an active and self-conscious historical subject, in opposition to other classes. Thompson, according to this argument, insofar as he

[2] G.A. Cohen, *Karl Marx's Theory of History: A Defence* (Princeton, 1978), p. 75.   [3] *Ibid.*
[4] Perry Anderson, *Arguments Within English Marxism* (London, 1980), p. 40.

defines class at all, identifies it with the latter. Before a class exists in this form, it is not a class at all.

As I have already suggested in the previous chapter, it can be argued that exactly the reverse is true: the great strength of Thompson's conception of class is that it is capable of recognizing, and giving an account of, the operations of class in the absence of class consciousness; while those who adopt the kind of structural definition his critics seem to have in mind have no effective way of demonstrating the efficacy of class in the absence of clearly visible self-conscious class formations, and no effective response to the claim that class is nothing more than an ideologically motivated theoretical construct imposed on historical evidence from without. I intend to elaborate that argument here but also to suggest that the failure to see this aspect of Thompson's work has less to do with his own neglect of objective structures than with his critics' understanding of what counts as a structural determination.

Where Thompson's critics see structures *as against* processes, or structures that *undergo* processes, Thompson sees structured processes. This distinction reflects an epistemological difference: on the one hand, a view that theoretical knowledge – the knowledge of structures – is a matter of 'static conceptual representation', while motion and flux (together with history) belong to a different, empirical sphere of cognition; and, on the other hand, a view of knowledge that does not oppose structure to history, in which theory can accommodate *historical* categories, 'concepts appropriate to the investigation of process'.[5]

It may be true that Thompson tells us too little about the relations of production and that he fails to define them with enough specificity. He may indeed take too much for granted. But to accuse him of defining class 'by reference to' or 'in terms of' class consciousness instead of production relations is quite simply to miss the point. It is not at all clear that Thompson's conception of class is incompatible with, for example, the following statement by Perry Anderson, although Anderson intends it as a rejoinder to Thompson, an attack on his excessively voluntarist and subjectivist definition of class, and an expansion of Cohen's criticism:

It is, and must be, the dominant mode of production that confers fundamental unity on a social formation, allocating their objective positions to

---

[5] E.P. Thompson, *The Poverty of Theory* (London, 1978), p. 237.

the classes within it, and distributing the agents within each class. The result is, typically, an objective process of class struggle ... class struggle is not a causal prius in the sustentation of order, for *classes are constituted by modes of production, and not vice versa*.[6]

Now unless the proposition that 'classes are constituled by modes of production' means – as in Anderson's case (or indeed Cohen's) it clearly does not – that modes of production immediately constitute active class formations or that the process of class formation is unproblematic and mechanical, Thompson (no doubt with some stylistic reservations) might readily accept it. His historical project presupposes that relations of production distribute people into class situations, that these situations entail essential antagonisms and conflicts of interest, and that they therefore create conditions of struggle. Class *formations* and the discovery of class consciousness grow out of the process of struggle, as people 'experience' and 'handle' their class situations. It is in this sense that class struggle precedes class. To say that exploitation is 'experienced in class ways and only thence give(s) rise to class formations' is to say precisely that the conditions of exploitation, the relations of production, are objectively *there* to be experienced.[7]

Nevertheless, objective determinations do not impose themselves on blank and passive raw material but on active and conscious *historical* beings. Class formations emerge and develop 'as men and women *live* their productive relations and *experience* their determinate situations, within "the *ensemble* of the social relations", with their inherited culture and expectations, and as they handle these experiences in cultural ways'.[8] This certainly means that no structural definition of class can by itself resolve the problem of class formation and that 'no model can give us what ought to be the "true" class formation for a certain "stage" of process'.[9]

At the same time, if class formations are generated by 'living' and 'experiencing', within a complex totality of social relations and historical legacies, they presuppose what is lived and experienced: productive relations and the determinate situations 'into which men are born or enter involuntarily'.[10] In order to experience things in

6 *Ibid.*, p. 55.
7 E.P. Thompson, 'Eighteenth-Century English Society: Class Struggle without Class?', *Social History* 3 (2) (May 1978), p. 149 n. 36.
8 *Ibid.*, p. 150.   9 *Ibid.*
10 E.P. Thompson, *The Making of the English Working Class* (Harmondsworth, 1968), p. 10.

'class ways' people must be 'objectively distributed' into class situations; but this is the beginning, not the end, of class formation. It is not a small, or theoretically trivial, point to distinguish between the constitution of classes by modes of production and the process of class formation. Nor is it unimportant to suggest that, however completely we may succeed in deductively situating people on a chart of class locations, the problematic question of class formation will remain and may yield answers that are both theoretically and politically more significant. The crucial point is that the main burden of a Marxist theory of class must be less on identifying class 'locations' than on explaining processes of class formation.

In effect, Thompson is being accused of voluntarism and subjectivism not because he neglects the objective, structural determinations of class, but on the contrary, because he refuses to relegate the process of class formation, which is his central concern, to a sphere of mere contingency and subjectivity set apart from the sphere of 'objective' material determination, as his critics appear to do. He does not proceed from a theoretical dualism which opposes *structure* to *history* and identifies the 'structural' explanation of class with the charting of objective, static class locations while reserving the process of class formation for an apparently lesser form of historical and empirical explanation. Instead, Thompson, taking seriously the principles of historical materialism and its conception of materially structured historical processes, treats the process of class formation as a *historical* process shaped by the 'logic' of material determinations.

Thompson could, in fact, turn the tables on his critics. One of his major objectives in refusing to define class as a 'structure' or 'thing', as he points out in *The Making of the English Working Class*, has been to vindicate the concept of class against those, especially bourgeois social scientists, who deny its existence except as 'a pejorative theoretical construct, imposed upon the evidence'.[11] He has countered such denials by insisting upon class as a relationship and a process, to be observed over time as a pattern in social relations, institutions and values. Class, in other words, is a phenomenon which is visible only in process.

The denial of class, especially where there is no historical clarity to force its reality upon our attention, cannot be answered simply by

[11] *Ibid.*

reciting the 'structural' definition of class. This is, in fact, no better than the reduction of class to a theoretical construct imposed on the evidence. What is needed is a way of demonstrating how the structuration of society 'in class ways' actually affects social relations and historical processes. The point, then, is to have a conception of class that invites us to discover how objective class situations actually shape social reality, and not simply to state and restate the tautological proposition that 'class equals relation to the means of production'.

The concept of class as *relationship* and *process* stresses that objective relations to the means of production are significant because they establish antagonisms and generate conflicts and struggles; that these conflicts and struggles shape social experience 'in class ways', even when they do not express themselves in class consciousness or in clearly visible formations; and that over time we can discern how these relationships impose their logic, their pattern, on social processes. Purely 'structural' conceptions of class do not require us to look for the ways in which class actually imposes its logic, since classes are simply *there* by definition.

Thompson has nevertheless been attacked on the grounds that, by failing to define class in purely 'structural' terms, he has rendered the concept inapplicable to all historical cases in which no class consciousness can be discerned.[12] Yet the emphasis on class as relationship and process is especially important precisely in dealing with cases where no well-defined expressions of class consciousness are available to provide uncontestable evidence of class. This applies in particular to social formations before industrial capitalism, which in nineteenth-century England for the first time in history produced unambiguously visible class formations, compelling observers to take note of class and provide conceptual instruments to apprehend it.

In fact, Thompson is arguably the one Marxist who, instead of evading the issue or taking class for granted, has tried to give an account of class which can be applied in such ambiguous cases. His purpose here has not been to deny the existence of class in the absence of class consciousness but, on the contrary, to answer such denials by showing how class determinants shape social processes, how people behave 'in class ways,' even before, and as a pre-

[12] For example, Cohen, *Marx's Theory*, p. 76; Anderson, *Arguments*, p. 40.

condition to, the 'mature' formations of class with their consciously class-defined institutions and values.[13]

So, for example, the formula 'class struggle without class', which Thompson tentatively proposes to describe English society in the eighteenth century, is intended to convey the effects of class-structured social relations upon agents without class consciousness and as a precondition to conscious class formations. Class struggle therefore precedes class, both in the sense that class formations *presuppose* an experience of conflict and struggle arising out of production relations, and in the sense that there are conflicts and struggles structured 'in class ways' even in societies that do not yet have class-conscious formations.

To argue that a purely structural definition is required to rescue the universal applicability of 'class' is to suggest that in the absence of class consciousness classes exist *only* as 'objective relations to the means of production', with no practical consequences for the dynamics of social process. So perhaps it is not Thompson but his critics who effectively reduce class to class consciousness. Thompson, in contrast, seems to be arguing that the 'objective relations of production' always matter, whether or not they are expressed in a well-defined consciousness of class – though they matter in different ways in different historical contexts and produce class *formations* only as a result of historical processes. The point is to have a conception of class that turns our attention to precisely how, and in what different modes, objective class situations matter.

Thompson, then, does indeed say that classes arise or 'happen' because people 'in determinative productive relations', who consequently share a common experience, identify their common interests and come to think and value 'in class ways';[14] but this does not mean that classes do not, in any meaningful sense, exist for him as objective realities before class consciousness. On the contrary, class consciousness is possible because 'objective' class situations already exist. His primary concern, of course, is to focus attention on the complex and often contradictory historical processes by which, in determinate historical conditions, class *situations* give rise to class *formations*. As for purely 'structural' definitions of class, since they cannot define completed class formations, either they are intended

[13] Thompson, 'Eighteenth-Century English Society', p. 147.
[14] See, for example, Thompson, *English Working Class*, pp. 9–10. See also Thompson, *Poverty of Theory*, pp. 298–9.

simply to denote the same determining pressures exerted by objective class distributions on variable historical processes – so that the difference between Thompson and his critics is largely a question of emphasis – or such definitions refer to nothing significant at all.

THE MAKING OF THE ENGLISH WORKING CLASS

The proposition that Thompson neglects objective determinations in favour of subjective factors has been put to a practical test by Perry Anderson in a particularly trenchant criticism of his major historical work, *The Making of the English Working Class*. Anderson argues that, in this work, the objective conditions of capital accumulation and industrialization are treated as secondary and external to the making of the English proletariat:

It is not the structural transformations – economic, political and demographic – ... which are the objects of his inquiry, but rather their precipitates in the subjective experience of those who lived through these 'terrible years'. The result is to resolve the complex manifold of objective-subjective determinations whose totalization actually generated the English working class into a simple dialectic between suffering and resistance whose whole movement is internal to the subjectivity of the class.[15]

In fact, suggests Anderson, the advent of industrial capitalism becomes merely a moment in a long and largely 'subjective' process, going back to Tudor times, in which the formation of the English working class appears as a gradual development in a continuous tradition of popular culture.[16] There is, according to Anderson:

no real treatment of the whole historical process whereby heterogeneous groups of artisans, small holders, agricultural labourers, domestic workers and casual poor were gradually assembled, distributed and reduced to the condition of labour subsumed to capital, first in the formal dependence of the wage-contract, ultimately in the real dependence of integration into mechanized means of production.[17]

So, Anderson argues, Thompson provides us with no means of testing his proposition that 'the English working class made itself as much as it was made', since he gives us no measure of the proportional relation between 'agency' and 'necessity'. What would be required is at least a 'conjoint exploration of the objective assemblage and transformation of a labour-force by the Industrial Revo-

[15] Anderson, *Arguments*, p. 39.   [16] *Ibid.*, p. 34.   [17] *Ibid.*, p. 33.

lution, and of the subjective germination of a class culture in response to it'.[18] By concentrating on the 'immediate experience of the producers rather than on the mode of production itself', Thompson gives us only the subjective elements of the equation.[19]

Anderson correctly isolates two of the most characteristic and problematic themes in Thompson's argument: his stress on the continuity of popular traditions cutting across the 'catastrophic' break of the Industrial Revolution; and his insistence on historically situating the critical moments in the formation of the English working class in such a way that the moment of fruition comes in the period 1790–1832, that is, before the real transformation of production and the labour force by industrial capitalism was very far advanced and with no account of the tremendous changes in the working class thereafter.[20]

Difficulties certainly do arise here, as Anderson suggests. The emphasis on the continuity of popular traditions – older traditions not specifically proletarian but artisanal and 'democratic' – may at first glance make it hard to perceive what is new about the working class of 1790–1832, what is specifically proletarian, or unique to industrial capitalism, in this class formation. What, exactly, has been 'made', and what role has the new order of industrial capitalism played in the making? The temporal parameters may also present problems. To end the process of 'making' in 1832, when industrial transformation was far from complete, may seem to imply that the developments in class consciousness, institutions and values outlined by Thompson occurred independently of 'objective' transformations in the mode of production.

There are no doubt many historiographical issues to be contested here about the nature and development of the English working class. But the immediate question is whether Thompson's insistence on the continuity of popular traditions and his apparently idiosyncratic periodization of working-class formation reflect a preoccupation with subjective factors at the expense of objective determinations. Is it Thompson's intention to set 'subjective' developments (the evolution of popular culture) against 'objective' factors (the processes of capital accumulation and industrialization)?

The first striking point about Thompson's argument is that, for all his insistence on the continuity of popular culture, he considers his

[18] *Ibid.*, p. 32.   [19] *Ibid.*, p. 33.   [20] *Ibid.*, p. 45.

argument not as a denial but as a reaffirmation of the view that the period of the Industrial Revolution represents a significant, indeed 'catastrophic', historical milestone, marked by the emergence of a class sufficiently new to appear as a 'fresh race of beings'. In other words, his object is not to assert the subjective continuity of working-class culture against the radical objective transformations of capitalist development but, on the contrary, to reveal and explain the changes within the continuities.

In part, Thompson's emphases are shaped to fit the specific terms of the debates in which he is engaged, debates about the effects of the Industrial Revolution such as the 'standard of living' argument, controversies between 'catastrophic' and 'anti-catastrophic' or 'empiricist' analyses, and so on. He is, among other things, responding to a variety of recent historical – and ideological – orthodoxies which question the importance of dislocations and disruptions entailed by industrial capitalism, or, if they admit to the existence of hardships within the generally progressive and improving tendencies of 'industrialization', attribute them to causes external to the system of production – for example, to 'trade cycles'. Such arguments are sometimes accompanied by denials that *the* working class, as distinct from several working classes, existed at all.

An emphasis on the diversity of working-class experience, on the differences between the 'pre-industrial' experience of domestic workers or artisans and that of factory hands fully absorbed into the new industrial order, can be particularly serviceable to capitalist ideology. It is, for example, especially useful in arguments that confine the hardships and dislocations engendered by industrial capitalism to 'pre-industrial' or traditional workers. In these interpretations, the degradation of such workers becomes simply the inevitable and impersonal consequence of 'displacement by mechanical processes', 'progress', and improved industrial methods, while the modern worker moves steadily onward and upward.

Thompson vindicates the 'catastrophic' view, as well as the notion of *the* working class, by confronting the evidence adduced by their critics. One of his tasks is to explain why, although by certain statistical yardsticks there may have been a slight improvement in average material standards in the period 1790–1840, this improvement was experienced by workers as a 'catastrophe', which they handled by creating new class formations, 'strongly based and self-conscious institutions – trade unions, friendly societies, edu-

cational and religious movements, political organizations, period-
icals' together with 'working-class intellectual traditions, working-
class community patterns, and a working-class structure of feel-
ing'.[21] These institutions and forms of consciousness are tangible
testimony to the existence of a new working-class formation, despite
the apparent diversity of experience; and their expressions in
popular unrest bear witness against the 'optimistic' view of the
Industrial Revolution.

Yet Thompson then faces the problem of accounting for the fact
that this class formation is already visibly in place when the new
system of production is still undeveloped; that large numbers of the
workers who constitute this class formation, and indeed initiate its
characteristic institutions, do not apparently belong to a 'fresh race
of beings' produced by industrialization, but are still engaged in
ostensibly 'pre-industrial' forms of domestic and artisanal labour;
and that factory hands probably did not (except in cotton districts)
form the 'nucleus of the Labour movement' before the late 1840s.[22]
In light of these facts, it would on the face of it be difficult to
maintain that the new working class was simply created by the new
forms of production characteristic of industrial capitalism. To
account for the incontestable presence of class formations that unite
new and traditional forms of labour – artisans, domestic workers,
factory hands – it becomes necessary to identify a unifying experience, one which also explains why the 'catastrophic' impact of the
Industrial Revolution was experienced in sectors apparently still
untouched by the transformation of industrial production.

Here Thompson's critics might argue – as Anderson's criticism
suggests – that Thompson relies too much on 'subjective' experiences, suffering and the continuity of popular culture to override the
objective diversity of artisans and factory hands without giving an
account of the processes that actually, objectively, united them into
a single class. Indeed, these critics might argue that for Thompson
no objective unity is necessary to identify the working class, as long
as it can be defined in terms of a unity in consciousness.

But criticisms like this concede too much to Thompson's anti-
Marxist opponents. For example, the 'optimistic' and 'empiricist'
arguments rely at least implicitly on setting up an opposition
between 'facts' and 'values', between their own 'objective' standards

and merely 'subjective' standards having to do with the 'quality of life'. This opposition can be used to obscure the issues by relegating problems of exploitation, relations of production and class struggle – which are the focus of Thompson's argument – to the sphere of subjectivity, while identifying objectivity with 'hard' 'impersonal' factors: trade cycles, technology, wage and price indices. Thompson, while certainly concerned with the 'quality of life', defines its conditions not simply in subjective terms but in terms of the objective realities of capitalist production relations and their expressions in the organization of life.

'OBJECTIVE' DETERMINATIONS

The single most important objective condition experienced in common by various kinds of workers during the period in question was the intensification of exploitation; and Thompson devotes the second and central section of *The Making of the English Working Class*, introduced by a chapter entitled 'Exploitation', to a description of its effects.[23] He is concerned not simply with its effects in 'suffering' but in the distribution and organization of work (as well as leisure), most especially its consequences for work discipline and the intensity of labour, for example in the extension of hours of work, increasing specialization, the break up of the family economy, and so on.[24] He also considers how the exploitive relationship was expressed in 'corresponding forms of ownership and State power', in legal and political forms, and how the intensification of exploitation was compounded by counter-revolutionary political repression.[25] These are factors that certainly cannot, from a Marxist point of view, be dismissed as 'subjective'; and Thompson sets them against the 'hard facts' of the 'empiricist' argument, not as subjectivity against objec-

[23] See, for example: *ibid.*, pp. 217–18, 226. The structure of the book as a whole is worth noting. Part One describes the political culture and traditions of struggle which people brought with them into the transforming experience of 'industrialization'. Part Two describes in great detail that transforming experience itself, the new relationship of exploitation and its multifarious expressions in every aspect of life, in work and leisure, in family and communal life. Part Three describes the new working-class consciousness, the new political culture, and the new forms of struggle that emerged out of that transformation. Part Two is the pivotal section, explaining the objective influences (as Thompson himself describes them), the transformations through which the old popular tradition was reshaped into a new working-class culture.

[24] See, for example: Thompson, *English Working Class*, pp. 221–3, 230.

[25] *Ibid.*, pp. 215–18.

tivity, but as the real objective determinations which underlie the 'facts':

> By what social alchemy did inventions for saving labour become agents of immiseration? The raw fact – a bad harvest – may seem to be beyond human election. But the way that fact worked its way out was in terms of a particular complex of human relationship: law, ownership, power. When we encounter some sonorous phrase such as 'the strong ebb and flow of the trade cycle' we must be put on our guard. For behind this trade cycle there is a structure of social relations, fostering some sorts of expropriation (rent, interest, profit) and outlawing some others (theft, feudal dues), legitimizing some types of conflict (competition, armed warfare) and inhibiting others (trade unionism, bread riots, popular political organization) . . . .[26]

The underlying objective determinations affecting the developments of 1790–1832 were, then, the working out of capitalist modes of expropriation, the intensification of exploitation this implied, and the structure of social relations, legal forms and political powers by which that exploitation was sustained. The significant point is that these factors affected *both* 'traditional' and new forms of labour; and their common 'experience', with the struggles it entailed – in a period of transition which produced a moment of particular transparency in relationships of exploitation, a clarity heightened by political repression – underlay the process of class formation.

The particular significance and subtlety of Thompson's argument lies in its demonstration that the apparent continuity of 'pre-industrial' forms can be deceptive. He argues that domestic and artisanal production were themselves transformed – even when they were not displaced – by the same process and the same mode of exploitation that created the factory system. In fact, it was often in outwork industries that the new relationship of exploitation was most transparent. This is, for example, how he answers arguments that attribute the hardships of 'industrialization' simply to 'displacement by mechanical processes':

> it will not do to explain away the plight of weavers or of 'slop' workers as 'instances of the decline of old crafts which were displaced by a mechanical process'; nor can we even accept the statement, in its pejorative context, that 'it was not among the factory employees but among the domestic workers, whose traditions and methods were those of the eighteenth century, that earnings were at their lowest'. The suggestion to which these statements lead us is that these conditions can somehow be segregated in

[26] *Ibid.*, pp. 224–5.

our minds from the true improving impulse of the Industrial Revolution – they belong to an 'older', pre-industrial order, whereas the authentic features of the new capitalist order may be seen where there are steam, factory operatives, and meat-eating engineers. But the numbers employed in the outwork industries multiplied enormously between 1780–1830; and very often steam and the factory were the multipliers. It was the mills which spun the yarn and the foundries which made the nail-rod upon which the outworkers were employed. Ideology may wish to exalt one and decry the other, but facts must lead us to say that each was a complementary component of a single process .... Moreover, the degradation of the outworkers was very rarely as simple as the phrase 'displaced by a mechanical process' suggests; it was accomplished by methods of exploitation similar to those in the dishonourable trades and it often preceded machine competition .... Indeed, we may say that large-scale sweated outwork was as intrinsic to this revolution as was factory production and steam.[27]

Thompson undermines the ideological foundations of his anti-Marxist adversaries simply by displacing the focus of analysis from 'industrialization' to *capitalism*.[28] In other words, he shifts our attention from purely 'technological' factors, as well as from trade cycles and market relations – the typical refuges of capitalist ideology – to the relations of production and class exploitation. From this (Marxist) standpoint, Thompson is able to account for the historical presence of working-class formations in the early stages of industrialization, on the grounds that the essential capitalist relations of production and exploitation were already in place, and indeed were the pre-conditions for industrialization itself.

For a variety of reasons, then, Thompson cannot accept the simple proposition that the factory system produced, out of whole cloth, a new working class, nor the suggestion that the objective 'assemblage, distribution, and transformation' of the labour force had to precede the emergence of a class consciousness and culture 'in response' to it. He cannot accept that the making of the working class out of 'heterogeneous groups' had to await the completion of the process in which they were 'assembled, distributed, and reduced to the condition of labour subsumed to capital, first in the formal

[27] *Ibid.*, pp. 288–9; see also pp. 222–3.

[28] Elsewhere, Thompson explicitly questions the 'suspect' concept of 'industrialism,' which obscures the social realities of industrial capitalism by treating them as if they belonged to some inevitable 'supposedly-neutral, technologically-determined, process known as "industrialization" ...', 'Time, Work-Discipline, and Industrial Capitalism,' now available in his collection of essays, *Customs in Common* (London, 1991).

dependence of the wage-contract, ultimately in the real dependence of integration into mechanized means of production'. For one thing, if the relations of production and exploitation are the critical objective factors in constituting a mode of production, and if they provide the impulse for the transformation of labour processes, then the 'formal subjection' of labour to capital assumes a special significance and primacy.

The 'formal subjection' represents the establishment of the capitalist relationship between appropriator and producer and the pre-condition to, indeed the motivating force for, the subsequent 'real' transformation of production, often called 'industrialization'. It acts as a determinative force upon various kinds of workers, and as a unifying experience among them, even before the process of 'real subjection' incorporatcs them all and 'assembles' them in factories.

In a very important sense, then, it is indeed 'experience' and not simply an objective 'assemblage' that unites these heterogeneous groups into a class – though 'experience' in this context refers to the effects of objective determinations, the relations of production and class exploitation. In fact, the connection between relations of production and class formation can probably never be conceived in any other way, since people are never actually assembled directly in class formations in the process of production. Even when the 'assemblage and transformation' of the labour force is complete, people are at best assembled only in productive units, factories, and so on. Their assemblage in class formations which transcend such individual units is a process of a different kind, one that depends upon their consciousness of, and propensity to act upon, a common experience and common interests. (More on this later.)

Thompson is perhaps being criticized for concentrating on the formal subjection at the expense of the real. There are indeed weaknesses in his arguments arising from his focus on the determinative and unifying force of capitalist exploitation and its effects on 'pre-industrial' workers, and his relative neglect of the specificity of 'industrialization' and machine production, the further 'catastrophe' occasioned by the completion of 'real subjection'. Perry Anderson, for example, refers to the profound changes in working-class industrial and political organization and class consciousness after the 1840s, when the transformation was more or less complete – changes which, he suggests, Thompson's argument cannot explain.[29] But this is not the same thing as saying that Thompson concentrates on subjective rather than objective determinations – unless it is from the standpoint of 'optimistic' and 'empiricist' orthodoxies or capitalist ideology, in which the very premises of Marxist theory, with its focus on relations of production and class exploitation, can be dismissed altogether as 'subjectivist'.

There are other more general theoretical and political reasons for denying that the making of the English working class was the 'spontaneous generation of the factory system'. The basic theoretical and methodological principle of Thompson's whole historical project is that objective determinations – the transformation of production relations and working conditions – never impose themselves on 'some nondescript undifferentiated raw material of humanity' but on historical beings, the bearers of historical legacies, traditions and values.[30] This means, among other things, that there are necessarily continuities cutting across all historical transformations, even the most radical, and indeed that radical transformations can be revealed and substantiated precisely – only? – by tracing them within continuities. Again, his own emphasis on the continuity of popular culture is intended not to deny but to identify and stress the transformations it undergoes.

This much is perhaps characteristic of any truly historical account, but there is more to Thompson's argument than this. It is essential to his historical materialism to recognize that 'objective' and 'subjective' are not dualistically separated entities (which lend themselves easily to the measurement of 'necessity' and 'agency'), related to one another only externally and mechanically, 'the one sequential upon the other' as objective stimulus and subjective response.[31] It is necessary somehow to incorporate in social analysis the role of conscious and active historical beings, who are 'subject' and 'object' at once, both agents and material forces in objective processes.

Finally, Thompson's mode of analysis makes it possible to acknowledge the active role of the working class, with its culture and values, in 'making' itself. This role may be obscured by formulations which speak, on the one hand, of 'the objective assemblage and

---

[29] Anderson, *Arguments*, pp. 45–7. Anderson refers here to Gareth Stedman Jones's discussion of the 're-making' of the English working class in the latter part of the nineteenth century, in 'Working-Class Culture and Working-Class Politics in London, 1870–1890: Notes on the Remaking of a Working Class', *Journal of Social History* (Summer 1974), pp. 460–508.

[30] Thompson, *English Working Class*, p. 213.   [31] Thompson, *Poverty of Theory*, p. 298.

transformation of labour force by the Industrial Revolution', and, on the other – sequentially? – 'the subjective germination of a class culture in response to it'. The acknowledgment of working-class self-activity is central not only to Thompson's historical project but to his political one.

CLASS AS RELATIONSHIP AND PROCESS

Thompson's concern, then, is to render class visible in history and to make its objective determinations manifest as historical forces, as real effects in the world and not just as theoretical constructs that refer to no actual social force or process. This means that he must locate the essence of class not simply in 'structural *positions*' but in *relationships* – the relationships of exploitation, conflict and struggle which provide the impulse to processes of class formation. Yet this very emphasis is often singled out as evidence of his voluntarism and subjectivism, his neglect of objective determinations. Clearly, his preference for treating class as relationship and process – rather than, for example, as a structure which *enters* relationships or *undergoes* process – demands closer scrutiny – and here I shall take more than the usual interpretive liberties in elaborating what may be more my own theory of class than Thompson's.

'Class as relationship' actually entails two relationships: that between classes and that among members of the same class. The importance of stressing the relationship between classes as essential to the definition of class is self-evident when considered against the background of 'stratification' theories which – whether they focus on income distribution, occupation groups, status, or any other criterion – have to do with *differences*, *inequalities* and *hierarchy*, not relations. It is surely unnecessary to point out the consequences, both sociological and ideological, of employing a definition of class (if class is admitted as a 'category of stratification' at all) which factors out relations like domination or exploitation. Even more fundamentally, such categories of stratification may render class itself invisible altogether. Where is the dividing line between classes in a continuum of inequality? Where is the qualitative break in a structure of stratification?[32]

[32] For an important discussion of this point, see Peter Meiksins, 'Beyond the Boundary Question', *New Left Review*, 157, pp. 101–20, and 'New Classes and Old Theories', in Rhonda Levine and Jerry Lembcke, eds., *Recapturing Marxism: An Appraisal of Recent Trends in Sociological Theory* (New York, 1987).

Even the criterion of relation to the means of production is not enough to mark such boundaries and can easily be assimilated to conventional stratification theory. It is possible, for example, to treat 'relations to the means of production' as nothing more than income differentials by locating their significance not in the exploitative and antagonistic social relations they entail but in the different 'market chances' they confer.[33] The differences among classes thus become indeterminate and inconsequential. If classes enter into any relationship at all, it is the indirect, impersonal relationship of individual competition in the market place, in which there are no clear qualitative breaks or antagonisms but only a quantitative continuum of relative advantage and disadvantage in the contest for goods and services.

It is explicitly against class as a 'category of stratification' that Thompson directs much of his argument about class as a relationship, and precisely on the grounds that stratification theories tend to render class invisible.[34] The most obvious target of this attack is conventional anti-Marxist sociology; but Thompson often points out that there are affinities between certain Marxist treatments of class and these sociological conjuring tricks, to the extent that they are more interested in abstractly defined structural class *locations* than in the qualitative social breaks expressed in the dynamics of class relations and conflicts.

While the identification of antagonisms in the relation between classes is a necessary condition for a definition of class, it is not sufficient. That brings us to class as an *internal* relationship, a relationship among members of a class. The idea of class as a relationship in this sense also entails certain propositions about how classes are connected to the underlying relations of production.

The proposition that production relations are the foundation of class relations is certainly the basis of any materialist theory of class; but it does not by itself advance the issue very far. If we cannot say that class is *synonymous* with production relations, we are still left with the problem (which is generally evaded) of defining precisely the nature of the connection between class and its foundation in production.

The relations of production are the relations among people who

[33] See, for example: Max Weber, *Economy and Society* (New York, 1968), pp. 927–8. Rational choice Marxism has some striking affinities with this view.

[34] For example, Thompson, *English Working Class*, pp. 9–10.

are joined by the production process and the antagonistic nexus between those who produce and those who appropriate their surplus labour. The division between direct producers and the appropriators of their surplus labour, the antagonism of interest inherent in this relationship, no doubt defines the polarities underlying class antagonisms. But class relations are not reducible to production relations. First, the clear polarities (when they *are* clear) inherent in the relations of production do not account neatly for all potential members of historical classes. More fundamentally, even if individual appropriators owe their exploitive power to the *class* power that stands behind them, it is not classes that produce and appropriate. To put it very simply: people who are joined in a class are not all directly assembled by the process of production itself or by the process of appropriation.

Workers in a factory, brought together by the capitalist in a cooperative division of labour, are directly assembled in the production process. Each worker also stands in a kind of direct relationship to the particular capitalist (individual or collective) who appropriates his or her surplus value, just as the peasant is directly related to the landlord who appropriates his rent. A direct relationship of some kind can also be said to exist, for example, among peasants who work independently of one another but who share the same landlord, even if they do not deliberately combine in opposition to him.

The relationship among members of a class, or between these members and other classes, is of a different kind. Neither the production process itself nor the process of surplus extraction actually brings them together. 'Class' does not refer simply to workers combined in a unit of production or opposed to a common exploiter in a unit of appropriation. Class implies a connection that extends beyond the immediate process of production and the immediate nexus of extraction, a connection that spans across particular units of production and appropriation. The connections and oppositions contained in the production process are the basis of class; but the relationship among people occupying similar positions in the relations of production is not given directly by the process of production and appropriation.

The links that connect the members of a class are not defined by the simple assertion that class is structurally determined by the relations of production. It still remains to be explained in what sense and through what mediations the relations of production establish connections among people who, even if they occupy similar positions in production relations, are not actually assembled in the process of production and appropriation. In *The Making of the English Working Class*, as we have seen, Thompson addressed himself to this very question. Here, he sought to account for the existence of class relationships among workers not directly assembled in the process of production and even engaged in widely divergent forms of production. In his account, it was indeed the relations of production that lay at the heart of these class relationships; but the determining structural pressures of production relations could be demonstrated only as they worked themselves out in a historical process of class formation, and these pressures could be apprehended theoretically only by introducing the mediating concept of 'experience'.

Class formation is particularly difficult to explain without resorting to concepts like Thompson's 'experience'. While people may participate directly in production and appropriation – the combinations, divisions and conflicts generated by these processes – class does not present itself to them so immediately. Since people are never actually 'assembled' in classes, the determining pressure exerted by a mode of production in the formation of classes cannot easily be expressed without reference to something like a common experience – a lived experience of production relations, the divisions between producers and appropriators, and more particularly, of the conflicts and struggles inherent in relations of exploitation. It is in the medium of this lived experience that social consciousness is shaped and with it the '*disposition* to *behave* as a class'.[35] Once the medium of 'experience' is introduced into the equation between production relations and class, so too are the historical and cultural particularities of this medium. This certainly complicates the issue; but to acknowledge, as Thompson does, the complexity of the mechanism by which production relations give rise to class is not to deny their determining pressure.

Thompson has been accused of idealism because of his emphasis on 'experience', as if this notion had slipped its material moorings. But his use of this concept is certainly not intended to sever the link between 'social being' and social consciousness or even to deny the primacy that historical materialism accords to social being in its

---

[35] Thompson, 'The Peculiarities of the English', in *The Poverty of Theory*, p. 85.

relation to consciousness. On the contrary, although Thompson sometimes distinguishes among levels of experience ('lived experience' and 'perceived experience'), his primary use of the term is as 'a necessary middle term between social being and social consciousness', the medium in which social being determines consciousness: 'it is by means of experience that the mode of production exerts a determining pressure on other activities'.[36] Experience in this sense is precisely 'the experience of determination'.[37] In fact, since Marx's concept of social being itself clearly refers not simply to the mode of production as an impersonal 'objective structure' but to the way that people live it (one can hardly avoid saying *experience* it), Thompson's 'experience' substantially overlaps with 'social being'.

The concept of 'experience', then, means that 'objective structures' do something to people's lives, and that this is why, for example, we have classes and not only relations of production. It is the task of the historian and the sociologist to explore what these 'structures' do to people's lives, how they do it, and what people do about it – or, as Thompson might put it, how the determining pressures of structured processes are experienced and handled by people. The burden of the theoretical message contained in the concept of 'experience' is, among other things, that the operation of determining pressures is a historical question, and therefore immediately an empirical one. There can be no rupture between the theoretical and the empirical, and Thompson the historian immediately takes up the task presented by Thompson the theorist.

Neither Marx nor Thompson nor anyone else has devised a 'rigorous' theoretical vocabulary to convey the effect of material conditions on conscious, active beings – beings whose conscious activity is itself a material force – or to comprehend the fact that these effects assume an infinite variety of historically specific empirical forms. But it can surely be no part of theoretical rigour to ignore these complexities merely for the sake of conceptual tidiness or a framework of 'structural definitions' which purport to resolve all important historical questions on the theoretical plane. Nor is it enough just to concede the existence of these complexities in some other order of reality – in the sphere of history as distinct from the

---

[36] Thompson, *Poverty of Theory*, p. 290; also pp. 200–1. A conception of 'determination' similar to Thompson's is given a systematic treatment in Raymond Williams, *Marxism and Literature* (Oxford, 1977), pp. 83–9.

[37] Thompson, *Poverty of Theory*, p. 298.

sphere of 'objective structures' – which belongs to a different level of discourse, the 'empirical' in opposition to the 'theoretical'. They must somehow be acknowledged by the theoretical framework itself and be embodied in the very notion of 'structure' – as, for example, in Thompson's notion of 'structured process'.

Deductive 'structural definitions' of class cannot explain how people sharing a common experience of production relations but not united by the process of production itself come by the 'disposition to behave as a class', let alone how the nature of that disposition – the degree of cohesion and consciousness associated with it, its expression in common goals, institutions, organizations, and united action – changes over time. Such definitions cannot take into account the pressures against class formation – pressures that may themselves be inherent in the structure, the objective determinations, of the prevailing mode of production – and the tension between the impulses towards and against coalescence and common action.

The notion of class as 'structured process', in contrast, acknowledges that while the structural basis of class formation is to be found in the antagonistic relations of production, the particular ways in which the structural pressures exerted by these relations actually operate in the formation of classes remains an open question to be resolved empirically by historical and sociological analysis. Such a conception of class also recognizes that this is where the most important and problematic questions about class lie, and that the usefulness of any class analysis – as either a sociological tool or a guide to political strategy – rests on its ability to account for the process of class formation. This means that any definition of class must invite, not foreclose, the investigation of process.

Thompson's insistence on class as process again puts in question the accusation that he equates class with class consciousness, that, to put it another way, he confuses the phenomenon of class itself with the conditions that make class 'an active historical subject'.[38] The first point to note about this accusation is that it is itself based on a confusion: it fails to take account of the difference between, on the one hand, class consciousness – that is, the active awareness of class identity – and, on the other hand, forms of consciousness that are shaped in various ways by class situations without yet finding expression in a self-aware and active class identity. Thompson is

[38] Cohen, *Marx's Theory*, p. 76.

especially concerned with the historical processes that intervene between the two.

More fundamentally, to equate class with a particular level of consciousness, or with the existence of class consciousness at all, *would* be to identify class with one stage of its development instead of stressing, as Thompson does, the complex processes that go to make up the 'disposition to behave as a class'. Thompson's conception of class as 'relationship' and 'process' is directed against definitions which, at best, imply that there is one point in the formation of classes where one can stop the process and say 'here is class, and not before', or at worst and, perhaps more commonly, seek to define classes outside the medium of time and historical process altogether. This can be done either by 'deducing' classes from 'structural positions' in relation to the means of production or by 'hypostasizing class identities – great personalized attributions of class aspirations or volition – which one knows are at best the metaphorical expression of most complex, and generally involuntary, processes'.[39] Thompson's object, then, is not to identify class with a particular level of consciousness or organization which makes it a conscious political force, but rather to focus our attention on class in the process of becoming, or making itself, such a force.

Class as 'structure' conceptualizes away the very fact that defines the role of class as the driving force of historical movement: the fact that class at the beginning of a historical mode of production is not what it is at the end. The identity of a mode of production is commonly said to reside in the persistence of its production relations: as long as the form in which 'surplus labour is pumped out of the direct producer' remains essentially the same, we are entitled to refer to a mode of production as 'feudal', 'capitalist', and so on. But *class* relations are the principle of movement *within* the mode of production. The history of a mode of production is the history of its developing class relations and, in particular, their changing relations to the relations of production. Classes develop within a mode of production in the process of coalescing around the relations of production and as the composition, cohesion, consciousness, and organization of the resulting class formations change. The mode of production reaches its crisis when the development of class relations within it actually transforms the relations of production themselves.

---

[39] Thompson, 'Peculiarities of the English', p. 85.

To account for historical movement, then, means precisely to deny that the relation between class and the relations of production is fixed.

The structural definition of class, as Thompson suggests, often tends to attribute a kind of personal volition to class as 'It'. The other side of that coin is the tendency to attribute failures to some kind of personality defect in 'It', like 'false consciousness'. There is more than a little irony, then, in the fact that Thompson, when countering conceptions of this kind, is accused of subjectivism and voluntarism. What is presented as an objectivist alternative to Thompson turns out to be a more extreme and idealist subjectivism and voluntarism, which merely transfers volition from human agency – a human agency bounded by 'determining pressures' and drawn into 'involuntary processes' – to a more exalted Subject, Class, a thing with a static identity, whose will is largely free of specific historical determinations.

This transfer upward of subjective volition reaches its highest point in structuralist arguments. Althusserians, for example, purport to expel subjectivity altogether from social theory and deny agency even to class-as-It; but, in a sense, they merely create an even more imperious Subject, the Structure itself, whose will is determined by nothing but the contradictions in its own arbitrary personality. Arguments which appear to Thompson's critics as subjectivist and voluntarist – his conception of human agency and his insistence on historical specificity apparently at the expense of 'objective structures' – are those which he marshals *against* subjectivism and voluntarism and for a recognition of the objective determining pressures that impinge upon human agency. Far from subordinating objective determining pressures to subjectivity and historical contingency, his point is to set historical investigation against the kind of inverted subjectivism, voluntarism and idealism that creep into analyses which lack a firm historical and sociological ground.

THE POLITICS OF THEORY

Thompson has always worked from the premise that theory has implications for practice. His definition of class, with its emphasis on class as an active process and a historical relationship, was certainly formulated to vindicate class against social scientists and historians who deny its existence; but it was also intended to counter both intellectual traditions and political practices that suppress human agency and in particular deny the self-activity of the working class in the making of history. By placing class struggle at the centre of theory and practice, Thompson intended to rescue 'history from below' not only as an intellectual enterprise but as a political project against both the oppressions of class domination and the programme of 'socialism from above' in its various incarnations from Fabianism to Stalinism.[40] His attacks on Althusserian Marxism were directed equally against what he perceived to be its theoretical deformations and against the political practice he found inscribed in them.

Thompson's critics have returned the compliment. In his concept of class and the historical project that rests upon it, they have often found a unity of theory and practice in which his 'subjectivist' theory of class underpins a 'populist socialism'. He has been criticized for being too quick to see, in any form of consciousness touched by class-determined life circumstances, the kind of class consciousness that suggests a readiness to act purposefully as a class. He exhibits, according to this criticism, a kind of 'populism' which treats as unproblematic the construction of a socialist politics out of popular culture.

Curiously, this judgment seems to unite defenders of 'orthodox' structural definitions of class with critics who maintain that Thompson has not gone far enough in pursuing the implications of his 'non-reductive' Marxism. So, for example, Stuart Hall has argued that Thompson conflates 'class-in-itself' with 'class-for-itself', and that inscribed in this confusion is a politics of 'too simple "populism"'.[41] The 'catch-all category of experience', Hall argues,

---

[40] Bryan Palmer, in his very useful book, *The Making of E.P. Thompson: Marxism, Humanism, and History* (Toronto, 1981), has provided an illuminating general discussion of the relationship between Thompson as a social historian and as a political activist. Palmer has warned me against describing Thompson's work as 'history from below', on the grounds that the phrase has misleading 'American populist' connotations and has lost favour with historians. He suggests that it obscures the extent of Thompson's concern for the relations between 'top' and 'bottom' and, in particular his increasing interest in the problem of the state. I accept the warning against misrepresenting the nature of Thompson's concerns, but want to retain the term in the sense in which it is (still) applied to a historiographical movement, deriving much of its early impetus from the British Communist Party Historians Group in the 1940s and 1950s, that has sought to explore the broad social foundations of historical processes and to illuminate the role of the 'common people' in shaping history.

[41] Stuart Hall, 'In Defense of Theory', in Raphael Samuel, ed., *People's History and Socialist Theory* (London, 1981), p. 384.

conflates the objective determinants of class with their appropriation in consciousness and seems to imply that '"the class" is always *really* in its place, at the ready, and can be summoned up "for socialism"', without facing up to 'all that is involved in saying that socialism has to be constructed by a real political practice'. Although it may not have been unambiguously obvious at the time of Hall's writing, in retrospect, and especially in the context of his affinities with 'post-Marxist' theories, it seems clear that this argument, which opened a wider gulf between 'objective structures' and class-conscious class formations, was coming close to the absolute 'non-correspondence' between the economic and the political proposed by post-Marxists; yet it is based on much the same account of Thompson's theory of class as that of Anderson or Cohen, and, apparently, on much the same dichotomy between structure and history. It is not insignificant, in view of the Althusserian flip of the coin to which I alluded in the previous chapter, that in this criticism of Thompson, Hall was writing in (qualified) defence of Althusser.

If, as I have argued, Thompson's historical project is opposed to the conflation – or, what is in effect the same thing, the simple equation – of objective determinations and their expressions in consciousness, and if his focus on the process of class formation presupposes a distinction between them since it is concerned with the changing relations between them, he cannot be accused of conflating the 'objective' and 'subjective' determinants of class, or structure and consciousness. The distinction between 'class-in-itself' and 'class-for-itself' is not, however, simply an analytic distinction between objective class structure and subjective class consciousness. It refers to two different stages in the process of class formation and two different historical modes of relationship between structure and consciousness – and, in this sense, Thompson certainly has a conception of 'class-in-itself', to which, for example, he alludes with his paradoxical formula, 'class struggle without class'.

The question then is whether Thompson crosses the line between these two modes of class too soon, whether he is too quick, as Hall suggests, to perceive, in any form of consciousness touched by class-determined life circumstances, a readiness to act purposefully as a class. This question is above all a political one, and there is undoubtedly a danger here. Romanticism about the customs and traditions of the 'people' and about the radical promise contained in the mere difference and separateness of popular culture is not the soundest foundation for building a socialist movement or assessing and overcoming the 'people's' own resistance to socialist politics. But Thompson surely has no illusions about this, whatever his successors in 'people's history' may think.

Thompson's message is indeed political; but there is something else in his recovery of popular consciousness and the 'making' of class than a failure to recognize the difference and barriers between, on the one hand, popular culture, which arises directly out of experience – an experience of work, exploitation, oppression, and struggle – and, on the other hand, an active socialist consciousness which is painfully crafted by political practice. His historical project, his reconstruction of history as it is made by the working class as active agents and not simply as passive victims, grows directly out of the basic political principle of Marxism and its particular understanding of socialist practice: that socialism can come only through the self-emancipation of the working class.[42]

This proposition implies that the working class is the only social group possessing not only an immediate interest in resisting capitalist exploitation but also a collective power adequate to end it. The proposition also implies a scepticism about the authenticity – or, indeed, the likelihood – of emancipation not achieved by self-activity and struggle but won by proxy or conferred by benefaction. There are no guarantees here; but however difficult it may be to construct socialist practice out of popular consciousness, there is, according to this view, no other material out of which it can be constructed and no other socialism that is consistent with both political realism and democratic values. Perhaps the point is simply that socialism will come about either in this way or not at all.

HEGEMONY AND SUBSTITUTIONISM

When Thompson launched his controversial attack on Althusserianism, one of his principal concerns was to counter the drift away

---

[42] Thompson, for example, opposes his own work to the 'Fabian orthodoxy, in which the great majority of working people are seen as passive victims of *laissez faire*, with the exception of a handful of far-sighted organizers (notably Francis Place)' (*English Working Class*, p. 12). This 'orthodoxy' is, of course, not unrelated to the Fabian political programme, with its view of the working class as passive victims requiring the imposition of socialism from above, not by means of class struggle but through piecemeal reform and social engineering by an enlightened minority of intellectuals and philanthropic members of the ruling class.

from this democratic understanding of the socialist project on the part of Western Marxism, towards a theoretical abandonment of the working class as the principal agent of social transformation through the medium of class struggle, and a transfer of that role to other social actors, most especially to intellectuals. 'There is no mark more distinctive of Western Marxisms', he wrote,

> nor more revealing as to their profoundly anti-democratic premises. Whether Frankfurt School or Althusser, they are marked by their very heavy emphasis upon the ineluctable weight of ideological modes of domination – domination which destroys every space for the initiative or creativity of the mass of the people – a domination from which only the enlightened minority or intellectuals can struggle free. ... it is a sad premise from which socialist theory should start (all men and women, except for us, are originally stupid) and one which is bound to lead on to pessimistic or authoritarian conclusions.[43]

This kind of theoretical 'substitutionism' in its most extreme form can be achieved by doing what Stuart Hall accuses some Althusserians, though apparently not Althusser himself, of doing: treating all 'classes as mere "bearers" of historical process, without agency: and historical process itself as a process "without a subject"'.[44] But much the same effect is produced, Thompson suggests, by conceiving of class as a static category, and being less concerned about the historical process of class formation than about the deductive charting of structural class locations or the theoretical construction of an ideal class identity. These are the kinds of formulation that lend themselves far too easily to the dismissal of actual historical, and hence imperfect, forms of class consciousness as 'false' and therefore in need of substitutes.[45] If there is a political message inscribed in Thompson's theory of class, it is against the theorization of a 'substitutionism' in which the working class is not merely represented but eclipsed by its substitute.

Much of Thompson's work has been directed, explicitly or implicitly, against the view that hegemony is one-sided and complete, imposing 'an all-embracing domination upon the ruled – or upon all those who are not intellectuals – reaching down to the very threshold of their experience, and implanting within their minds at birth categories of subordination which they are powerless to shed and

[43] Thompson, *Poverty of Theory*, pp.377–8   [44] Hall, 'In Defense of Theory', p. 383.
[45] See, e.g., Thompson, 'Eighteenth-Century English Society', p. 148.

which their experience is powerless to correct'.[46] This, as he suggests, is a dominant theme in Western Marxism, this tendency to identify hegemony with the thorough absorption of subordinate classes into ruling class ideology and cultural domination (probably with the assistance of Ideological State Apparatuses), so that the construction of a counter-hegemonic consciousness and culture and the establishment of working-class hegemony must apparently be accomplished by free-spirited intellectuals.[47]

Such a definition of hegemony accords well with theoretical constructions of class in which nothing exists between the objective constitution of classes by modes of production, on the one hand, and an ideal revolutionary class consciousness, on the other, except a vast empirical-historical (and hence impure and theoretically indigestible) spectrum of 'false' consciousness. But there is an added irony here, as I suggested in the previous chapter (and elsewhere): the flip side of this brand of Marxism is the post-Marxist abandonment of class politics altogether and its replacement by the politics of 'discourse'.

For Thompson, in contrast, hegemony is not synonymous with domination by one class and submission by the other. Instead, it embodies class *struggle* and bears the mark of subordinate classes, their self-activity and their resistance. His theory of class, with its emphasis on the process of class formation, is intended to permit the recognition of 'imperfect' or 'partial' forms of popular consciousness as authentic expressions of class and class struggle, valid in their historical circumstances even if 'wrong' from the standpoint of later, or ideal, developments.

It is one thing to mistake the mere *separateness* of popular culture for radical opposition, ready to be harnessed immediately to the struggle for socialism; it is quite another simply to mark out the space where the cultural writ of the dominant class does not run, and to identify 'popular' consciousness – however resistant it may be to the formation of 'true' class consciousness – as the stuff out of which a complete class consciousness must and can nonetheless be made. To deny the authenticity of 'partial' class consciousness, to treat it as false instead of as a historically intelligible 'option under pressure',[48] has important strategic consequences. We are invited

---

[46] *Ibid.*, p. 164.   [47] See *ibid.*, p. 163 n. 60.
[48] Raymond Williams, 'Notes on Marxism in Britain since 1945', *New Left Review*, 100 (November 1976–January 1977), p. 87.

either to look for surrogate agents of class struggle and historical change, or to abandon the field altogether to the hegemonic enemy. It is against these political alternatives, and their theoretical foundations in a concept of class as 'structure' or ideal identity, that Thompson sets his own theory of class as process and relationship.

Raymond Williams, in his 'Notes on British Marxism in Britain since 1945', wrote of his own stance in relation to the available choices confronting British Marxists in the 1950s and his rejection of the rhetorical populism which complacently ignored the implications of 'consumer' capitalism and the 'powerful new pull' it exerted upon the people. At the same time, he continued:

because I saw the process as options under pressure, and knew where the pressure was coming from, I could not move to the other available position: that contempt of the people, of their hopelessly corrupted state, of their vulgarity and credulity by comparison with an educated minority, which was the staple of cultural criticism of a non-Marxist kind and which seems to have survived intact, through the appropriate alterations of vocabulary, into a formalist Marxism which makes the whole people, including the whole working class, mere carriers of the structures of a corrupt ideology. . . .[49]

Against this trend, Williams insisted that 'there were still, and still powerful, existing resources':

To stay with the existing resources; to learn and perhaps to teach new resources; to live the contradictions and the options under pressure so that instead of denunciation or writing-off there was a chance of understanding them and tipping them the other way: if these things were populism, then it is as well that the British Left, including most Marxists, stayed with it.[50]

Edward Thompson, for one, certainly stayed with it. His theory of class, the discovery of authentic expressions of class in popular consciousness and culture, represent an effort 'to live the contradictions and options under pressure . . . instead of denunciation or writing-off'. His insistence on a historical and sociological account of working-class 'reformism', for example, instead of the ritual excommunication which denounces it from a vantage point outside

---

[49] *Ibid.* For a similar view, see Thompson, 'Peculiarities of the English', pp. 69–70, where he attacks schematic, unhistorical and unsociological conceptions of class, in particular, those which have produced ritual denunciations of working-class reformism, instead of an understanding of its 'deep sociological roots,' and have thus neglected a vital datum confronting any socialist political practice.

[50] Williams, 'Notes on Marxism', p. 87.

of history as the 'false consciousness' of a working class 'It', implies that we must understand the 'existing resources' in order to 'tip them the other way'.

There are, of course, dangers here too. 'To stay with the existing resources' can become an excuse for not looking beyond them; to acknowledge the 'deep sociological roots' of 'reformism' as a political reality that must be confronted may lead to accepting it as a limit on the horizons of struggle. It is one thing to acknowledge the authenticity of working-class 'options under pressure' and to be wary of the notion of false consciousness as an invitation to 'write off'. It is quite another to pass over the failures and limitations in many forms of working-class organization and ideology. There is certainly room for debate on the Left about where the line is to be drawn between accepting 'existing resources' as a challenge to struggle and submitting to them as a limit upon it.

CHAPTER 4

History or technological determinism?

We need to be reminded why Marxism ascribes a determinative primacy to class struggle. It is not because class is the only form of oppression or even the most frequent, consistent, or violent source of social conflict, but rather because its terrain is the social organization of production which creates the material conditions of existence itself. The first principle of historical materialism is not class or class struggle, but the organization of material life and social reproduction. Class enters the picture when access to the conditions of existence and to the means of appropriation are organized in class ways, that is, when some people are systematically compelled by differential access to the means of production or appropriation to transfer surplus labour to others.

The compulsion to transfer surplus labour can take different forms, with varying degrees of transparency. Capitalism undoubtedly represents a special case, because capitalist appropriation is not a distinctly visible act – like, say, the serf's payment of dues to the lord, which constitutes a separate act of appropriation, after the fact of the serf's labour and in the context of a transparent relationship between appropriator and producer. In contrast, there is no immediately obvious way of separating the act of capitalist appropriation from the process of production or from the process of commodity exchange through which capital realizes its gains. The concept of surplus *value* – as distinct from the more general category of surplus *labour*, which applies to all forms of surplus appropriation – is meant to convey this complex relation between production, realization in commodity exchange and capitalist appropriation.

There has been no shortage of critics, including Marxist economists, who have been keen to point out the difficulty of explaining these relations in quantitative terms – that is, of measuring 'value' and 'surplus', or of relating 'value' to 'price'. It is unlikely that

Marx's concept of surplus labour or surplus value was ever intended to provide the kind of mathematical measure these critics require; but, in any case, this shortcoming – if shortcoming it is – has no bearing on the historical significance of 'surplus labour'. The fundamental insight encased in this concept concerns the conditions in which people have access to the means of subsistence and reproduction and the proposition that a decisive historic break occurs when the prevailing conditions systematically compel some to transfer part of their labour or its product to others.

The critical datum in explaining the role of class in history is not, then, the quantitative measure of the 'surplus' but the specific nature of the compulsion to transfer it and the specific nature of the social relation in which that transfer takes place.[1] In cases where direct producers – like feudal peasants – remain in possession of the means of production, the transfer of surplus is determined by direct coercion, by means of the appropriator's superior force. In capitalism, the compulsion is of a different kind. The direct producer's obligation to forfeit surplus is a pre-condition for access to the means of production, the means of sustaining life itself. What compels direct producers to produce more than they will themselves consume, and to transfer the surplus to someone else, is the 'economic' necessity which makes their own subsistence inseparable from that transfer of surplus labour. Wage labourers in capitalism, lacking the means to carry on their own labour, only acquire them by entering into a relationship with capital. This need not, of course, mean that those who are obliged to transfer surplus labour will get *only* the bare necessities; it simply means that the transfer is a necessary condition for their access to the means of survival and reproduction – and whatever they can acquire above and beyond that with those means. Such relations can be shown to exist even in the absence of any means of quantifying a 'surplus' or measuring the relative gains of producers and appropriators. We need only acknowledge that the producer's self-reproduction has among its necessary conditions a relation to an appropriator who claims part of his or her labour or product.

[1] Marx's classic statement of this principle occurs in *Capital* III (Moscow, 1971), pp. 791–2, where he explains that the key to every social form, 'which reveals the innermost secret, the hidden basis of the entire social structure', is 'the specific economic form, in which unpaid surplus labour is pumped out of direct producers', though the same 'economic basis' can take an infinite variety of empirical forms 'which can be ascertained only by analysis of the empirically given circumstances'.

It is no doubt possible to identify transfers of surplus labour which are not determined by coercive imperatives (e.g., gifts, the fulfilment of kinship obligations), but these are not the kind to which the concept of class specifically refers. It is also important to acknowledge that class may not always entail direct relationships, in the sense of face-to-face confrontations, between exploiter and exploited, and that in the absence of such confrontations, class relations may not generate conflict as readily as other, more direct non-class antagonisms may do. But class conflict has a particular historical resonance because it implicates the social organization of production, the very basis of material existence. Class struggle has a distinctive potential as a transformative force because, whatever the immediate motivations of any particular class conflict, the terrain of struggle is strategically situated at the heart of social existence.

How, then, do relations between producers and appropriators figure in the materialist explanation of historical movement? I shall distinguish between two broad categories of Marxist explanation, illustrated by two of their most important recent exponents. The first situates production relations and class within a larger, transhistorical context of technological development. The other seeks specific principles of motion in every social form and its dominant social property relations. The distinction I am drawing is not simply that between Marxist theories which give primacy to 'forces of production' and those that give priority to 'relations of production' and class struggle. Instead, I want to emphasize the difference between theories that posit some general, transhistorical and universal law of historical change – which invariably means some kind of technological determinism – and those that stress the specificity of every social form – which generally means an exploration of the specific 'laws of motion' set in train by the prevailing social relations between appropriators and producers.

Two especially important examples from recent Marxist scholarship will suffice to illustrate the point. From their respective theoretical vantage points, both offer an account of the major historical transformation that has preoccupied Marxist historians, the transition from feudalism to capitalism. The first comes from the influential school of 'Rational Choice Marxism', in the person of John Roemer, who has joined his distinctive theory of exploitation and class with a theory of history indebted to G.A. Cohen's powerful defence of Marxism conceived as a technological determinism.[2] The other example is the Marxist historian Robert Brenner and his work on the origins of capitalism.

History, according to John Roemer, takes the form of an evolution in property relations, in which 'progressively fewer kinds of productive factors remain acceptable as property'.[3] For example, property in persons is eliminated as slave society passes into feudalism, leaving some property rights in the labour of others and property in alienable means of production. The transition from feudalism to capitalism eliminates property rights in the labour of others while still allowing property in the alienable means of production, and so on. This 'progressive socialization of property' occurs for reasons 'related to efficiency', that is, the advancement of the forces of production. 'The mechanism that brings about this evolution is class struggle', but 'the reason such an evolution occurs lies somewhere deeper: evolution occurs because *the level of development of the technology outgrows the particular form of the social organization, which comes to constrain and fetter it*'.[4]

The connection between the mechanism (class struggle) and the deep cause (technological determinism) can be explained in the following way. Class struggle serves as a 'facilitator' in the transition from one social form to another, when the 'dissonance' between the level of development of productive forces and the old economic structure reaches a crisis point. So, for example, Roemer asks us to 'imagine' (his word) a feudal system, with lords and serfs, but one in which 'a nascent capitalist economy is emerging alongside' the feudal system.[5] 'Now there is an option: capitalists and feudal lords can compete for control of the working population. If the technology or forces of production that the capitalists are using enables them to pay higher real wages than serfs can earn, then there is an economic advantage to the liberation from serfdom that did not formerly exist.' Serfs can become independent peasants, taking advantage of

---

[2] G.A. Cohen, *Karl Marx's Theory of History: A Defence* (Princeton, 1978).
[3] John Roemer, *Free to Lose* (London, 1988), p. 126.
[4] *Ibid.*, p. 6. Emphasis in the original.   [5] *Ibid.*, p. 115.

the trade opened up by the capitalists, or they can become artisans or proletarians in the towns. 'The competition between feudalism and capitalism now enables class struggle against feudalism to be successful even though formerly it was not.'

We now have three levels of explanation: (1) the deep cause (technological determinism); (2) the historical process (the successive elimination of forms of exploitation or the progressive socialization of property); (3) the 'facilitator' (class struggle – though this only 'facilitates' a process that was 'bound to come sooner or later'[6]). It is not entirely clear at what level the 'rational choice' model should be introduced. The most obvious place is in class struggle, which implies that change occurs when (if not because) people are in a position to choose the available option of the next, more progressive mode of production. At the same time, there appears to be an overarching rational choice, at the level of the deep cause, having to do with 'the ceaseless effort of rational human beings to alleviate their conditions of scarcity'[7] – though they do not actually choose the next available economic structure *because* it is conducive to technological progress. In either case, the necessary link between the rational-choice model and the theory of history is the presupposition that there is a direct correspondence between the self-interested actions of individual rational actors and the requirements of technical progress and economic growth.

This three-layered structure raises rather more questions than it answers, not least about the connections among its three levels. Are rational individuals, insofar as they are the makers of history (but are they?), motivated by the desire to alleviate scarcity through technological improvement or by the wish to escape exploitation – or neither? Is class struggle necessary or not; and if not, what is the mechanism of historical change? Or does the deep cause somehow make mechanisms and facilitators redundant, since change is somehow 'bound to come sooner or later' anyway, behind the backs of rational individuals? And where, in any case, is the *struggle* in class struggle? We have lords and capitalists competing to give more attractive terms to producers, to serfs who might want to become proletarians; and we have serfs escaping from lords – apparently without constraints, and willingly giving up their rights of possession – as soon as a more attractive option comes along; but *struggle....*?

[6] *Ibid.*, p. 124.   [7] *Ibid.*, p. 123.

What, indeed, is the 'economic advantage' that would impel serfs to prefer a wage which, by some sophisticated statistical measure, was higher than their 'earnings' as serfs, at the cost of losing their rights of possession, giving up the land which provides them with full and direct access to the means of subsistence in exchange for the uncertainties of the proletarian condition? For that matter, even if serfs choose this option, how do they manage to achieve it? If the lords' property 'rights' in the labour of others have anything to do with the 'control' – i.e., the power – that they exercise over the serfs, how is it that when the critical moment of transition comes, serfs can simply choose to escape the lord's control just because a more eligible option has presented itself? Has feudalism no self-sustaining logic and resources of its own to resist this easy transition?

All this is quite apart from the fact that the whole edifice is constructed without benefit of evidence. Roemer has chosen his words carefully when he asks us to 'imagine'. We can hardly do anything else. ('Imagine' and 'suppose' are the basic vocabulary of this game-theoretic discourse.) We are not (or not always) being asked to believe that this is how things actually happened, or even that it was historically possible for them to happen in this way, only that it is logically conceivable that they did (though it is never made clear why we should be interested in such imaginary logical possibilities).

Indeed, it is very unlikely that Roemer himself believes his own imaginary account of the transition to capitalism; and it is a measure of the price exacted by his game-theoretic model that it obliges him to set aside everything he undoubtedly knows about the power relations between lords and serfs, the dispossession of small producers and the concentration of landlordly property which were the conditions of the transition; everything, that is, about coercion, compulsion, imperatives, or indeed about the *social relations* of exploitation. This process of transition which Roemer asks us to 'imagine' evidently has little to do with history, and it would serve no purpose to counter this imaginary story with evidence. History is, apparently, a subject about which we can say anything we like.

BEGGING THE QUESTION OF HISTORY

There is one thing that Roemer asks us to 'imagine' that is inescapably critical to his argument, an assumption upon which the whole shaky edifice rests. We must accept that capitalism already exists as an 'option', that a 'nascent capitalist economy is emerging alongside' the feudal system. We must also never ask how this came to be so, though for Roemer this evidently presents no problem:

According to historical materialism, feudal, capitalist, and socialist exploitation all exist under feudalism. At some point feudal relations become a fetter on the development of the productive forces, and they are eliminated by the bourgeois revolution.... Historical materialism, in summary, claims that history progresses by the successive elimination of forms of exploitation which are socially unnecessary in the dynamic sense.[8]

He goes on to characterize this interpretation as 'a translation of the technological determinist aspect of historical materialist theory into the language of the theory of exploitation'. According to this interpretation of historical materialism, all successive forms of exploitation are already contained in the preceding ones (his account of the progress from slave society to capitalism suggests that this retrospective analysis goes back beyond feudalism), so that all forms of exploitation which have emerged in the course of history have apparently been present since the beginning; and history proceeds by the process of elimination.

Each form of exploitation is in turn eliminated as it obstructs the development of productive forces. In this sense, technological determinism, for Roemer, supplies the mechanism (deep cause?) of elimination. But the irreducible first premise of the argument is that each successive social form exists simultaneously with the one that precedes it. In this respect, Roemer's theory of elimination is simply a more ingenious variation on an old theme.

It has been a favourite ploy of theorists who have trouble with *process* to beg the question of history by assuming that all historical stages – and especially capitalism – have in effect existed, at least as recessive traits, since the beginning. Such accounts of history typically invoke some *deus ex machina*, some external factor, to explain the process that brings these recessive or embryonic traits to fruition. Traditionally the most popular 'external' forces have been trade (markets enlarging and contracting, with trade routes opening and closing) and/or technical progress, both conceived as exogenous to the systems being transformed, either in the sense that they are determined by alien intrusions such as barbarian invasions, or in the

---

[8] Roemer, *A General Theory of Exploitation and Class* (Cambridge, Mass., 1982), pp. 270–1.

sense that they operate according to some universal natural law (progress, the natural development of the human mind, or perhaps, more scientifically, demographic cycles) not specific or instrinsic to the existing social form.

Assumptions such as these have been a staple of bourgeois ideology, which I shall take up in a subsequent chapter. For the moment, it is enough to note that Marxists too have often gone in for this kind of thing by conjuring up images of aspirant modes of production lurking in the interstices of previous ones, waiting only for the opportunity to establish their 'dominance' when certain obstacles are removed (it seems so much easier somehow to account for the demise of what already exists than to explain its coming into being). The Althusserian concept of 'social formation', for example, in which any and all modes of production can coexist without any need to explain their emergence, serves exactly this purpose.

There can be no doubt that this kind of conceptual conjuring has far too often served in place of a Marxist theory of history; and, no doubt, Marx's more formulaic aphorisms about the stages of history and successive modes of production could be read as invitations to evade the issue of historical processes in this way. It was Marx, after all, who first spoke of 'fetters' and 'interstices'. But there is much more in Marx which demands that we look for the key to historical change in the dynamic logic of existing social relations without assuming the very thing that needs to be explained.

Robert Brenner's primary purpose has been to break the prevailing habit of begging the central historical question, the practice of assuming the existence of the very thing whose emergence needs to be explained. He distinguishes between two kinds of historical theories in Marx's own work, the first still heavily reliant on the mechanical materialism and economic determinism of the eighteenth-century Enlightenment, the second emerging out of Marx's mature critique of classical political economy. The first is characterized by its begging of the question, invoking the self-development of productive forces via the division of labour which evolves in response to expanding markets, a 'nascent' capitalism in the womb of feudal society.

The paradoxical character of this theory is thus immediately evident: ... there really is no *transition* to accomplish: since the model starts with bourgeois society in the towns, foresees its evolution as taking place via bourgeois mechanisms [i.e. change and competition leading to the adoption of the most advanced techniques and to concomitant changes in the social organization of production. EMW], and has feudalism transcend itself in consequence of its exposure to trade, the problem of how one type of society is transformed into another is simply assumed away and never posed.[9]

Later, Marx was to pose the question very differently. He substantially revised his views on property relations in general and pre-capitalist property relations in particular: 'In the *Grundrisse* and *Capital*, Marx defines property relations as, in the first instance, the relationships of the direct producers to the means of production and to one another *which allow them to reproduce themselves as they were*. By this account, what distinguishes pre-capitalist property relations ... is that they provided the direct producers with the full means of reproduction.' The condition for maintaining this possession was the peasant community, and its consequence was that the lords required 'extra-economic' means of taking a surplus, which in turn demanded the reproduction of their own communities. The structure of these property relations was thus reproduced 'by communities of rulers and cultivators which made possible the economic reproduction of their individual members'.[10] Given these property relations, reproduced by communities of rulers and direct producers in conflict, the individual lords and individual peasants adopted the economic strategies that would best maintain and improve their situation – what Brenner calls their rules for reproduction. The aggregate result of these strategies was the characteristic feudal pattern of development.

The transition to a new society with new developmental patterns thus entailed not simply a shift from one mode of production to another alternative mode, but a transformation of existing property relations, from feudal rules of reproduction to new, capitalist rules. According to these new rules, the separation of direct producers from the means of production, and the end of 'extra-economic' modes of extraction, would leave both appropriators and producers subject to competition, and able – indeed obliged – to move in response to the requirements of profitability under competitive pressures. This inevitably raised a new and different question about the transition from feudalism to capitalism: 'it was the problem of

[9] Robert Brenner, 'Bourgeois Revolution and Transition to Capitalism', in A.L. Beier *et al.*, eds., *The First Modern Society* (Cambridge, 1989), p. 280.
[10] *Ibid.*, p. 287.

accounting for the transformation of pre-capitalist property relations into capitalist property relations via the action of pre-capitalist society itself'.[11]

This is the challenge that Brenner has taken up: to offer an explanation of the transition to capitalism which relies entirely on the dynamics of feudal relations, and their conditions of reproduction, without reading capitalism back into its predecessor or presenting it as an available option.[12] This project also requires an acknowledgement that pre-capitalist property relations have a logic and tenacity of their own, which cannot be conjured away by the convenient assumption that people are driven by an urge to take the next available (capitalist) option, an urge that existing structures cannot resist.

This is something that Roemer's model is systematically unable to take into account; and, in this respect, it is no different from a long tradition going back to Adam Smith, a tradition that has included Marxists (indeed, the young Marx himself) as well as non-Marxists. It has, in fact, been the rule rather than the exception to assume the existence of capitalism in order to explain its coming into being, to explain the transition from feudalism to capitalism by already assuming capitalist structures and capitalist motivations. But the relations of capitalism and the associated compulsions of capital accumulation, the specific logic of capitalism and its systemic imperatives, can in no way be deduced from the dominant relations of feudalism nor discovered in its 'interstices'. Nor can the relations and imperatives of capitalism be deduced from the mere existence of towns, on the assumption – unwarranted both logically and historically – that towns are by nature capitalist.

[11] *Ibid.*, p. 293.

[12] Brenner's contribution to the collection on *Analytical Marxism* (Cambridge, 1986) edited by Roemer, which presents his account of the transition in a schematic form, argues that the conventional explanation of the development of capitalism, based largely on Adam Smith, assumes precisely the extraordinary phenomenon that needs to be explained; that property relations must be understood as 'relations of reproduction'; that pre-capitalist economies have their own logic and 'solidity', which are in effect denied by the conventional view; that capitalist development is a more historically limited and specific occurrence than is allowed by theories that attribute it to some universal law of technical progress; and that the history of the transition cannot be explained by assuming that there is a necessary correspondence between the self-interested actions of individual actors and the requirements of economic growth. In these respects, his argument runs directly counter to Roemer's basic assumptions, and to Cohen's technological determinism. It is worth adding that his schematic argument in this volume, in contrast to the contributions of rational choice Marxists, is grounded in historical research and is based on the premise that the work of historical *explanation* needed to be done in advance of the analytic *presentation*.

A GENERAL THEORY OF HISTORICAL SPECIFICITY

There will be more on the subject of towns, capitalism and the begging of historical questions in the next chapter. Here, we need simply to take note of the differences between Brenner and Roemer and the implications they have for the Marxist theory of history. First, the empirical differences: Brenner's history of capitalist development puts in question nearly every point in Roemer's imaginary scenario. Capitalism does not, in his account, simply exist, miraculously, 'alongside' the feudal economy, nor is it here a product of mercantile interests in the towns competing with feudal interests in the countryside. Direct producers do not join the capitalist economy by fleeing the countryside to become artisans or proletarians. While the development of capitalism certainly presupposes the existence of markets and trade, there is no warrant for assuming that markets and trade, which have existed throughout recorded history, are inherently, or even tendentially, capitalist. In Brenner's account, the transition to a distinctively *capitalist* form of society is a process set in train by the transformation of agrarian relations themselves, in particular conditions which have little to do with the mere expansion of trade.

Indeed, this account (like others in the famous 'Transition Debate'[13]) begins by casting doubt on the inherent antagonism of markets and trade to the feudal order. It is not capitalism or the market as an 'option' or *opportunity* that needs to be explained, but the emergence of capitalism and the capitalist market as an *imperative*. Brenner gives an account of the very special conditions in which direct producers in the countryside were subjected to market imperatives, rather than the emergence of 'options' for direct producers, opportunities offered them by trading interests in the towns.

In the traditional models of technological determinism and 'bourgeois revolution', together with their non-Marxist counterparts, an already present capitalist society simply grows to maturity. In Brenner's model, 'one type of society is transformed into another'. The point is not that city is replaced by countryside in his analysis nor that trade and commerce play only a marginal role but rather that Brenner acknowledges the *specificity* of capitalism and its dis-

[13] Rodney Hilton, ed., *The Transition from Feudalism to Capitalism* (London, 1976). See also Hilton, 'Towns in English Feudal Society', in *Class Conflict and the Crisis of Feudalism: Essays in Medieval Social History* (London, 1985).

tinctive 'laws of motion', which also means acknowledging the necessity of explaining how trade and commerce (not to mention cities), which have existed throughout recorded history, became something other than they had always been. It goes without saying that the existence of cities and traditional forms of trade throughout Europe (and elsewhere) was a necessary condition for England's specific pattern of development, but to say this is far from explaining how they acquired a distinctively *capitalist* dynamic. Brenner has yet to explain the role of cities and the urban economy in European economic development; but, by explaining how the *market* acquired a qualitatively new role in agrarian production relations, as direct producers were deprived of non-market access to the means of their own self-reproduction, he has established the context in which the systemic role of cities and trade was transformed.

This account has significant theoretical implications, especially in challenging the assumptions of technological determinism. Brenner's history suggests that there is no historical necessity for less productive 'economic structures' to be followed by more productive ones and stresses the historical specificity of the conditions in which the process of 'self-sustaining' growth was first established. Roemer's response to this challenge is simply that capitalism did eventually spread to other parts of Europe, even if it first emerged in England, so that Brenner's evidence does not contradict Cohen's version of historical materialism, with its universal law of technological determinism. But quite apart from its cavalier treatment of historical time, and a similar treatment of geographical space, this response depends on treating the historically specific process of capitalist expansion, a priori, as a transhistorical law of nature.

When Roemer invokes the universality of capitalist development, at least its eventual spread to other parts of Europe, he takes it for granted that this bespeaks a universal process of technological advance. Yet this simply begs the question. Capitalism itself has, since its inception, displayed a distinctive capacity for expansion and universalization, a capacity rooted in its specific pressures for accumulation, competition and the improvement of labour productivity. The point of Brenner's argument, in contrast to technological determinism, is to avoid simply taking for granted the universal development of capitalism by subsuming it under some universal law of technological change, and instead to explain how historically specific conditions produced capitalism's *unique* technological imperatives and its *unique* expansionist drive.

In seeking the moving force for the transition from feudalism within the dynamic of feudalism itself, not by reading capitalist principles and motivations back into history, nor by assuming some transhistorical 'general theory' of motion, Brenner challenges the whole notion of historical theory as a general account of universal laws which move in a predetermined direction. Not only does he question the historical-materialist credentials of such a theory by attributing it to an undeveloped phase of Marx's work, still uncritically bound to classical bourgeois thought; but his whole historical project testifies to a view that a theory of history subsuming the entire developmental process from classical antiquity to capitalism (let alone the whole of world history) under one universal and essentially unidirectional law of motion would need to be so general as to be vacuous. How useful, after all, is a 'theory' of technological progress that claims to be equally compatible with moments of rapid technical improvement and long epochs of stagnation or 'petrification'?[14]

It is one thing to say that capitalism uniquely fosters technological development. It is quite another to contend that capitalism developed *because* it fosters technological development, or that capitalism *had* to develop because history somehow requires the development of productive forces, or that less productive systems are necessarily followed by more productive ones, or that the development of productive forces is the only available principle of historical movement from one mode of production to another. Once the specific imperative of capitalism to improve the forces of production is conceded – as it is by even the most uncompromising technological determinist – it seems both more efficient (on the principle of Ockham's razor) and less question begging to say that the universality of capitalism demonstrates the *specificity* of its drive to improve productive forces, its competitive and expansionist drive and capacity, rather than the *generality* of technological determinism.

[14] It was Marx himself who insisted that capitalism is unique in its drive to revolutionize productive forces, while other modes of production have tended to conserve existing forces, and that 'petrification' may have been the rule rather than the exception. See, for example, *Capital* 1 (Moscow, 1971), pp. 456–7. A similar view appears even in the *Communist Manifesto*, which in other respects still adheres to the early, uncritical theory of history.

This proposition is, at any rate, more consistent with the variety of developmental patterns which have manifested themselves throughout history.

The most distinctive feature of historical materialism – that which distinguishes it most radically, in form as well as substance, from conventional 'bourgeois' theories of progress – is not its adherence to a general law of technological determinism. It is, rather, a focus (such as that which characterizes the most complete and systematic of Marx's own works, his actual practice in the critique of political economy and the analysis of capitalism) on the specificity of every mode of production, its endogenous logic of process, its own 'laws of motion', its characteristic crises – or, to use Brenner's formula, its own rules for reproduction.

This is not simply a matter of distinguishing between a 'general theory' of history and a 'special' theory of capitalism. It is rather a different (and general) theory of history of which the theory of capitalism, with its specific laws of motion, is the prime example. While technological determinism takes the form of retrospective or even teleological predictions, with the benefit of hindsight, with such a degree of generality that no empirical evidence could possibly falsify it, historical materialism demands empirical specification which does not assume a predetermined outcome. But if the mark of a theory is the existence of 'fixed points' which remain constant throughout its specific applications, there are more than enough fixed points here – in particular, the principle that at the foundation of every social form there are property relations whose conditions of reproduction structure social and historical processes.

DOES MARXISM NEED A UNILINEAR VIEW OF HISTORY?

One of the most serious and frequent criticisms levelled against Marxism has been that it subscribes to a mechanical and simplistic view of history according to which all societies are predestined to go through a single, inexorable sequence of stages from primitive communism to slavery to feudalism, and finally to capitalism which will inevitably give way to socialism. What is at issue in such criticisms is not simply the value of Marxism as a theory of history and its alleged inability to account for the variety of historical patterns on display in the world, but also the viability of the socialist project itself. Since

Marxism is so clearly wrong about the unilinear course of history, surely it is equally wrong about the inevitability – indeed, the possibility – of socialism.

This criticism of Marxism as a theory of history has become increasingly hard to sustain in the face of all the good Marxist history that clearly contradicts it. While the characterization of Marxism as a unilinear determinism has been tenacious, the large and growing body of distinguished Marxist historiography has forced the critics to open another front of attack. Even before the collapse of Communism, we were being told that without a mechanically deterministic and unilinear history, Marxism cannot exist at all. Having lost hold of its lifeline, its albeit profoundly mistaken conception of history, Marxism is dead. And whither Marxist history, so too goes the socialist project, since there can no longer be any grounds for believing that history has laid the foundation for socialism.

It must be said, however, that critics of Marxism have not been alone in believing that something vital is lost with the unilinear conception of history and that socialist conviction must suffer a grievous injury with the abandonment of the simple belief in a universal pattern of history, characterized in particular by an inexorable growth of productive forces. This consideration must certainly have figured, for example, in G.A. Cohen's attempt to revive a technological-determinist Marxism (and in Roemer's adaptation of Cohen). There are both critics and advocates who are convinced that the socialist project must be weakened by the loss of faith in a theory of history according to which socialism is the culmination of one universal pattern of historical evolution. Marxism, according to this view, needs a (more or less) unilinear conception of history conceived as a universal pattern of systematic and constant growth of productive forces; and, without it, the socialist project is deeply compromised, because on this conception of history depends the conviction that the inevitable rise of capitalism will prepare the ground for socialism with equal inevitability.

I have been arguing here that historical materialism is not, now or in its origins, a technological determinism; that its great strength lies not in any unilinear conception of history but, on the contrary, in a unique sensitivity to historical specificities. It remains to be shown that the socialist project has nothing of any consequence to lose from a repudiation of a unilinear technological determinism; and this requires, first, a closer look at the Marxist theory of history and the difference between technological determinism and historical materialism.

Here is how one severe critic of Marxism has characterized one of the 'most disastrous errors' of Marxist thought. Although Marx professed to acknowledge the particularities of specific cultures and the unevenness of economic development, this critic maintains, he nevertheless 'subscribed to a belief in something like a law of the increasing development over human history of productive forces. He asserted this not just as a brute historical fact nor yet as a mere trend, but as the unifying principle of human history.'[15] On this rock, the whole Marxist project has foundered. Any attempt to sustain such a view

has to confront, however, the inconvenient fact that the systematic and continuous expansion of productive forces over many centuries appears to have occurred within capitalist Europe and its offshoots and nowhere else. Explaining the singularity of capitalist development generates a most fundamental criticism of the Marxian scheme of historical interpretation. For, contrary to [G.A.] Cohen's attempted reconstruction of historical materialism in Darwinian functionalist form, a mechanism for filtering out inefficient productive arrangements exists *only within the capitalist mode of production.* Within a capitalist market economy, there is a powerful incentive for enterprises to innovate technologically, and to adopt innovations pioneered by others, since firms which persist in using less efficient technologies will lose markets, reap dwindling profits and eventually fail. Nothing akin to this selective mechanism of market competition existed in the Asiatic mode of production, and it has no replica in existing socialist command economies. Cohen's defence of the Development Thesis is bound to fail because it attempts to account for the replacement of one productive mode by another by invoking a mechanism which features internally in only a single mode of production, market capitalism.

John Gray is here so precisely on the mark in his insistence on the singularity of capitalism and his characterization of that system as uniquely driven by a 'powerful incentive' to revolutionize productive forces, that it seems churlish to point out that Marx thought of it first.[16] Indeed, this insight into the specificity of capitalism is the

---

[15] John Gray, 'The System of Ruins', *Times Literary Supplement*, 30 December 1985, p. 1460.

[16] There is often a tendency to exaggerate the degree of 'stagnation' characteristic of other, non-Western societies. Nevertheless, it remains true that the development of capitalism in the West has been marked by a unique drive to revolutionize the forces of production, specifically to develop technologies and means of labour whose object is to increase labour

essence of Marx's critique of political economy. His account of capitalism has as one of its principal objects an explanation of this 'powerful incentive', the unique imperatives that impel capital to constant self-expansion and that create the uniquely capitalist drive to increase labour productivity. The uniqueness of capitalism in this respect, far from constituting an embarrassment to Marxism, is the very core of its theoretical being. It was Marx who first provided a systematic explanation of this unique phenomenon; indeed it was Marx who recognized that it required an explanation and could not be taken for granted as inscribed in human nature – whether in the natural development of human reason, or in the inclination to 'truck, barter and exchange', or in human acquisitiveness and/or indolence. And it is still Marxists who are making the most serious efforts to develop and improve this explanation.

In contrast, the conventional 'bourgeois' accounts of economic and technological development have, since the very beginnings of classical political economy, tended to rely, implicitly or explicitly, on unilinear, 'stagist' conceptions of progress in which the improvement of the 'practical arts' and material prosperity has inexorably accompanied the unfolding of human nature, as humanity has evolved from primitive pastoralism (or whatever) to modern 'commercial' society. Contemporary economists may have jettisoned the historical and moral perspectives of their predecessors, but they are if anything even more dependent on hidden assumptions about the natural acquisitiveness of human beings, the 'unlimited' character of human desires, the necessity of accumulation, and hence the natural tendency to improve the forces of production.

UNIVERSAL HISTORY OR THE SPECIFICITY OF CAPITALISM?

Throughout *Capital* and elsewhere, Marx emphasizes the particularity of the capitalist drive to revolutionize productive forces: 'modern industry', created by capital, is 'revolutionary' 'while all other modes of production were essentially conservative',[17] having instruments, techniques, and methods of organizing labour which, once established, tended to 'petrify';[18] the capitalist class requires constant change in production, while previous classes required stability:

productivity and to cheapen commodities (as distinct, for example, from enhancing their durability or aesthetic qualities).
[17] Marx, *Capital* I, p. 457.   [18] *Ibid.*, p. 456.

'The bourgeoisie cannot exist without continually revolutionizing the instruments of production, and thereby the relations of production and all the social relations. Conservation, in an unaltered form, of the old modes of production was on the contrary the first condition of existence for all earlier industrial classes.'[19]

Even more significant than all this is Marx's view that the particular object of technological change under capitalism is specific to that system, differing from any universal object that might be attributed to humanity in general, such as 'economizing effort' or 'lightening toil'. Marx repeatedly insists that the capitalist development of productive forces is not intended to decrease 'labour-time for material production in general', but to increase 'the surplus labour-time of the working classes'.[20] 'So far as capital is concerned, productiveness does not increase through a saving in living labour in general, but only through a saving in the *paid* portion of living labour...'.[21] Commenting on J.S. Mill's remark that 'It is questionable if all the mechanical inventions yet made have lightened the day's toil of any human being', Marx observes that this is 'by no means the aim of the capitalist applications of machinery. Like every other increase in the productiveness of labour, machinery is intended to cheapen commodities, and, by shortening that portion of the working-day in which the labourer works for himself, to lengthen the other portion that he gives, without an equivalent, to the capitalist. In short, it is a means of producing surplus-value.'[22]

In other words, even if there is a general tendency inherent in human nature to seek means of 'economizing effort' or 'lightening toil', the specific drive of capitalism to revolutionize productive forces is not reducible to it. We are still left with the problem of determining the source of an impulse specific to capitalism. In short, we must distinguish fundamentally between any general tendency toward the improvement of productive forces (about which more in a moment) and the specific tendency of capitalism to revolutionize the forces of production.

A stress on the uniqueness of capitalism and its developmental drive – and the denial of unilinearism that this implies – is therefore not an aberration or a momentary, if fatal, lapse in Marxism. It is deeply embedded in and intrinsic to Marx's own analysis from the

---

[19] *Communist Manifesto*, also quoted in Marx, *Capital* I, p. 457.
[20] Marx, *Capital* III, p. 264.
[21] *Ibid.*, p. 262.   [22] Marx, *Capital* I, p. 351.

start. This alone should put us on guard against any easy assumption that the 'abandonment' of a unilinear technological determinism strikes at the heart of the Marxist project. How, then, can this emphasis be made to accord not only with a general Marxist theory of history but also with the Marxist conviction that socialism is the 'logical end' of a general historical process?

There are those who claim that when it comes to a theory of history, at least for Marxists, it is all or nothing, unilinearism or chaos, predestination or the abyss. If Marxists cannot spell out a universal and inexorable sequence of specific historical stages, they cannot claim, it would seem, to explain historical processes at all. They can discover no patterns or logic in history; they can only describe a chaotic and arbitrary mixture of contingencies:

The abandonment of unilinearism raises problems which are very deep. If it is disavowed and not replaced by anything, one may well ask whether one is left with any theory at all, or merely with the debris of a theory. Marxism is supposed to be a theory of historical change, providing a key to its motive force and, presumably, its overall pattern. If any kind of society can follow any other kind, without any constraints, if societies may stagnate forever, what kind of meaning can be attached to the attribution of primacy to the forces of production, or indeed to anything else? If there are no constraints on the possible patterns of change, what point is there in seeking the underlying mechanism or the secret of constraint, when no constraint exists to be explained? If anything is possible, what could a theory explain, and what theory could be true? Those Western Marxists who blithely disavow unilinealism, as a kind of irritating and unnecessary encumbrance, without even trying to replace it with something else, do not seem to realize that all they are left with is a label, but no theory. Though unilinealism is indeed false, its unqualified abandonment leaves Marxism vacuous.[23]

This seems an extraordinary misunderstanding not only of Marxism but of what is entailed by historical theory and explanation. Is it really true that, in the absence of unilinearism, 'any kind of society can follow any other kind, without constraints'? Does the 'abandonment' of unilinearism really mean that 'anything is possible'? If Marxists refuse to accept that human history consists of an inexorable progress from primitive communism through slavery and feudalism to capitalism, are they really obliged to accept, for example, that capitalism can emerge from a pastoral society, that

[23] Ernest Gellner, 'Along the Historical Highway', *Times Literary Supplement*, 16 March 1984, p. 279. This account has much in common with post-Marxist views of Marxism and history.

'modern industry' can spring directly from primitive agriculture, that a hunting and gathering economy can sustain a feudal structure? Are they obliged to acknowledge that a system of production that generates little surplus can sustain a massive state or religious establishment and a luxurious material culture? Is there really nothing left in Marxist theory, failing unilinearism, that would deny the possibility of all these historical anomalies?

With such a Manichaean view of the alternatives, it is hard to see how any theory – or indeed any historical explanation – is possible at all. Does Marxism really need unilinearism in order to have a 'theory of historical change'? In fact, is unilinearism a theory of change at all, or is it just an attempt to avoid explaining historical change by preempting the question with a mechanical sequence of stages, while the object of Marxist theory *without* unilinearism is precisely to offer a 'key' to the motive forces of historical process?

Marx's theory of history does not take the form of propositions like 'primitive communism is (must be) followed by slavery. . . . etc.', but rather something like 'the fundamental key to the development of feudalism (say) and the forces at work in the transition to capitalism is to be found in the specific mode of productive activity characteristic of feudalism, the specific form in which surplus labour was pumped out of the direct producers, and the class conflicts surrounding that process of surplus-extraction'. This kind of proposition gives full recognition both to historical specificity and to structural constraints. It is both general and specific in that it provides a *general* guide to discovering the *specific* 'logic of process' in any given social form; and Marx himself, of course, applied his general principles – about the centrality of productive activity and the specific form in which 'surplus labour is pumped out of the direct producers' – in a monumentally detailed and fruitful analysis of capitalism and its very specific 'laws of motion'.

'CONTRADICTION' AND THE DEVELOPMENT OF PRODUCTIVE FORCES

Where, then, do the forces of production figure in all this?[24] The proposition that history is simply the inexorable progress of productive forces is vacuous and by itself inconsistent with Marx's analysis

---

[24] The concept of productive forces can include more than simply 'material' forces and technologies; but what is usually in question in these debates are the instruments, techniques and organizational forms which have the effect of increasing productive capacity.

of capitalism. It can accommodate a whole range of possibilities, from the revolutionizing of productive forces under capitalism to the tendency of productive forces to 'petrify' in pre-capitalist societies. The sense in which it is true is very limited in its explanatory value and begs the critical question of capitalist development. Of course it is indisputable that in a very long perspective there has been a broadly evolutionary development of material productive forces; but this need mean no more than that changes in the forces of production tend to be progressive and cumulative, that once an advance occurs it is seldom completely lost, and that regression is over the long term exceptional. If this is so, it is still possible to characterize these developments as evolutionary and 'directional' (*not* teleological), in the sense that there is a general progressive tendency and each development is accompanied by new possibilities, as well as new needs.[25] But this tells us nothing about the likelihood, frequency, rapidity or extent of change; nor does it contradict the view, expressed by Marx, that 'petrification' has been more the rule than the exception.

Technological change and improvements in labour productivity are not the only ways in which societies have adapted to their material needs, or even to the exploitative demands of dominant classes; and systems of production do not necessarily contain a compulsion to be succeeded by more 'productive' systems. It is, again, a specific characteristic of capitalism to demand the constant transformation of productive forces as its principal form of adaptation. If that compulsion has become a more general rule, it is because one of the chief consequences of the capitalist impulse has

---

[25] Erik Olin Wright, in a reply to Anthony Giddens's critique of Marx's theory of history ('Giddens's Critique of Marx', *New Left Review*, 138 (1983), especially pp. 24–9), shows how a more limited proposition about the development of productive forces (such as the one being proposed here), which makes no excessive explanatory claims and no unwarranted assumptions about the compulsion of less productive social forms to be succeeded by more productive ones, is still consistent with the cumulative, evolutionary and 'directional' character of social development. He offers some cautious suggestions about why the development of productive forces is cumulative, without making claims for a universal drive to improve productive capacities; and, while he accepts that direct producers in general have an interest in reducing unpleasant toil, he denies that there is any 'systematic pressure'. In fact, he suggests that, if in pre-class societies such an impulse – albeit a 'very weak' one – may have the effect of encouraging the improvement of productive forces, or at least the acceptance of those introduced from elsewhere, the desire to lighten toil is not the operative principle where class exploitation exists (p. 28). In other words, his account of Marxist evolutionism seems generally compatible with the argument outlined here. At any rate, it is a useful corrective to the extravagant claims often made for the development of productive forces.

been an unprecedented capacity – and need – to drive out, or impose its logic upon, other social forms.

So, while the evolution of productive forces is an important datum in the understanding of historical process, there are strict limits to its explanatory force. Above all, the observation that history has been generally marked by a progressive development of productive forces cannot be taken to mean that historical movement and social change are impelled by a drive to improve the forces of production, or that social forms rise and decline according to whether they promote or obstruct such improvement.[26]

What, then, of the proposition that history is propelled forward by the inevitable *contradictions* between forces and relations of production? This proposition is often regarded as the central tenet of Marx's theory of history and deserves close and critical scrutiny.

The principle in question goes something like this: Forces of production tend to develop. At some point, they come up against the limits imposed by production relations which make further development impossible. This contradiction compels productive forces to break through the restrictive integument, requiring relations of production to change and allowing forces to advance. The main canonical source for this proposition is Marx's 1859 Preface to *The Critique of Political Economy*, and I have no intention of denying this textual warrant; nor do I intend to enter into a debate about the textual evidence or about its significance, except to say that both Marxists and their critics have placed an enormous theoretical burden upon Marx's short-hand aphorisms – notably those about the contradictions between forces and relations of production, and those about 'base' and 'superstructure' – without taking account of their rarity or their poetic allusiveness and economy of expression, and without putting into the balance the weight of his whole life's work and what it tells us about his theoretical principles. But with or without Marx's imprimatur, the principle of contradiction between forces and relations of production demands exploration.

Let me begin with an example cited against my version of historical materialism by a Marxist critic who has castigated me for giving inadequate attention to *contradiction*, specifically the contradiction between forces and relations of production, as the chief

[26] See Robert Brenner, 'The Origins of Capitalist Development', *New Left Review*, 104 (1977), pp. 59–60.

mechanism of major social transformations. The case of ancient Rome is invoked to illustrate how such systemic contradictions (as distinct from some 'voluntaristic' agency like class struggle) produce historical change.

Here, first, is how the relevant systemic contradiction is described in the interpretation of Roman history on which this critic relies: 'a decline in the supply of slave labour consequent on low rates of internal reproduction, leading to off-setting attempts at slave-breeding, decreasing the rate of exploitation, which then necessitated complementary depression of free labour to sustain overall levels of surplus extraction'.[27] Whether or not this is an adequate explanation of the transition from antiquity to feudalism, what does it tell us about the meaning of the contradiction between forces and relations of production, and does it support the proposition that history advances as developing productive forces break through the fetters of restrictive production relations?

Here is a case where the primary appropriating class reached the limits of surplus extraction and sought to compensate for a declining rate of exploitation by depressing the condition of peasant producers in order to widen the range of its appropriative powers. This was not a case where dynamic forces taxed the limits of restrictive relations. If productive forces were 'fettered', it is not in the sense that their inherent tendency to develop was thwarted, but rather that such a tendency was largely absent, or very weak, in the prevailing production relations, which encouraged the extension of extra-economic surplus extraction instead of the improvement of labour productivity.

Nor can it be said that production relations were compelled to assume a new form more conducive to the development of productive forces. On the contrary, it was more a matter of relations of production adapting to the limits of productive forces, a reorganization of surplus extraction to accommodate the limitations of production. As the imperial infrastructure – its cities, its road systems, its wealth, its population – disintegrated, and as the Empire became

---

[27] This example is cited against me by Alex Callinicos in 'The Limits of "Political Marxism"', *New Left Review*, 184 (1990), pp. 110–15. The quotation is from Perry Anderson, 'Class Struggle in the Ancient World', *History Workshop Journal*, 16 (Autumn 1983), p. 68. Although questions could be raised about this explanation of Roman imperial history, this is not the place for a debate about the decline and fall of the Empire. Suffice it to say that the comments I am about to make concerning the decline of Rome's productive forces would apply to any other plausible account of the decline.

increasingly vulnerable to 'barbarian' invasions (by peoples with less-developed productive forces), the apparatus of surplus appropriation was effectively scaled down to the level of existing productive forces.

Although evidence is sparse, it can even be argued (as Marx and Engels, incidentally, did argue, for example in *The German Ideology*), that the result was a *destruction* of productive forces, a regression from the development of Roman antiquity. At any rate, long after the 'crisis', indeed after the better part of a millennium, the level of material life remained very low; and economic growth, when it did occur, for a long time was based not so much on the improvement of productivity as on the 'extra-economic' logic of a war economy, the logic of coercive appropriation and pillage.[28] Feudalism did eventually bring about technical developments (though their extent remains a subject of controversy); but by this time, surely, the causal thread between the crisis of antiquity and the development of productive forces has worn rather thin. The connections would be exceedingly tenuous even if the order of causality were reversed, from developing productive forces which strain the fetters of restrictive production relations, to production relations changing in order to encourage the advancement of stagnant productive forces.

If we are prepared to accept this kind of time scale, we can probably claim a direct causal link between almost any two widely separated historical episodes, without regard to the duration and complexity of intervening processes; but how informative would such a causal explanation be? And it still remains a question whether the availability (which by no means guaranteed the widespread *utilization*[29]) of technical innovations when they did occur determined social change – the more so as differences in the rate and direction of social transformations between, say, England (where agrarian capitalism eventually emerged) and France (where agrarian stagnation eventually set in) simply did not correspond to differences in their respective feudal technologies.

We can certainly call the Roman pattern an example of the contradiction between forces and relations of production; but if we

[28] See, for example, Georges Duby, *The Early Growth of the European Economy* (Ithaca, 1974), p. 269.

[29] See Robert Brenner, in T.H. Aston and C.H.E. Philpin, eds., *The Brenner Debate: Agrarian Class Structure and Economic Development in Pre-Industrial Europe* (Cambridge, 1985), pp. 32, 233.

do, we must mean something different from even the weakest formulation of this principle, for example, that a 'weak impulse' for the
forces to develop creates 'a dynamic asymmetry' between the forces
and relations such that 'eventually the forces will reach a point at
which they are "fettered", that is, a point at which further development is impossible in the absence of transformation in the relations
of production'.[30] In the case of Rome, the 'contradiction' served as a
mechanism of change not because forces were developing beyond
the capacity of existing relations, nor even by bringing about an
enabling transformation of social relations which had the effect of
shifting stagnant forces of production, but, on the contrary, by
compelling relations to sink to the level of productive forces. To
accommodate this example, then, we would have to include among
the possible outcomes of the contradiction the adaptation of production relations to the 'fetters' of productive forces, and perhaps
even the destruction of those forces.

These difficulties cannot be overcome simply by adopting some
version of a 'functional' explanation (as proposed by G.A. Cohen),
which allows a temporal priority to changes in production relations
as long as we assume that the underlying reason for such changes is
the need to advance the forces of production. This kind of 'explanation' works as a general account of history only if we are prepared
to interpret it with such vacuous generality as to include every
possibility from the revolutionary improvement of productive forces
to their stagnation, or even regression. This is not, of course, to deny
that technical innovations occurred in pre-capitalist societies, or
even that there were incremental and cumulative developments.
The question is whether these developments constituted the
dynamic force that motivated historical change – either (causally)
before or ('functionally') after the fact.[31] This is not an issue that can

---

[30] See Wright, 'Giddens's Critique of Marx', p. 29.

[31] In his criticism of me cited above, Callinicos makes no distinction between propositions
having to do with the occurrence of technical innovations and those concerning the causes
of historical change. For example, he accuses Brenner of acknowledging no differences in
levels of development among various pre-capitalist societies, but Brenner says nothing of
the kind. His argument is not that all pre-capitalist societies are on the same level of
technological development, but rather that their various property relations have in
common a tendency to encourage the expansion of extra-economic surplus extraction
rather than the improvement of labour productivity. This is why (see, for example, the
passages cited in note 29 above) any failure to improve agricultural productivity in such
cases may have less to do with the unavailability of new techniques than with the
underutilization even of existing technologies.

be resolved by invoking a priori, universalistic and question-begging assumptions about the progressive directionality of history.

It would be better not to talk about the forces of production as if they represented an autonomous principle of historical movement, somehow external to any given system of social relations. Even if over the long term there is a cumulative directionality in the progress of human knowledge and technology, the cumulative continuities of history do not alter the fact that each distinct mode of production has its own specific connections between forces and relations of production, its own specific contradictions – or perhaps we should say, to use Brenner's formulation, its own specific 'rules for reproduction'.

Let us take the Roman case again, accepting, for the sake of argument, the account of the decline in the supply of slave labour cited above. What is at stake here is a crisis of appropriation. What makes it a crisis is not that sluggish production relations restrict the further development of (more or less) dynamic productive forces. It is rather that, within the limits of existing conditions, within the prevailing ensemble of productive forces and relations, the principal classes can no longer successfully pursue their normal strategies of self-reproduction. Class struggle enters into the process here, and not simply at the point of transition, since strategies of reproduction are determined not in isolation but in relations between appropriators and producers. When they reach their viable limits, the strategies are likely to change.

This does not, however, necessarily imply the adoption of strategies more conducive to the advancement of productive forces. In pre-capitalist societies generally, the outcome is more likely to be an adjustment in the scope and methods of surplus extraction, or a reorganization of the extra-economic forces that constitute the power of appropriation, whether by direct exploitation or by pillage and war: the state, the military apparatus, and so on. (This also means, incidentally, that the advantage which any particular society may have in relation to others need not be directly proportional to the level of its productive forces.[32] We cannot generalize throughout history the rules of international capitalist competition which give the competitive advantage to more productive economies

---

[32] For a somewhat different view, see Christopher Bertram, 'International Competition in Historical Materialism', *New Left Review*, 183 (1990), pp. 116–28.

– and even here, geopolitical or military superiority may not neatly coincide with productivity. At any rate, in pre-capitalist societies, the effective organization of extra-economic resources is likely to be decisive.) The available productive capacities certainly establish the limits of the possible, but to say this is to say neither that less productive systems must necessarily be followed by more productive ones, nor even that the developmental impulses of productive forces determine the necessity and direction of historical change.

Since the principle of contradiction between forces and relations of production, at least in its conventional interpretation, begs the question, without asking whether and to what extent productive forces do and must develop in the first place, it may seem, on the face of it, hardly less vacuous than the general law of technological development in its simpler form. It can certainly be said that there is a minimum level of productive forces without which any set of production relations cannot be sustained, and it is also true that any set of production relations can permit or encourage only so much change in the forces of production and only in a limited range of forms. But it is quite another matter to suggest that there is a particular set of productive forces to match every set of production relations (or vice versa), or that development in one must go step by step in tandem with the other.

Productive forces establish the ultimate conditions of the possible, and no doubt the emergence of capitalism in particular requires that the forces of production be to *some* degree developed and concentrated (though we need to recall just how modest the level of productive forces was in late medieval Europe, while, conversely, other at least equally advanced technological regimes – for instance, in China – did not give rise to capitalism). Nevertheless, at any given stage of development the available productive forces can sustain a wide range of production relations; and the various changes in production relations that have occurred in history cannot be explained simply by reference to the development of productive forces, either in the sense that the former have followed the latter or in the sense that the former have changed 'in order to' remove obstacles to the development of the latter.

THE SPECIFIC CONTRADICTIONS OF CAPITALISM: HISTORY
AGAINST TELEOLOGY

Still, the principle of contradiction between forces and relations of production may have a more specific and fruitful meaning, if we cease to treat it as a general law of history – a law so general as to be vacuous – and regard it as a law of *capitalist* development, a principle internal to the capitalist mode of production from its inception to its decline, a statement about its specific dynamic and internal contradictions. Indeed it is precisely, and only, in this specific application that the principle received any detailed elaboration from Marx himself – and in such a way that it appears not as a general law but as a characteristic specific to capitalism, an account of those very contradictions that are associated with the uniquely capitalist drive to revolutionize productive forces.

For example:

The *real barrier* of capitalist production is *capital itself*. It is that capital and its self-expansion appear as the starting and the closing point, the motive and the purpose of production; that production is only production for *capital* and not vice versa, the means of production are not mere means for a constant expansion of the living process of the *society* of producers. The limits within which the preservation and self-expansion of the value of capital resting on the expropriation and pauperization of the great mass of producers can alone move – these limits come continually into conflict with the methods of production employed by capital for its purposes, which drive towards unlimited extension of production, towards production as an end in itself, towards unconditional development of the social productivity of labour. The means – unconditional development of the productive forces of society – comes continually into conflict with the limited purpose, the self-expansion of the existing capital. The capitalist mode of production is, for this reason, a historical means of developing the material forces of production and creating an appropriate world market and is, at the same time, a continual conflict between this its historical task and its own corresponding relations of social production.[33]

The formula thus sums up both the unique principles of motion within capitalism, its dynamic internal contradictions, and also the possibilities contained within capitalism for the transformation of society:

[33] Marx, *Capital* III, p. 250.

The contradiction between the general social power into which capital develops, on the one hand, and the private power of the individual capitalists over these social conditions of production, on the other, becomes ever more irreconcilable and yet contains the solution of the problem, because it implies at the same time the transformation of the conditions of production into general, common, social conditions. This transformation stems from the development of the productive forces under capitalist production, and from the ways and means by which this development takes place.[34]

This principle of contradiction can, with caution, be used to illuminate retrospectively the transition from feudalism to capitalism. It suggests that a mode of production whose internal principle of motion was to revolutionize productive forces could not have come about without a transformation in the relations of production and class. But the meaning of such restrospective formulations, in which historical *consequences* are described as if they were causes, should not be misconstrued. This is one of Marx's favourite ploys – as in the famous proposition that 'Human anatomy contains a key to the anatomy of the ape'; and it is often mistaken for teleology. In this case, Marx's formulation simply means that the drive to transform productive forces was not the cause but the result of a transformation in the relations of production and class.[35]

If the formula is fruitful as an account of capitalism, as a general law of history it is rather empty and is not rendered more informative by the teleological proposition that capitalism emerged because history requires the development of productive forces and the development of productive forces requires capitalism. Nor is this question-begging formulation Marx's own. When he speaks of the

---

[34] *Ibid.*, p. 264.

[35] 'The production of relative surplus-value revolutionizes out and out the technical processes of labour, and the composition of society. It therefore presupposes a specific mode, the capitalist mode of production, a mode which, along with its methods, means, and conditions, arises and develops spontaneously on the foundation afforded by the formal subjection of labour to capital. In the course of this development, the formal subjection is replaced by the real subjection of labour to capital.' (Marx, *Capital* III, pp. 477–8.) In other words, a transformation in the social relations of production that gives rise to the 'formal subjection' of labour to capital – the transformation of producers into wage labourers directly subject to capital without at first transforming the means and methods of production – set in train a process that had as its eventual consequence the revolutionizing of productive forces. Capitalist relations carried a compulsion to increase surplus value; and as the production of absolute surplus value gave way to relative surplus value, the need to increase labour productivity was met by completely transforming the labour process, the 'real subjection' of labour to capital. The revolutionizing of productive forces was thus only the end of a complex process that began with the establishment of capitalist social relations.

'historical task' of capitalism, he is not identifying the causes or explaining the processes that gave rise to capitalism; he is making a statement about the *effects* of capitalist development, and specifically from the point of view of socialism. 'The capitalist mode of production presents itself to us historically, as a necessary condition to the transformation of the labour-process into a social process'[36] tells us something about what capitalism has done to make possible the transition to socialism. It tells us little about the laws of history in general – nor does it explain how a system came to be established in which the transformation of productive forces was indeed a basic 'law of motion'.

It is surely significant that in Marx's own accounts of historical transitions the development of productive forces plays little role as the primary motor. This is true even in his explanation of the transition from feudalism to capitalism. His most comprehensive accounts of pre-capitalist societies in the *Grundrisse*, and of the historical transition to capitalism – especially in the section on 'Primitive Accumulation' in *Capital* – do not invoke the development of productive forces as the motivating impulse of historical change. They are, in fact, based on the premise that what needs to be explained is precisely the origin of capitalism's distinctive drive to improve the forces of production.

There are two ways of looking at this curious fact. One is to say that there is a fundamental inconsistency between, on the one hand, his 'general theory' – as stated baldly, for example, in the 1859 Preface – which treats the advancement of productive forces as the motivating force of history in general, and, on the other hand, his analysis of capitalism as *unique* in its drive to advance technological development.[37] The alternative, as I have already suggested, is to reconsider what is 'general' in his general theory. But what needs to be kept in mind at all times is that, if there is any single theme that predominates over all others in Marx's historical materialism, and in the critique of political economy which formed the core of his life's work, it is an insistence on the specificity of capitalism. If there is a consistent 'general theory' in his work, it must be one that can

---

[36] Marx, *Capital* I, p. 317.

[37] This is the position adopted, for example, by Jon Elster, who, while correctly noting that Marx did not invoke the development of productive forces in his account of historical transitions, insists that Marx's theory of history is inherently inconsistent. See *Making Sense of Marx* (Cambridge, 1985), chap. 5.

accommodate this overriding principle. And *that* general theory is, again, likely to consist of those theoretical instruments – applied to such remarkable effect in the critique of political economy – which allowed him to identify the specificity of capitalism and its distinctive 'laws of motion'.

There is no doubt that Marx never bothered to resolve the inconsistencies between his aphorisms about the forces of production and his insistence on the specificity of capitalism. But even in the context of the technological 'general theory' (if such it is), there is room for a specifically capitalist dynamic. The critical issue for Marx was always the *specific compulsion* of capitalism to revolutionize the forces of production, which differs from any more general tendency to improve productive forces that may be ascribed to history as a whole. In that sense, it was possible for him consistently to hold both the view that history displays a general tendency to improve the forces of production and the view that capitalism had a special need and capacity to revolutionize productive forces.

Beginning early in his career, Marx never deviated from the view that the capitalist drive is specific and unprecedented and that, whatever progressive tendencies may be generally observable in history, the specific logic of capitalism and its specific compulsion to improve the productivity of labour by technical means are not reducible to these general tendencies. They require a specific explanation. He also made it very clear that the capitalist impulse to improve the productivity of labour is quite distinct from, and often in opposition to, any general human inclination to curtail labour. The capitalist impulse is, again, to increase the portion of *unpaid labour*. He devoted much of his life's work to explaining this specifically capitalist dynamic.

Marx conducts his critique of political economy, the core of his mature work, by differentiating himself from those who take for granted and universalize the logic and dynamic of capitalism without acknowledging the historical specificity of its 'laws' or seeking to uncover what produces them. Marx, unlike the classical political economists, and indeed a host of other ideologues of 'commercial society', did not assume that the 'progress' embodied in modern society was simply the outcome of a drive inherent in human nature or natural law, but insisted on the specificity of the capitalist demand for productivity and the need to find an explanation for it.

It was Marx's identification of that specific dynamic that made it possible even to raise the question of the 'transition' to capitalism, to seek an explanation of how that dynamic was set in train, something that remained impossible as long as people assumed the very forces that needed to be explained. Marx himself never produced a systematic account of the historical process of transition, and his discussions of pre-capitalist modes of production were never more than retrospective analyses, part of a strategy to explicate the workings of capitalism and emphasize the historicity of its laws and categories. But he took the qualitative leap that was required to make an explanation of the transition possible, and he thereby established a basis for a general theory of history which would also treat other modes of production on their own specific terms.

It is especially ironic that the strategy adopted by Marx to highlight the specificity of capitalism has been mistaken for a teleological account of history. So, for example, his famous aphorism that 'Human anatomy contains a key to the anatomy of the ape' from the *Grundrisse* has been described as a statement of his 'teleological stance' which is 'closely related to the propensity for functional explanation . . .'.[38] This misunderstanding is compounded by the suggestion that the aphorism applies to the 'teleological' relationship between Communism and capitalism in the same way that it does to the relationship between capitalist and pre-capitalist modes of production.

Marx does, of course, sometimes analyse capitalism from the standpoint of socialism – that is, by identifying the potentiality within capitalism for a socialist transformation. But his procedure in treating capitalism in its relation to pre-capitalist societies necessarily has a different purpose. Capitalism can provide the 'key' to pre-capitalist society, in the sense here intended, only because it actually exists and because it has given rise to its own historically constituted categories, whose historical specificity Marx is trying to demonstrate by *critically* applying them to pre-capitalist forms. That is precisely the meaning of his *critique* of political economy.

The point is not that capitalism is *prefigured* in pre-capitalist forms but on the contrary that capitalism represents a historically specific *transformation*. Marx adopts this paradoxical strategy in order to counter 'those economists who smudge over all historical differences

[38] *Ibid.*, p. 54.

and see bourgeois relations in all forms of society'[39] – that is, against
what might be called the teleological tendencies of classical political
economy, for which 'bourgeois relations' are the natural and universal order of things, the destination of progress already present in all
earlier stages of history. Since Marx's point of departure is a refusal
to incorporate capitalism into the historical process that produced
it, and especially with a theory of history in which every mode of
production is propelled by its own distinctive laws of motion, his
characteristic procedure is exactly the reverse of teleological or even
functional explanation.

The transition to capitalism, then, is historically unique because it
represents the first case in which a crisis in the 'rules for reproduction' produced not simply a transformation in modes of appropriation but a process the result of which was a wholly new and
continuous drive to revolutionize the forces of production. It is
specifically in capitalism that the dynamic impulse of productive
forces can be regarded as a primary mechanism of social change.
Capitalism is also unique in its particular systemic contradictions
between forces and relations of production: its unprecedented drive
to develop and socialize the forces of production – not least in the
form of the working class – constantly comes up against the limits of
its primary purpose, the self-expansion of capital, which is sometimes impelled even to destroy productive capacities, as advanced
capitalist countries have learned all too well in recent years.

HISTORY AND THE 'NECESSITY' OF SOCIALISM

If the contradiction between forces and relations of production does
not provide an explanation for the *emergence* of a social form in which
that contradiction *does* play a central role, where is such an explanation to be found? On this score, Marx suggests that the critical
factor is 'the historical process of divorcing the producer from the
means of production', in particular, the process whereby peasant
producers were expropriated from the soil.[40] Although he has a few
things to say about this process, it has remained for later historians
to explain how and why it took place and how it generated specifically capitalist imperatives to revolutionize the material forces of
production. These questions have, in fact, been the subject of some

---

[39] Marx, *Grundrisse* (Harmondsworth, 1973), p. 105.   [40] Marx, *Capital* I, p. 317.

of the most fruitful work in Marxist historiography, notably in the 'Transition Debate' and in the work of Robert Brenner.

If there is in Marx a systematic statement of a very 'general trend' in history, a single direction in which all human history has tended, then his remarks on the increasing separation of direct producers from the means of their own labour, subsistence, and reproduction are both more systematically developed (see, in particular, the discussion of pre-capitalist formations in the *Grundrisse*) and more useful than technological determinism. And they also set the terms for his conception of socialism.

Technological-determinist Marxism tends to suggest that the object of socialism is to perfect the development of productive forces. It is not surprising that this version of Marxism was most congenial to a Soviet regime overwhelmingly preoccupied with rapid industrialization, at any price. The other version of Marxism, which takes its inspiration from Marx's own account of (Western) history as the increasing separation of direct producers from the means of production, suggests a different project for socialism: the reappropriation of the means of production by direct producers. The first project, even apart from Stalinist deformations, was likely to be driven by undemocratic impulses, as the forced acceleration of economic development proceeded at the expense of working people. The other project has at its core the highest democratic aspirations, summed up in Marx's definition of socialism as, in its foundations, 'a free association of the producers'.

Treating the process of expropriation as a 'general trend', at least in Western history, has much to recommend it politically; and, as a guide to history, it certainly tells us something essential about the long historical process, stretching back to classical antiquity, that created the conditions for the emergence of capitalism. But it is no substitute for Marx's method of discovering historical specificities, not only the specificity of capitalism, but by extension, non-capitalist forms. And even as a 'general trend', the process of expropriation is itself affected by the specificity of every social form, the particular relation between appropriators and direct producers. Indeed, this process is especially difficult to formulate as a 'law' – at least in a form that would satisfy those for whom a 'general theory' of history must take the form of transhistorical laws – because it is a process of class struggle, whose specific outcome must, by definition, remain unpredictable. Marxist theory can point us in the direction of class struggle as a principle of historical movement and provide the tools for exploring its effects, but it cannot tell us a priori how that struggle will work out.

And, indeed, why should it? What Marxist theory tells us is that the productive capacities of society set the limits of the possible, and, more specifically, that the particular mode of surplus extraction is the key to social structure. It tells us, too, that class struggle generates historical movement. None of this makes history accidental, contingent, or indeterminate. For example, if the outcome of class struggle is not predetermined, the specific nature, conditions, and terrain of struggle, and the range of possible outcomes, certainly are historically determinate: struggles between wage labourers and industrial capitalists over the extraction of surplus value are, needless to say, structurally different from struggles between peasants and feudal landlords over the appropriation of rent. Each of these struggles has its own inner logic, quite apart from the additional specificities of time and place. A specific application of these principles has provided an explanation of how capitalism emerged, how capitalist relations have generated a compulsive drive to revolutionize productive forces (among other things), how the imperatives of capital accumulation have tended to generalize the logic of capitalism and to submerge other modes of production, while creating the conditions that place socialism on the agenda.

Socialism can no doubt be understood as building upon the developments of capitalism, while resolving its specific contradictions; but to acknowledge the specificity of capitalism is at the same time to insist on the specificity of socialism, not simply as an extension of, or an improvement upon, capitalism but as a system of social relations with an inherent logic of its own: a system not driven by the imperatives of profit maximization, accumulation and so-called 'growth', with their attendant waste and degradation – material, human and ecological – a system whose values and creative impulses are not circumscribed by constricted notions of technological progress.

The dynamic of capitalism and its specific drive to transform production have created contradictions and possibilities for further transformations. Not the least important consideration, of course, is that capitalism has brought about a development in productive forces which establishes an unprecedented material foundation for human emancipation. But under capitalism, driven by the logic of profit, there is no necessary correspondence between productive capacity and the quality of human life. A society with the most advanced productive forces, with the capacity to feed, clothe, house, educate and care for the health of its population to a degree undreamt of in the most visionary utopias, may nevertheless be riddled with poverty, squalor, homelessness, illiteracy and even the diseases of malnutrition. The socialist project would have as one of its principal goals the elimination of such disparities between productive capacity and the quality of life. Socialism can even be regarded as the means by which the forces of production will break the 'fetters' of capitalism and develop to a higher level, provided that we understand precisely what this means: socialism will liberate the creative capacities of humanity from the imperatives of exploitation and specifically the compulsions of capitalist self-expansion – which is something different from simply continuing capitalist development by permitting an even more 'unconditional' revolutionizing of productive forces of the kind that capitalism has set in train.

In fact, socialism is intended to develop the forces of production by putting an end to this specifically capitalist impulse. This is worth stressing, just to dissociate the socialist project from the logic of capitalist accumulation and from the technological determinism according to which the historic mission of socialism is apparently just to improve upon capitalist development and 'progress'. This kind of misunderstanding not only puts in question the liberating effects of socialist production but also, among other things, creates a suspicion among people increasingly sensitive to environmental dangers that Marxism, no less than capitalism, is an invitation to indiscriminate 'productivism', unsustainable 'growth' and ecological disaster.

How, then, is the socialist project affected by the denial of unilinearism and technological determinism? Without such a view of history, does it follow that the socialist movement lacks certain vitally important convictions, notably that socialism is not simply the arbitrary conclusion of a unique and contingent historical process but the outcome of a universal historical logic as well as a response to universal needs and aspirations? 'Marxism', writes one of its recent critics

is a collective soteriology. It is a faith which, though it promises no salvation to individuals, does very emphatically offer it to humanity at large. It differs from Christianity in at least two further respects: salvation is not selective, nor conditional on merit or selection, but will descend upon all of us without distinction, if we are still here when the time comes. It will come without conditions or, for that matter consultation. We will be saved whether we like it or not.... The potential for an eventual and indeed inescapable salvation is built into the present. The entelechy of salvation, the acorn/oak tree vision of social change, is central to Marxism, and constitutes an important part of its appeal.[41]

With the 'newer model Marxism', which disowns unilinearism, history, according to this argument, becomes pure accident; and 'the *promise* of salvation is replaced by a merely contingent, humiliatingly accidental and extraneous *possibility* of salvation'.

There is much in this statement that is both wrong and objectionable (where, incidentally, does class struggle come into it?); but the main objection to it must be that it attaches so little weight to *history*. If what we are dealing with is not *teleology* but *history*, then the relevant category in characterizing the socialist project is not inevitablity, not inescapability, not 'entelechy', not *promise*, but precisely *possibility*. And is this such an inconsiderable thing? It is not 'merely contingent, humiliatingly accidental and extraneous possibility' but *historical* possibility, that is, the existence of determinate social and material conditions which make something *possible* that was *im*possible before, conditions in which socialism can indeed be a political project and not simply an abstract ideal or a vague aspiration.

As for the *universality* of the socialist project, it is because socialism is the end of all classes, and not because it is the terminus of technological determinism, that it has a universal sweep. We need not relinquish the universality of the socialist 'promise' simply because we conceive it less as the *telos* of all history than as a historical product of, and specific antithesis to, capitalism. What is most significant about capitalism in this respect is not simply that it represents the highest development of productive forces to date, but also that it is, so to speak, the highest development of exploitation, the last stage in the separation of producers from the means of production, beyond which lies the abolition of all classes and the reappropriation of the means of production by a 'free association of direct producers'. The historical trajectory that produced the capitalist configuration of classes may have been relatively local and

---

[41] Ernest Gellner, 'Stagnation Without Salvation', *Times Literary Supplement*, January 1985, p. 27.

specific, but class struggle and the aspiration to be free of exploitation have not. Furthermore, as capitalism has drawn the whole world into the ambit of its expansionary logic, the conditions and terrain of class struggle everywhere have changed, and every class struggle has come closer to the threshold of the last one. The definition of socialism as the abolition of class contains all the universal 'logic' that the socialist project requires.

We are not obliged to accept a Manichaean choice between determinism and contingency. The real alternative to both is *history*. Even a complete repudiation of 'grand narratives' in the 'postmodern' manner does not dispose of historical causality. And even at a time when history seems to be defying socialist aspirations in the most dramatic and decisive way, we need not – should not – choose between the promise of historical inevitability and the denial of any historical foundation to the socialist project.

I do actually think that 'history is on our side' – but not in the sense that socialism has been inscribed in the inexorable laws of progress since the dawn of history, or that its coming is inevitable. For me, it is more a matter of the historically specific and unique possibilities and tensions created by capitalism which have put socialism on the agenda and produced the conditions for bringing it about. Even in Eastern Europe, where there are already signs of a return to old contradictions and class conflicts as the 'discipline' of the market takes hold, there may yet be an opportunity for the first time to test the proposition that the conditions of socialist emancipation reside in the specific contradictions of capitalism.

CHAPTER 5

History or teleology? Marx versus Weber

Marx versus Weber has long been a favourite fixture among academics – or, to be more precise, Weber has been a favourite stick with which to beat Marxists: Marx is a reductionist, an economic determinist; Weber has a more sophisticated understanding of multiple causes, the autonomy of ideology and politics; Marx's view of history is teleological and Eurocentric, Weber's more attuned to the variability and complexity of human culture and historical patterns. Weber is the greater sociologist and a better historian because, where Marx over systematizes, reducing all cultural and historical complexities to a single cause and one unilinear historical process, Weber, with his methodology of 'ideal types', acknowledges complexity and multi-causality even as he subjects them to some kind of conceptual order.

Yet is it really so? Or should the shoe be on the other foot? In what follows, it will be argued that it is Weber, not Marx, who looked at the world through the prism of a unilinear, teleological and Euro-centric conception of history, which Marx had done more than any other Western thinker to dislodge. Far from advancing social theory beyond the alleged crudities of a Marxist determinism, Weber reverted to a pre-Marxist teleology, in which all history is a drive – though sometimes, perhaps more often than not, thwarted – toward capitalism, where the capitalist destination is always prefigured in the movements of history, and where the differences among various social forms have to do with the ways in which they encourage or obstruct that single historical drive.

PROGRESS AND THE RISE OF CAPITALISM

The idea of progress commonly associated with the Enlightenment was made up of two distinct but related strands. On the one hand, there were variations on the theme of human improvement as an essentially cultural and political phenomenon, the rise of reason and freedom. On the other, there was a kind of materialism which represented history as stages in the evolution of 'modes of subsistence', and specifically the maturation of 'commercial society', the last and most perfect stage. The two strands were united by a conception of technical progress, in which the development of the human mind was manifested in the improvement of techniques for the provision of material subsistence, not only the perfection of the instruments of production but above all an increasingly refined division of labour, between town and country, among specialized crafts, and ultimately within the workshop itself. These material improvements were accompanied on the cultural plane by a growing rationality and the decline of superstition, and on the political plane by advances in liberty.

As this idea of progress was elaborated, certain underlying assumptions became increasingly obvious – in particular, the assumption that the seeds of 'commercial society' were already present at the beginning of history, indeed in the depths of human nature itself. It was not simply that, as Adam Smith maintained, there was a deep-seated inclination in human nature to 'truck, barter and exchange' but that the modern property relations we now describe as capitalist were rooted in the most primitive practices of exchange between rationally self-interested producers, becoming increasingly specialized in an evolving division of labour which promoted a natural process of economic development.[1] Capitalism, in other words, was simply a maturation of trade and the division of labour by this natural process of growth.

A typical corollary of this thesis was that European feudalism represented a hiatus, an unnatural break in the natural development of commercial society, which had already been established in the ancient Mediterranean, only to be interrupted by extraneous factors in the form of barbarian invasions. The 'Dark Ages' represented a regression, both in material terms, as the economy reverted to subsistence principles, and in culture, as the rationality of the ancients gave way once more to the forces of irrationalism and superstition. Economic development was stopped in its tracks,

[1] For a discussion of this view, especially in the work of Adam Smith, see Robert Brenner, 'Bourgeois Revolution and Transition to Capitalism', in A.L. Beier *et al.*, eds., *The First Modern Society* (Cambridge, 1989), especially pp. 280–2.

fettered by the *political* parasitism of landlordly power. But with the reestablishment of order, and with the growth of towns, the obstacles to commerce were once again lifted, human nature was once again given free rein and the natural progress of history resumed.

Until the French Revolution, it was not unambiguously clear that the principal agents of this progress were the bourgeoisie, an urban class of merchants and industrialists. For British thinkers like Adam Smith or David Hume, the example of English agrarian capitalism suggested a more interactive process, in which the principles of commercial society were rooted in the countryside as much as in the town, as the ancient barons gave way to more forward-looking farmers who managed their land with an eye to profit. Just as the resumption of trade encouraged these landlords to reorganize agriculture, so they in turn encouraged the growth of cities and commerce, and improved the condition of 'the middle rank of men'. But adapted to the different experience of France, in the absence of agrarian capitalism and against the background of the bourgeoisie's political struggle, progress became more or less unambiguously a bourgeois project, in opposition to an unambiguously backward aristocracy. The antithesis between these two classes and the different forms of property they represented – the passive rentier aristocracy as against the productive and progressive bourgeoisie – came to be seen as the principal driving force of history.[2]

The effect of all this was to give an account of economic development which assumed the very thing that needed to be explained. The very particular dynamic of modern capitalism, with laws of motion very different from any earlier social form – the imperatives of competition and profit maximization, the subordination of production to the self-expansion of capital, the ever-increasing need to improve labour productivity by technical means – was simply treated as a natural extension of age-old practices, only a maturation of impulses already present in the most primitive acts of exchange, indeed in the very nature of *Homo oeconomicus*. What was needed was not an explanation of a unique historical process but simply an account of *obstacles* and their removal. Left to itself, self-interest guided by reason would produce capitalism. The existence

---

[2] This 'bourgeois paradigm' of historical development is discussed in my book, *The Pristine Culture of Capitalism: A Historical Essay on Old Regimes and Modern States* (London, 1991), chap. 1.

of capitalism, in other words, was assumed in order to explain its coming into being.

Marx was, at first, very much a part of this tradition. In his earlier accounts of history, there are many of the same assumptions about the existence of a rudimentary capitalism in the ancient world and its interruption by external forces, together with, of course, many of the Continental assumptions about the bourgeoisie as the agent of progress. Here too the existence of capitalism was assumed in order to explain its coming into being, as capitalist impulses, present 'in the interstices of feudalism', were liberated by breaking the 'fetters' of the feudal system.

But sometime between the *German Ideology* and *Capital*, with a critical milestone in the *Grundrisse*, a radical change took place.[3] Marx was no longer willing to assume the very thing that needed to be explained. He was increasingly inclined to insist on the specificity of capitalism and its laws of motion, and this obliged him to recognize that the establishment of this distinctive dynamic could not be taken for granted. The specific imperatives of capitalism, its competitive drive for accumulation by means of increasing labour productivity, was something different from the age-old logic of commercial profit taking, and the principles of capitalism could not be read back into all history. Although Marx never fully developed these historical insights, their fruits can be seen in the *Grundrisse*, which contains his most systematic discussion of pre-capitalist societies and where he faces the problem of accounting for the transformation of pre-capitalist into capitalist property relations without assuming the pre-existence of capitalism. The same is true of *Capital*, especially in the discussion of the 'so-called primitive accumulation'. In neither of these cases is the natural division of labour, or the natural process of technological development, nor the maturation of trade and bourgeois practices the primary moving force. Instead, the transformation is rooted in the agrarian relations of feudalism itself, not even just in its urban interstices but in its primary property relations, in a transformation of the relations between landlords and peasants which has the effect of subjecting direct producers to market imperatives in unprecedented ways.

It is only in these new formulations that we can see the concept of

---

[3] See Brenner, 'Bourgeois Revolution' pp. 285–95 for a discussion of the transformation in Marx's conception of historical materialism and its implications for the transition from feudalism to capitalism.

'mode of production' in its distinctive Marxist sense. It is here that
Marx elaborates the idea that every social form has its own specific
mode of economic activity, with its own laws of motion, its own logic
of process. This is something quite different from earlier conceptions
of economic development as, in effect, the natural progress of *one*
universal economic logic. According to this pre-Marxist view,
shared to some extent by Marx in his earlier work, societies can
certainly vary, but their differences are less a matter of specific forms
with their own inherent logic than of stages in the development of
one social form, or, at best, of variations in the nature and degree of
encouragement afforded to, or impediments imposed upon, the
unfolding of this one natural historical logic. Marx's mode of production challenged the view that there is only one kind of economic
logic, albeit one that can be fettered or suppressed by *non*-economic,
and especially political, factors.

Marx's new insights were informed by the critique of political
economy. His analysis of capitalism was conducted not only as an
investigation of its specific economic practice but also, at the same
time, as what might now be called a deconstruction of capitalist
theory, by means of a critical and subversive application and transcendence of the very categories employed by classical political
economy in its own – increasingly ideological – account of the
capitalist economy.

Marx's *critique* of political economy made it possible for him not
only to avail himself of his predecessors' insights but to liberate
himself from their self-limiting assumptions. In the *Grundrisse*, the
implications for historical analysis are especially evident. His analysis of pre-capitalist economic formations begins with the deceptive
principle that 'human anatomy contains a key to the anatomy of the
ape'.[4] His purpose, as we have seen, is exactly antithetical to the
kind of teleology sometimes read into this aphorism. His stated
objective is to free political economy from the habit of reading
capitalist principles back throughout history. That habit is manifested above all in the application of categories derived from capitalism
and imposed on other social forms in such a way as to submerge both
their own specificity and that of capitalism itself. Marx achieves his
purpose by turning those categories against themselves. The result is
not to universalize their application, so that the economic activities

---

[4] Marx, *Grundrisse* (Harmondsworth, 1974), p. 105.

of pre-capitalist formations appear as merely rudimentary or imperfect capitalisms, but, on the contrary, to reveal their *differences* and, in so doing, inescapably to raise the question of how capitalism, as a specific and unprecedented social form, came into being – not simply as a maturation of earlier forms but as a transformation.

The power of Marx's method lies in the fact that, while focussing on the specificity of every economic formation, it also obliges us to look for principles of motion from one to another not simply in some transhistorical and universal moving force nor only in some *deus ex machina* nor merely in the removal of fetters and obstacles, but within the dynamics of each social form itself. Marx never completed the project he set himself in the *Grundrisse*; but he did begin to construct a new explanation of the transition from feudalism to capitalism in volume I of *Capital*, where he sketched out the processes by which peasant producers, specifically in England, were expropriated, creating, on the one hand, a class of capitalist tenant farmers subject to market imperatives and, on the other, a proletariat of agricultural labourers obliged to sell their labour power for a wage.

There is very little left here of his earlier explanations. The transformation of agrarian relations, which brings an end to feudalism and sets in train a capitalist dynamic, occurs within those relations themselves, not by means of a force external to those primary feudal relations, not by means of a bourgeoisie breaking asunder the fetters of feudalism, not by some further refinement of the division of labour. This was already a significant departure from the prevailing explanations and from Marx's earlier accounts; but it has remained for others working in the historical materialist tradition to develop the insights contained in Marx's critique of political economy and in his own sketchy application of those insights to the problems of history.

Marx's critique of political economy, while devoted essentially to the analysis of capitalism, laid the foundation for a view of history liberated from the categories of capitalist ideology. It provided a means of access to the specificities not only of capitalism but also of other social forms. It was no longer necessary to impose assumptions derived from capitalism upon social forms with different laws of motion or to treat history as a linear urge toward 'commercial society'. And, by extension, it was no longer necessary to generalize the Western experience – unless it was to acknowledge that capitalism, once established, has a unique expansionary drive and a capacity to eclipse all other social forms.

The old bourgeois teleology was, however, to survive elsewhere in a whole range of variations on the basic theme: in various versions of history as the rise of the 'middle classes', in various accounts of the rise of capitalism as the simple outcome of growing markets, the reopening of trade routes, the increase of trade, the liberation of the bourgeoisie from the fetters of feudalism, and so on. What all of these accounts have in common is the assumption that capitalism exists in embryo in any form of trade and commerce, that markets and trade were the solvents of feudalism, that merchant classes were the natural bearers of the capitalist spirit, and that what requires explanation is not the emergence of a new historical dynamic but the liberation of an old one.

Among the more obvious examples is Henri Pirenne, in whose work these assumptions are most explicitly stated:[5] The civilization of the ancient Mediterranean had seen the development of an advanced commercial system centred on maritime trade conducted by professional classes of merchants. This development was dramatically cut short – not, as Pirenne's predecessor would have it, by barbarian incursions into the Roman Empire but later, as the Islamic invasion closed off the Mediterranean and cut the trade routes between East and West, replacing the old 'economy of exchange' with an 'economy of consumption'. By the twelfth century, commerce had revived, with the growth of cities and a new class of professional merchants. This new commercial expansion 'spread like a beneficent epidemic over the whole Continent'.[6] But now, for the first time, there emerged cities more completely devoted to commerce and industry and a class more completely urban than ever before, the medieval burgher. The maturation of earlier capitalist classes which had been thwarted in Europe by the closing of trade routes following the Muslim invasions was now made possible by the revival of trade and the inevitable expansion of markets. The growth of medieval cities and the liberation of the burgher class was, in short, enough to account for the rise of modern capitalism.

The 'Pirenne thesis' has been controversial and generally super-

---

[5] Henri Pirenne's argument is neatly summarized in a series of his lectures published as *Medieval Cities: The Origins and the Revival of Trade* (Princeton, 1969).

[6] *Ibid.*, p. 105.

seded, but critics have seldom questioned the tacit assumptions on which it rested. Even in the more recently dominant demographic explanations of European economic development, often very critical of Pirenne and the 'rise of markets' model, the cycles of population growth work their effects on development through the mechanisms of the market, its perennial laws of supply and demand. There has seldom been an inclination to question the nature of the drive toward capitalism (and often the word 'capitalism' has been studiously avoided), or the assumption that the quantitative expansion of market opportunities, even if complicated by the cyclical patterns of population growth and Malthusian blockages, is the key to the transition from a feudal to a capitalist economy in Europe – together, perhaps, with an autonomous and transhistorical process of technological improvement.

With the notable exception of the economic historian, Karl Polanyi (whose affinities to Marxism were always greater than he seemed willing to acknowledge), it has been Marxists who have questioned these basic assumptions – and even they have not done so consistently.[7] It is primarily Marxists who have acknowledged the specificity of modern capitalism, its distinctive laws of motion, and the inadequacy of any explanation that treats capitalism as simply a maturation or expansion of age-old economic activities, the traditional practices of commercial profit taking, markets and trade.

WEBER ON WORK AND THE SPIRIT OF CAPITALISM: THE CONFLATION OF PRODUCTION AND EXCHANGE

In Max Weber, the bourgeois teleology takes a much more subtle form. Perhaps more than any other thinker in the canon of Western social science, Weber displays a global range of interests and knowledge, from antiquity to modernity, from East to West. The typologies for which he is famous acknowledge a broad spectrum of social forms, varieties of social action, political leadership and domination. On the face of it, these typologies argue strongly against the proposition that Weber, like so many before him, was inclined to generalize from the experience of Western Europe and to read into all times

---

[7] Some of the most important contributions to the debate are contained in Rodney Hilton, ed., *The Transition from Feudalism to Capitalism* (London, 1976) and T.H. Aston and C.H.E. Philpin, eds., *The Brenner Debate: Agrarian Class Structure and Economic Development in Pre-Industrial Europe* (Cambridge, 1985).

and places the social logic of modern Western capitalism. If anything, his life-long project was to identify the specificity of Western
civilization as one among many historical patterns. He was even
critical of Western conceptions of progress. And yet, if the critique of
political economy and a transcendence of capitalism's own self-
validating categories was Marx's first methodological principle, the
opposite is true of Weber; for at the heart of his historical sociology is
a conceptual framework that filters all history through the prism of
the modern capitalist economy.

The point is best illustrated by Weber's account of the origins of
capitalism. His most famous explanation has to do with the 'Protestant ethic', the ways in which the growth of European capitalism
was spurred on by the Reformation and the encouragement it gave
to the ethic of hard work and economic rationality. The idea of the
'calling', the values of asceticism, the glorification of hard work
associated with Calvinism – the psychological effects of the doctrine
of pre-destination – were all conducive to the 'spirit of capitalism'.
This, however, was only part of Weber's explanation and must be
read against the background of his other work, especially on the
distinctive character of the Western city. The Reformation had its
particular effects because its influences acted upon a civilization in
which the principles of economic rationality were already well
developed, where a bourgeoisie imbued with a commercial ethic
had already become especially powerful in the context of the urban
autonomy that was a unique characteristic of the Western city. The
emergence of Protestantism in this distinctive urban context facilitated the union of economic rationality with the 'work ethic',
against the grain of traditional conceptions of labour as a curse
rather than a virtue and a moral obligation. And out of that union
was born modern capitalism.

Attempts to characterize Weber in relation to Marx have generally concerned the extent to which Weber intended to treat
religious ideas, together with political forms, as autonomous and
primary, as against material determinants in the Marxist manner.
But the critical issue here is not whether Weber was an idealist
rather than a materialist, or whether he subordinated economic
interests to other motives. Underlying his 'Protestant ethic and the
spirit of capitalism' there are assumptions that have little to do with
the primacy or autonomy of non-economic determinants and that
reveal not so much his idealism as his bourgeois teleology.

The critical question is not whether Weber correctly identifies the roots of the Protestant ethic, whether the work ethic is cause or effect of the economic developments we associate with capitalism, whether ideas are prime movers or consequences. Weber's account of cause and effect is undoubtedly more complex than any simple dichotomy of idealism and materialism suggests. But there is an even more basic question: how much does the 'Protestant ethic' actually *explain* and how much does Weber's account of it, like other theories of 'commercial society', simply *assume* the very thing that needs to be explained?

Let us begin more or less at the beginning. Weber shared with his predecessors the conviction that the rudiments of capitalism existed in the ancient world, and like them, he treated Western feudalism as a hiatus in the evolution of the capitalist economy as in the progress of Western culture. With the decline of the Roman Empire, he writes:

the natural economy imposed its pressures toward feudalism on the once commercialized superstructure of the ancient world.

Thus the framework of ancient civilization weakened and then collapsed, and the intellectual life of Western Europe sank into a long darkness. Yet its fall was like that of Antaeus, who drew new strength from Mother Earth each time he returned to it. Certainly, if one of the classic authors could have awoken from a manuscript in a monastery and looked out at the world of Carolingian times, he would have found it strange indeed. An odour of dung from the courtyard would have assailed his nostrils.

But of course no Greek or Roman authors appeared. They slept in hibernation, as did all civilization, in an economic world that had once again become rural in character. Nor were the classics remembered when the troubadours and tournaments of feudal society appeared. It was only when the mediaeval city developed out of free division of labour and commercial exchange, when the transition to a natural economy made possible the development of burgher freedoms, and when the bonds imposed by outer and inner feudal authorities were cast off, that – like Antaeus – the classical giants regained a new power, and the cultural heritage of Antiquity revived in the light of modern bourgeois civilization.[8]

The rebirth of commerce and the revival of Western civilization in the context of new burgher liberties was, however, to be enhanced by a wholly new element, the union of economic rationality with a radically new attitude toward labour, a work ethic contrary to all

---

[8] Max Weber, *The Agrarian Sociology of Ancient Civilizations*, tr. R.I. Frank (London, 1988), pp. 410–11.

traditional denigrations of labour as a curse and a burden. It was this new cultural ensemble that was eventually to permit the maturation of capitalism into its modern industrial form.

Weber's theory of the Protestant ethic can certainly be read as a comment on the transformation of commerce from simply a mechanism of exchange and circulation to the organizing principle of *production*. In that sense, he may have moved beyond the old theories of 'commercial society' in an effort to explain the emergence of capitalism as a *mode of production*. But *does* he offer an explanation of that epochal development? Does the 'Protestant ethic' (either by itself or as part of a larger, transhistorical process of 'rationalization') add a fundamentally new element to the old assumptions about the evolution of commercial society? Or does it beg the question yet again?

The evolution of an economic system in which all production is subordinated to the self-expansion of capital, to the imperatives of accumulation, competition and profit maximization, required something more than the simple growth of markets and the traditional practices of buying cheap and selling dear. It even required something more than widespread production for exchange. The very specific integration of production and exchange entailed by this system – in which the economy is driven by competition, and profit is determined by improving labour productivity – presupposed a transformation of social property relations which subjected direct producers to market imperatives in historically unprecedented ways, by making their very access to the means of subsistence and self-reproduction market dependent. Weber does not so much explain as assume this historically unique formation. The Protestant work ethic cannot *explain* the specifically capitalist connection between trade and productivity because their union is already contained in his definition of 'work'.

Weber's idea of the work ethic exemplifies a conceptual habit that has long been a staple of economic discourse in Western capitalist societies and that has served as a cornerstone in the ideological justification of capitalism: the conflation of labour with capitalist enterprise. In the conventional discourse of modern economics, for example, it is capitalists, not workers, who *produce*. So, for example, the financial pages of major newspapers routinely talk about conflicts between, say, automobile *producers* and trade unions. This conflation goes back at least to the seventeenth century and to the beginnings of a more or less self-conscious capitalism. The earliest notable manifestation of this ideological practice occurs in John Locke's *Second Treatise of Government*, in a famous and much debated passage. Explaining how property held in common in the state of nature is taken out of common possession and becomes private property, Locke writes:

We see in *Commons*, which remain so by Compact, that 'tis the taking of any part of what is common, and by removing it out of the state Nature leaves it in, which *begins the Property*; without which the Common is of no use. And the taking of this or that part, does not depend on the express consent of all the Commoners. Thus the Grass my Horse has bit; the Turfs my Servant has cut; and the Ore I have digg'd in any place where I have a right to them in common with others, become my *Property*, without the assignation or consent of any body. The *labour* that was mine, removing them out of the common state they were in, hath *fixed* my *Property* in them.[9]

This passage has been the cause of much controversy, and there is much to be said about it – about Locke's attitude toward the process of enclosure in early modern England, about his views on wage labour, and so on. But one thing is beyond dispute, even if commentators tend to neglect its significance. The appropriation of another's labour ('the Turfs my Servant has cut') is being treated as exactly equivalent to the activity of labour itself ('the Ore I have digg'd'). This means not only that the master lays claim to the fruits of his servant's labour (the servant in question is a contractual wage labourer) but that the activity of labour, and all its attendant virtues, are attributes of the master. This is so, furthermore, in a sense quite different from the way in which, say, a slaveowner might claim the labour of his slave. The point here is not that the master owns the labour of the servant, as he would if the servant's very body were his chattel property. Nor is it simply that, as Marx would acknowledge, the master's purchase of the servant's labour power in exchange for a wage gives the former title to whatever the latter produces in the time stipulated by the wage contract. It is rather that the virtues of labour and 'industry' have been displaced from the activity of labour itself to the *employment* of labour and to the

[9] John Locke, *Second Treatise of Government*, para. 28. For a discussion of Locke's views on 'improvement', see Neal Wood, *John Locke and Agrarian Capitalism* (Berkeley and Los Angeles, 1984). See also E.M. Wood, 'Locke Against Democracy: Consent, Representation and Suffrage in the *Two Treatises*', *History of Political Thought*, 13(4) (1992), especially pp. 677–85, and E.M. Wood, 'Radicalism, Capitalism and Historical Contexts: Not Only a Reply to Richard Ashcraft', *History of Political Thought*, 15(3) (1994).

productive utilization of property. Throughout Locke's discussion of property, it is not the activity of labour itself that carries the rights and virtues of labour, but *improvement*, the productive use of property which gives it value, as against its passive enjoyment in the traditional manner of a rentier class.

The identification of labour with the economic activity of the capitalist is deeply rooted in Western culture, and with it goes a view of history in which the principal opposition – the social contradiction that gives history its momentum – is not between producing and appropriating classes, between exploiters and exploited, but rather between two different kinds of appropriating class, two antithetical forms of property, the passive property of the rentier and the active, productive property of the bourgeois/capitalist.

It is a short step from here to the eclipse of labour altogether by the economic activity of the capitalist. In an economic system where commodity production is generalized, where all production is production for exchange, where all production is subordinated to the self-expansion of capital, where all production *is* the production of capital, and where surplus labour is appropriated not by direct coercion but through the mediation of commodity exchange, the activity of production becomes inseparable from the activity of market exchange. Exchange, not productive labour, is likely to be defined as the essence of economic activity. Something like this conceptual framework – where 'economic' activity is market exchange and where 'labour' is capitalist appropriation and production for profit – underlies Weber's understanding of the work ethic and the rise of capitalism.

THE CITY AS CENTRE OF CONSUMPTION OR PRODUCTION

The full effect of Weber's question-begging definition of 'production', with all its implications for his conception of history and the development of capitalism, is most evident in his critical distinction between cities as centres of *production* and centres of *consumption*. If there is any single factor that weighs more heavily than any other in his account of the rise of modern capitalism, it is the nature of the Western medieval city. And one characteristic which crucially distinguishes that city from the town of, say, classical antiquity – a characteristic that permitted the medieval city to serve as a launching pad for the development of capitalism beyond its ancient limitations to its modern industrial form – is that, while the ancient Greek or Roman city tended to be a centre of consumption, in medieval Europe there emerged towns that were mainly centres of production.

The crucial issue here is not simply that such medieval cities produced more than did ancient towns, nor that more people were engaged in production in one than in the other, but rather that, according to Weber, the medieval city gave greater political and cultural weight to the interests of 'producers', while in classical antiquity it was 'consumer' interests that held sway. The medieval city in the West, then, not only established the conditions of urban autonomy which gave free rein to trade, commerce and the pursuit of gain but also, by encouraging the interests of producers and placing an ideological premium on them, prepared fertile ground for the 'work ethic'.

Weber's characterization of the ancient city as a centre of consumption has much to recommend it. Although he confuses the issue by insisting on the existence of 'capitalism' in ancient society (about which more in a moment), and although he may underestimate the extent to which the urban patriciates of medieval Europe remained essentially rentiers, his formulation has the virtue of pointing to the predominance of rentier property – the property of landlords, slaveowners, creditors – and a rentier mentality in the ancient world, as distinct from the entrepreneurial, productivist culture of modern capitalism. It is certainly true that the dominant property relations of classical antiquity did not encourage expansion of production for the market, or the 'rationalization' of production demanded by it. And while the status of wealthy entrepreneurs or privileged guild masters may tell us little about the condition of producers as *labourers*, it is no doubt true that in the Greek polis there never existed a clear manufacturing interest, not even the kind represented by the medieval guilds with their protectionist functions. Similarly, while it may obscure as much as it reveals to conflate rentier landlords with debtors or the poor beneficiaries of the Roman grain dole in the single category of 'consumer' interests, it is nevertheless true that the ancient Roman 'proletariat' was a 'consumer proletariat, a mass of impoverished petty bourgeois' whose primary material interests were bound up with the distribution

of grain by the state, as distinct from the modern proletariat which is
'a working class engaged in production'.[10]

Yet if Weber is pointing to something true about the ancient city,
we may have to look again at precisely what his message is and what
it tells us, by contrast, about the specific character of the medieval
city and the ways in which it laid the foundations of modern
industrial capitalism. The fact that the categories 'consumer' and
'producer' cut across huge differences of wealth and class turns out
to be critically significant. More specifically, it turns out to be
significant that the category of 'producer' is capable of accommodating both labourer and entrepreneur; for, in the end, it is the
status of the latter that represents for Weber the standing of the
category as a whole. It is, in other words, the social and cultural
location of the entrepreneur, not of the labourer, that determines for
Weber the social and cultural status of 'production' and 'labour'. It
gradually becomes clear that the difference between a centre of
production and a centre of consumption does not depend primarily
on the number of the city's inhabitants engaged in production, nor
even on the volume, range or quality of goods produced, nor on the
cultural evaluation of productive labour as such, but rather on the
identity of the classes with whom production is associated and, more
specifically, the extent to which production is controlled by a 'true'
bourgeoisie and hence subordinated to the requirements of commercial profit.

Ambiguities still remain in Weber's earlier work on the ancient
world, but by the time of his most mature and influential work,
Economy and Society, the message is clear. Recapitulating much of his
earlier argument about the differences between the ancient and
medieval cities, he finally spells out its implications in unmistakable
terms:

The great structural difference between the fully developed ancient and
medieval city, during the period of the rule of the *demos* here and the *popolo*
there, is manifested in this [neglect of artisan producer interests]. In the
ancient city of early Democracy, dominated by the hoplite army, the
town-dwelling craftsman – i.e., a man not settled on a 'citizen's parcel'
(*kleros*) and not economically capable of self-equipment for military service
– played a politically negligible role. In the Middle Ages the city was led by
the *popolo grasso*, the *grande bourgeoisie* of the large entrepreneurs, *and* by the
small capitalists, the tradesmen of the *popolo minuto*. But within the ancient

[10] Weber, *Agrarian Sociology*, p. 42.

citizenry these strata had no – or at least no significant – power. If ancient capitalism was *politically* oriented, so was ancient Democracy. . . .[11]

The principal difference between ancient and medieval cities is that the latter represented the interests of *producers* in a sense that the former did not. This is not, however, to say that the medieval city represented the interests of *labourers* while the ancient polis did not. If anything, the reverse is true. In the golden age of Athenian democracy, for example, the polis *was* dominated, Weber suggests, by the interests of an 'urban *petite bourgeoisie*', the mass of small producers – craftsmen and labourers who, together with peasants, constituted the majority of the citizen body. What the democracy lacked was a powerful '*bourgeoisie* in the modern sense'.[12] The hallmark of 'producers' is not the extent to which they are engaged in production, and even less in labour, but the extent to which production is attached to commerce and trade.

A true bourgeois, then, whether or not he engages in productive labour himself, is a producer; and to complete the paradox, the lower classes of Athens, even when they were engaged in productive labour, are defined by Weber less as producers than as consumers. This is so partly because, according to Weber, the main axis of social conflict ran not, as in the modern world, between an industrial proletariat and industrial employers but between debtors and creditors. But if, as debtors, the lower classes embodied essentially 'consumer' interests, they were consumers also in another sense, as recipients of public payments for performance of civic duties – and it is here that the implications of Weber's 'producer' interests stand out in sharp relief.

Seen from a vantage point different from Weber's – that is, from the vantage point of producers as *labourers* rather than as capitalists – the civic fees which facilitated participation in politics by labouring citizens might be conceived as precisely a manifestation of producer interests. The civic status of peasants and craftsmen in the democracy served the interests of labouring classes by giving them a certain immunity to exploitation by landlords and states, the kind of exploitation by direct political and military coercion typical of all pre-capitalist societies. Within Weber's conceptual framework, however, the interests of labourers in this sense are not the relevant issue. So civic fees become merely a form of unearned 'rentier'

---

[11] Weber, *Economy and Society* (New York, 1968), p. 1346.   [12] *Ibid.*, p. 1347.

income, structurally indistinguishable in this respect from the passive, 'consumer' income of unproductive landlord rentiers. In this sense, too, the interests of landlords, peasants and the urban 'petite bourgeoisie' in the polis are *political* rather than economic. *Homo politicus* predominates over *Homo oeconomicus*.

Weber even maintains that labour was socially degraded in the polis, including the democracy, in contrast to the position of the handicrafts in the later middle ages. He is not, of course, alone in this. It has become something of a convention that Athenians held labour in contempt because of its association with slavery. And while this proposition is itself debatable, there would be nothing remarkable about Weber's repetition of it.[13] But Weber has in mind something more than the effects of slavery on the culture of classical antiquity. By far the most significant expression of labour's oppressed social position in ancient Greece is, for him, the absence of guild associations and the various legal rights associated with them. This is a point to which he repeatedly returns in explaining the differences between the ancient polis and the medieval city.

Yet what does the presence of guilds actually tell us about the social status of labour? The history of guilds in medieval and early modern Europe can be divided into two major phases: at first, they represented the aspiring economic and political power of crafts and trades against patricians who retained their separateness, their status, privilege, and an important degree of autonomy; later, the guilds became strong enough to subject even patricians to their regulations and to dissolve what Weber calls 'extra-urban status differences' in both directions of the social hierarchy. In the first instance, if guild associations could be regarded as representative of *workers'* interests, they expressed their weakness as much as their strength. The associations of common producers were what they were because the patricians remained to a significant extent what they had been. By the time the guilds became truly powerful, as associations of monopolists and even of employers for whom apprentices constituted cheap labour, they could no longer be considered *labourers'* associations in any meaningful sense.

In this perspective, the absence of guilds in ancient Greece testifies more to the strength of the common people than to their

---

[13] I discuss Athenian attitudes toward labour in *Peasant-Citizen and Slave: The Foundations of Athenian Democracy* (London, 1988), pp. 137–45.

weakness and more to the relatively high status of labour than to its social degradation. Even in the most democratic medieval and Renaissance cities – such as republican Florence – ordinary artisans and labourers, as distinct from more prosperous craftsmen and merchants, had no such civic rights as the Athenian *demos*. The labouring citizen in Athens did not require the kind of legal protection afforded by medieval guilds because he had the protection of the polis and his status as a citizen. Just as the legal status of medieval guilds reflected the failure of medieval cities to destroy the patrician status, the absence of guilds in ancient Athens reflected the success of the polis, and the democracy in particular, in subjecting patricians to the jurisdiction of the civic community as a whole.[14] The medieval guilds had something in common with the Roman division between patricians and plebs, which reflected both the power of the plebs to make their will felt and their failure to subordinate the aristocracy; while in the democratic polis, where the victory of the *demos* was more complete, no distinct association of the 'common' people existed. The democracy itself was an association of the *demos*.

Weber, of course, knows all this. He even points out that craft guilds began in precisely those periods and places in which democracy had declined or never triumphed. But it remains significant that the absence of guilds in the democratic polis and their presence in the medieval city represents for him the low status of labour in the first and its elevation in the second. The touchstone, as always, is the status of labour as an attribute not of workers but of the *bourgeoisie*. This, again, tells us a great deal about the question-begging definition of Weber's 'work ethic'; for just as the medieval city was a 'center of production' not because it answered to the interests of labourers but because it encouraged the entrepreneur, so too the glorification of labour in the 'work ethic' would represent not so much the cultural elevation of the labourer or the activity of productive labour itself as the subjection of work to the requirements of profitable exchange.

---

[14] The nineteenth-century historian of ancient Greece, George Grote, drew an illuminating contrast between ancient and medieval societies on the grounds that guilds as formally recognized associations grew out of the failure of medieval cities to destroy the patrician status, while the reforms of Cleisthenes in Athens, often cited as the true foundation of the democracy, succeeded in eliminating the separate political identity of patrician families all at once, 'both as to the name and as to the reality', in his *History of Greece*, chap. xxxi.

THE RISE OF MODERN CAPITALISM

This, then, is the background against which Weber constructed his argument about the 'spirit of capitalism' in the West. The medieval centre of production with burgher liberties allowed free play to economic rationality, and its productive ethos paved the way for the ethic of 'work'. But the full realization of the tendencies already present in the medieval city, the full application of economic rationality not only to trade but to the organization of production, the maturation of a true bourgeoisie as an agent of production, apparently required a further liberation of economic rationality from the political and cultural impediments that stood in its way. Production in the medieval city may already have been subordinated to the requirements of trade, but the organization of work itself, the labour process, its disciplines, techniques, and instruments, had yet to be entirely transformed by the rationality of capital. Just as the political parasitism of the feudal aristocracy had to be decisively replaced by the economic activity of the true, modern *bourgeoisie*, so the traditional consumer or rentier mentality had to be entirely displaced by the values of productivity. The requisite cultural transformation was achieved by the Protestant ethic.

Weber's Protestant ethic, however, cannot account for the 'spirit of capitalism' without, again, already assuming its existence. The idea of the 'calling', the values of asceticism, even the glorification of hard work in themselves have no necessary associations with capitalism. What makes the work ethic capitalist is not the glorification of work itself but its identification with productivity and profit maximization. Yet that identification already presupposes the subordination of labour to capital and the generalization of commodity production, which in turn presuppose the subordination of direct producers to market imperatives.

Neither of the major terms in Weber's equation – the tradition of bourgeois autonomy or Protestant theology – nor both of them together can *explain* these presuppositions without begging the question. If there was nothing in the concept of 'work' that required its association with commerce and trade, neither was there anything in the traditional economic practices of burghers that would account for the subjection of labour to capital, nothing in the rationality of commercial profit taking that would explain how it came about that all production became production for exchange and that direct producers were compelled to enter the market in order to gain access to their means of self-reproduction. And there is certainly nothing to explain how production became subject to the imperatives of competition, the maximization of surplus value and the self-expansion of capital. It was Marx, not Weber, who acknowledged that this was what required explanation and that the explanation could be found only in the primary relations of feudalism and the process by which they were internally transformed.

For Weber, as for many before him, the bourgeois ethic was antithetical to, and impeded by, the rentier/consumer mentality of feudalism, while, at the same time, feudalism permitted the development of capitalism in its urban interstices. The autonomy of the urban commune provided a space – created by a 'natural economy' and a fragmented political power – in which the capitalist spirit could develop with some degree of freedom from these parasitic constraints. But while there can be little doubt that the distinctive autonomy of the Western city had something to do with the evolution of capitalism, there is here again a begging of the question. To say that feudalism permitted the rise of capitalism simply by leaving spaces in which urban autonomy and burgher liberties could flourish is to assume that towns and burghers are by nature already capitalist. Yet if anything, the economic activity of the medieval burgher was parasitic on feudalism, dependent on the lordly consumption of luxury goods and on the fragmentation of markets which were integral to the feudal order and which were the source of pre-capitalist commercial profits, as merchants bought cheap in one market and sold dear in another.[15]

Even in an advanced 'center of production' like Florence, the economy continued to operate on essentially feudal principles, which would prove to be self-limiting as an impetus to economic development. So, for example, economic advantage continued to be determined less by productivity than by political, juridical and military power – whether the traditional powers of the landed aristocracy or the political dominance of urban elites; while wealth was in large part expended in luxury consumption or in enhancing the political and military powers of the ruling classes, improving the

[15] See, for example, John Merrington, 'Town and Country in the Transition to Capitalism', in Rodney Hilton ed., *The Transition from Feudalism to Capitalism*, pp.170–95; and Hilton, 'Towns in English Feudal Society', in *Class Conflict and the Crisis of Feudalism* (London, 1990), pp. 102–13.

means of *appropriation* rather than developing the means of *production* (despite some advances in specialization). Nor was there much expansion of consumption by direct producers, peasants and petty craftsmen. In the first instance, the autonomous urban commune was not a community of modern 'bourgeois' so much as a 'collective lordship', dominating and exploiting the surrounding countryside, particularly as a source of taxes, military service and grain.

Even later, when trade and industry expanded, the great merchants, who traded the products of others at least as much as those of their own city, depended on their political dominance for access to the means of appropriation, while prosperous 'producers' typically relied on politically constituted property in the form of monopolistic privilege rather than on economic superiority in the form of competitive advantages in productivity. In any case, the primary vocation of the mercantile burgher was not so much production as circulation, buying cheap in one market and selling dear in another. And even where production and circulation were united in a single enterprise, the economic logic was the same, having to do with profit upon alienation rather than the maximization of surplus value in the capitalist manner. It was not this kind of economic rationality that led to the dissolution of feudalism and its replacement by different principles of economic action.

A mature capitalist economy did not emerge in the most advanced and autonomous urban communes – like the city-states of central and northern Italy. Without exception, their economic development sooner or later ran into a dead end. Not even the synthesis of burgherdom and Protestantism had the required effect, in, say, Germany or Switzerland, while in France the same Calvinist doctrines were deployed by the Huguenots to support not the 'spirit of capitalism' but, among other things, the independent feudal powers of the provincial nobility. Even the Netherlands failed to produce an integrated capitalist economy, with mutually reinforcing agricultural and industrial sectors. There was, in the Dutch Republic, no shortage of Calvinist repression; but the Protestant Ethic, typically embodied here in hardworking small farmers or prosperous merchants, never impelled the Republic beyond what some historians have called (teleologically) a 'failed transition'. Only England gave rise to a fully developed capitalist economy, and this was the Western European state which (as Weber sometimes seems to acknowledge) least fits the model of autonomous civic communes with a powerful burgher class. *This* capitalist economy was born in the countryside, and none of Weber's assumptions can explain how agrarian relations between landlords and peasants in England set in train the dynamic of capitalist development.

It should be clear from these examples that the issue here is not the transition from a rural to an urban economy, or from agriculture to industry. Before we even raise the question of 'industrialization' there needs to be an explanation of how relations between appropriators and producers, whether urban or rural, were transformed in such a way as to subject production to the imperatives of capitalist competition and profit maximization and the compulsion to accumulate by means of increasing labour productivity. This transformation in social property relations is assumed rather than explained by the presumption that capitalist imperatives exist in embryo in any urban economy, waiting to be released by the removal of political or cultural impediments; nor is the issue advanced very much by simply positing a long-term, transhistorical process of 'rationalization' which, in the absence of obstructions, will take hold of production.

'ECONOMIC ACTION' AND THE 'PURELY ECONOMIC' DEFINITION OF CAPITALISM

Weber is not on the whole interested in social property relations or their historic transformations. Although he does not fail to acknowledge that the emergence of modern industrial capitalism involved major social changes, especially the proletarianization of the labour force, his tendency is to regard that transformation as yet another manifestation of a more or less impersonal and transhistorical *technical* process, another stage in the process of rationalization (aided, admittedly, by a measure of coercion) which subjected the organization of production to the stringent requirements of economic rationality. In general, the transformation of social relations between appropriating and producing classes, whether urban or rural, lies outside his conceptual framework. In fact, neither production nor appropriation figures among Weber's *economic* activities. 'Economic' action is market exchange. Productive activity can be accommodated in Weber's conception of the 'economic' only when it is subsumed under market transactions. And Weber is less interested in the process of appropriation – the process by which the

surplus labour of primary producers becomes another's property –
than in the use of property already appropriated, its utilization
either in passive consumption or in active profit seeking.

The same inclination to identify the 'economy' with markets is
evident in his conception of class. As a purely 'economic' category,
class is defined by the market – not by exploitative relations
between appropriators and producers but by unequal 'market
chances'. Where there is no market, other forms of stratification,
notably 'status', will predominate; wherever there are markets there
are classes. This does not, however, mean that class is an important
principle of stratification only in capitalist societies. Quite apart
from the fact that 'capitalism' (as we shall see) appears to exist in
various forms of society, ancient and modern, there also appear to
be various systems of class, defined by different kinds of 'market'.
Thus if *modern* capitalism differs fundamentally from other social
forms, it is because here the *labour* market determines 'market
chances' while in other cases it is some other kind of market – as, for
example, in classical antiquity, where the credit market determined
the division between creditors and debtors.

The labour market, however, is not, for Weber, a defining feature
of capital ism as such (which can exist, as it did in the ancient
world, in the absence of a labour market, though to the detriment of
further capitalist development, because the absence of its disciplines
in controlling the lower classes impeded large accumulations of
bourgeois property). The modern labour market, like modern proletarianization, is in effect just another *technical* development, yet
another manifestation of the autonomous process of rationalization
and the division of labour which gave rise to the industrial organization of production.

The market, the processes of circulation and exchange, not
labour and its appropriation, defines the 'economy' for Weber, not
just in his historical work but at the very heart of his conceptual
apparatus. 'Action will be said to be "economically oriented"', he
writes:

so far as, according to its subjective meaning, it is concerned with the satis-
faction of a desire for 'utilities' (*Nutzleistungen*). 'Economic action' (*Wirt-
schaften*) is a peaceful use of the actor's control over resources, which is
rationally oriented, by deliberate planning, to economic ends.[16]

[16] Weber, *Economy and Society*, p. 63.

'Utilities' may be:

the services of non-human or inanimate objects or of human beings. Non-human objects which are the sources of potential utilities of whatever sort will be called 'goods'. Utilities derived from a human source, so far as this source consists in active conduct, will be called 'services' (*Leistungen*). Social relationships which are valued as a potential source of present or future disposal over utilities are, however, also objects of economic provision.[17]

Karl Polanyi, in a brief but telling comment on Weber's concept of the 'economic', makes a significant observation about this distinction between 'goods' and 'services' as, respectively, useful services provided by *things* and *human beings*:

The human being is thus brought into formal analogy with things. Man is being treated as a service-rendering thing. Thus only can the term 'useful services' be effectively detached from things and persons alike. Such a separation is necessary for the purpose of economic theory which employs the 'useful services' as a unit; for only so can economic analysis be made to apply to *all* types of goods and their various relationships such as substitutability, complementarity, etc. Yet, from the viewpoint of economic *history*, this definition is useless. In the realm of economic institutions, the useful services of things and those rendered by human beings must be sharply distinguished. The first are attached to a dead object, the other to a live person; from the point of view of economic *institutions* they are therefore in an entirely different category.[18]

The point, of course, is that Weber has simply universalized the economic principles of *capitalism*. The formal analogy between men and things reflects accurately, if abstractly, the social realities of this historically specific economic system, in which labour power is a commodity. The result is a universalization of 'an analytic method devised for a special form of the economy, which was dependent upon the presence of specific market elements'.[19] Weber's definition of 'economic action' is guilty of what Polanyi calls the 'economistic fallacy', the uncritical generalization of a historically specific economic form.

The generalization of capitalist principles is reinforced by Weber's concept of 'rationality' and the role that it plays in his

---

[17] *Ibid.*, p. 68.
[18] George Dalton, ed., *Primitive, Archaic, and Modern Economies: Essays of Karl Polanyi* (Boston, 1971), p. 137.
[19] *Ibid.*, p. 141.

definition of 'economic action'. The consequence of applying the criterion of rational choice to the definition of what constitutes 'economic action' is that workers are engaged in economic activity only in the process of selling their labour power. The activity of work itself is not 'economic'. Just as slaves are tools of their masters and therefore not economically active, so factory workers, having sold their labour power for a wage, cannot be said to be economic actors while they are working. This, remarks Polanyi, is logical enough, since workers, no longer masters of their labour power, cannot be said to be choosing or disposing of their own scarce resources. 'However', he continues:

common usage is very different. To argue that the worker in the factory is *not* engaged in any kind of economic activity is not only contrary to common usage, but sounds like a paradox of questionable taste. The exclusion of everyday activities of producers from the scope of economic activities, is utterly unacceptable to the student of economic institutions. That the only economic activity carried on in a mine or a factory should be that of the shareholder who sells his shares, is a useless proposition to the student of the institution of the mine or the factory.[20]

And it is an even more useless proposition to the student of non-capitalist economic formations, where Weber's 'tasteless paradox' cannot even serve as a formally abstract account of the prevailing economic realities.

In keeping with this conceptual framework, Weber insists on defining *capitalism* in purely 'economic' terms, that is, in clear opposition to Marx, without reference to apparently extraneous social relations. 'Capital', according to Weber, 'is the money value of the means of profit-making available to the enterprise at the balancing of the books; "profit" and correspondingly "loss", the difference between the initial balance and that drawn at the conclusion of the period.'[21] 'The concept of capital has been defined strictly with reference to the individual private enterprise and in accordance with private business accounting practice . . . .'[22] On this basis, Weber insists that a 'capitalist economy' not only existed but played an important role in antiquity. The concept of capitalist enterprise, he argues in his work on the ancient world, tends now to be defined, misleadingly, in terms derived from the modern large-scale enterprise employing free labour:

---

[20] *Ibid.*, pp. 137–8.   [21] Weber, *Economy and Society*, p. 91.   [22] *Ibid.*, p. 94.

From this point of view it has been argued that capitalist economy did not play a dominant role in Antiquity, and did not in fact exist. However, to accept this premise is to limit needlessly the concept of capitalist economy to a single form of valorization of capital – the exploitation of other people's labour on a contractual basis – and thus to introduce social factors. Instead we should take into account only economic factors. Where we find that property is an object of trade and is utilized by individuals for profit-making enterprise in a market economy, there we have capitalism. If this be accepted, then it becomes perfectly clear that capitalism shaped whole periods of Antiquity, and indeed precisely those periods we call 'golden ages'.[23]

In this 'purely economic sense', then, a 'capitalist economy' exists wherever people are engaged in commercial profit taking. This kind of 'capitalism' certainly existed in the ancient world. Yet the exclusion of 'social factors' forecloses any possibility of explaining the specific dynamics of a capitalist mode of production, any possibility of accounting for the historically specific imperatives that set in train a distinctive pattern of self-sustaining economic growth in early modern Europe. Modern capitalism becomes simply more of the same old thing – freer, more mature, but not fundamentally different. To explain the rise of modern capitalism is then simply to account for the removal of impediments.

Much of Weber's discussion of classical antiquity, especially in *Economy and Society*, is indeed devoted to explaining why these early capitalist forms did not evolve into a mature capitalist system, with substantial accumulations of bourgeois wealth and, ultimately, the organization of production in its fully developed industrial-capitalist form. Weber here displays his affinities with the bourgeois-teleological conception of economic development; for the issue, as he presents it, is not how a historically unique social dynamic, characterized by specific imperatives of competition and accumulation, was set in train, but rather how the impulses of capitalism were *impeded*.

Among the greatest obstacles to the evolution of capitalism were political factors of one kind or another. In the ancient monarchies, 'capitalism was gradually checked by bureaucratic regulation'.[24] In the city-states, opportunities for capitalist accumulation tended to be greater, but here too there were political impediments. In democratic Athens, for example, 'All accumulations of burgher wealth of

[23] Weber, *Agrarian Sociology*, pp. 50–1. [24] *Ibid.*, p. 64.

any significance were subject to the claims of the polis of Democracy.'[25] Various juridical and political practices

subjected bourgeois accumulation of wealth to great instability. The absolute arbitrariness of justice administered by the people's courts – civil trials in front of hundreds of jurymen untrained in the law – imperilled the safeguards of formal law so much that it is the mere continued existence of wealth which is to be marvelled at, rather than the violent reversals of fortunes which occurred after every political mishap.

The people of Athens (and even Rome), free of the kinds of restraints imposed by the modern labour market, 'recklessly' applied 'arbitrary' and 'irrational' principles of 'substantive' rather than 'formal' justice, to questions of property. And their *political* interests outweighed the requirements of economic rationality.

What is particularly significant here is the manifest assumption that, left to its own unimpeded logic, commercial profit taking and the accumulation of 'bourgeois' wealth would eventually produce a mature industrial capitalism. As for the Protestant Ethic, it simply accelerated processes that were already at work where burgher wealth was left free to develop.

The issue for Weber, then, is always how the development of economic rationality is accelerated or retarded by non-economic institutions and values. In classical antiquity as in various other times and places, bourgeois economic activity was constrained by forces external to itself, especially the obstruction of *economic* by *political* principles, or religious beliefs inimical to economic rationality. The Athenian *demos* is in this respect the functional equivalent of the feudal aristocracy, a passive class of consumers, its political power parasitic on, and inimical to, the economic force of bourgeois wealth. Weber's accounts of other civilizations – Islamic or Asiatic – which have failed to produce a mature capitalism proceed along much the same lines, explaining the obstacles and impediments – whether in the form of religious doctrines, kinship principles, systems of justice, forms of political domination and other extra-economic factors – which have restrained or deflected the natural developmental logic of commerce and trade.

So, for instance, in China, despite well-developed cities which were centres of trade and production, including even guild organizations, and despite a number of developments which might have

[25] Weber, *Economy and Society*, p. 1361.

been expected to promote the maturation of a capitalist economy from the seventeenth century – the accumulation of great private fortunes, improvements in agricultural production, a vast increase in population, and so on – China never overcame the impediments that stood in the way of capitalism: notably a kinship system based on the extended family, a patrimonial state, the mentality of the mandarin, and a religious tradition that placed a premium on 'status', aestheticism and familial obligations, instead of an activist asceticism in the Puritan manner. What these various factors had in common which above all else impeded the evolution of capitalism was that by reinforcing kinship, on the one hand, and bureaucratic centralization, on the other, they obstructed the development of urban autonomy and a true bourgeoisie.

Elsewhere in Asia too the dominance of kinship principles, or the importance of a centralized officialdom, and/or religious systems that cultivated either aestheticism or mysticism (or both) were decisive above all because they obstructed the development of a particular class, a self-conscious, autonomous and politically powerful urban bourgeoisie. Again, the problem here is not Weber's attribution of great historical importance to urban autonomy in the West or 'patrimonialism' and kinship elsewhere but rather the underlying assumption that the principles of capitalism are secreted in the city and burgherdom, and that only some external impediment prevents them from coming to fruition in a modern capitalism.

WEBER'S METHOD: MULTI-CAUSALITY OR TAUTOLOGICAL CIRCULARITY?

Weber's admirers single out for special praise his multi-dimensional conception of social causation. Recently, for example, two neo-Weberians, Michael Mann and W.G. Runciman, have offered different but equally global totalizing visions of the social world based on elaborations of Weber's causal pluralism, applying what they take to be his greatest insight: that there is no single source of social power, no single principle of social causation like Marx's economic determinism, nor even a fixed hierarchy of social causes.[26]

---

[26] Michael Mann, *The Sources of Social Power* (Cambridge, 1986), and W.G. Runciman, *A Treatise on Social Theory*, 2 vols. (Cambridge, 1983 and 1989). Runciman's debt to Weber is more explicit, while Mann purports to strike some kind of balance between Marx and

Instead, the various sources of social power – economic, political, military, ideological – may combine and recombine in a variety of historically specific causal hierarchies. This causal pluralism, it is argued, makes for better history than Marx's monistic approach.

Yet Weber's causal pluralism has been won at considerable cost. It is not just, as some critics might argue, that a causal pluralism as eclectic as this is tantamount to denying causation altogether. It is rather that the complexity of Weber's theory of social causation is to a large extent spurious. The autonomy, indeed the definition, of, say, political or military as against 'economic' power as Weber understands them depends upon universalizing a conception of the 'economic' that is peculiar to a specific – capitalist – social form which already presupposes a distinctive separation of 'economic' from political and military power. This conception of the 'economic' is further constricted by the exclusion of both production and appropriation or at least their absorption into the processes of market exchange, in a way that is appropriate only to the economic realities of capitalism – and even here only as a formal and one-sided abstraction.

Such a conceptual framework is ill-suited to apprehending the economic organization – the production, appropriation and distribution of material goods – of any society (and this includes all pre-capitalist societies) in which politically constituted property, or appropriation by 'extra-economic' means through direct political and military coercion, plays a dominant role and in which relations between appropriators and direct producers are juridically and politically defined – that is, where material life is organized in 'non-economic' ways. In Weber's schema, there can be no means in such cases of determining the relation between the 'political' and the 'economic' (in the broad, non-capitalist sense), nor is there any way of establishing whether the organization of material life – the mode of production, appropriation and exploitation – is any less determinative in such societies than in the 'purely economic' order of capitalism, since in this conceptual schema the 'economic' exists *only* in its capitalist sense. All we can say, more or less tautologically, about non-capitalist economies is that the 'economic' in the formal and autonomous sense specific to capitalism is not dominant. And if

Weber, among others. But Mann's conception of 'social power', as well as his account of multiple causality, has more in common with Weber than he seems willing to concede.

'economic' power is not dominant, then some form of 'non-economic' power must be. This is not complex causality so much as simple circularity.

This same circularity is implicated in some of the most common criticisms of Marxist historiography. Marxist historians are, apparently, bad historians to the extent that they are good Marxists, and vice versa. Either their Marxism compels them to sacrifice historical specificity to theoretical reductionism, or else they compromise their Marxist purity in order to acknowledge the complexity of social causation. So, for example, if Marxist historians offer an explanation of feudalism in which juridical forms and parcellized sovereignty play a primary role, or an explanation of French history in which the absolutist state is a primary agent, then they are clearly abandoning the Marxist dogma of economic determinism in favour of the autonomy and primacy of 'extra-economic' factors. What such criticisms fail to acknowledge is that, since Marxist materialism distinguishes between pre-capitalist and capitalist societies precisely on the grounds that in the former surplus labour is 'pumped out' of the direct producer by various forms of 'extra-economic' domination, the specification of those 'extra-economic' forms must from the first enter into the definition of the 'economic base'.

In this respect, Marx's concept of the mode of production is more sensitive to historical specificity and variability than is Weber's conceptual schema derived and universalized from the experience of capitalism. The first premise of Marx's critique of political economy is that every distinct social form has its own distinctive mode of economic activity with its own systemic logic, its own 'laws of motion' and developmental patterns, and that capitalism is only one of several, or indeed many, such forms. For Weber, there is only one, essentially capitalist, mode of economic activity, which may be present or absent in varying degrees. For Marx, the various forms of 'extra-economic' social power – political, juridical, military – can play a constitutive role in the definition of the 'economic' and produce a wide variety of economic formations. For Weber, these extra-economic forms are in effect externalities which impinge upon, encourage or inhibit, accelerate or retard, but never fundamentally transform the single, universal and transhistorical mode of truly *economic* action. Who, then, is the Eurocentric, teleological reductionist?

HISTORY, PROGRESS AND EMANCIPATION

Max Weber may turn out to be the prophetic ideal type of the (post-)modern intellectual in our *fin de siècle*. In his work are prefigured two of the principal themes in Western intellectual culture at the close of the twentieth century, what might be called the end of Enlightenment progressivism in two antithetical (or not?) modes: the triumphalist conviction that Progress has reached its destination in modern capitalism and liberal democracy – the glorification of 'the market' and the 'end of History'; together with post-modernist irrationalism, pessimism and the assault on the 'Enlightenment project', its conceptions of reason and progress.

Weber, his criticism of concepts of progress notwithstanding, was still deeply indebted to the Enlightenment tradition with its belief in the advance of reason and freedom. Yet he ended with a much narrower and more pessimistic vision, and with a profound ambivalence toward Enlightenment values. The rise of capitalism certainly represented for him the progress of reason, but 'rationalization' was a two-edged sword: progress and material prosperity, on the one hand, the iron cage, on the other; the progress of freedom and liberal democracy, on the one hand, the inevitable loss of freedom, on the other – to which the only available response may be the embrace of irrationalism.

Ambivalence is not an unreasonable stance to adopt in relation to the fruits of modern 'progress'. What makes Weber's attitude more problematic is that his is an ambivalence that preserves the teleology of Enlightenment triumphalism while giving up much of its critical and emancipatory vision. The consequences are visible in his profoundly ambiguous response to the crises of his time. The Russian Revolution and Germany's defeat in World War I confirmed his fear that Western civilization as a whole was under threat. His reaction was not only deeply pessimistic but anti-democratic and irrationalist. Human emancipation was eclipsed in his political vision by German nationalism, even by the historic mission of the German nation as the bulwark against barbarian (especially Russian) threats to Western civilization. In this, he joined what was to be a long tradition – still flourishing today – of German conservatism (though this strand in his thought no doubt had a longer history, since even his earlier association with German liberalism had represented less a commitment to the advancement of freedom than to the liberals' nation-building project[27]). Finally, his main political legacy to the German nation was the provision in the Weimar Constitution which called for a popularly elected 'plebiscitary' president invested with vast powers, whose primary function was to command the blind obedience of the masses. In this new type of 'charismatic' leader, irrationalism was to be harnessed against the threat of revolution.

If Weber's thought is shot through with an ambivalence toward the fruits of Enlightenment progress, there is nonetheless a certain logic in that ambivalence which may tell us something, *mutatis mutandis*, about our current 'post-modern' condition, in which a submission to the inevitability of capitalism, together with an uncritical acceptance of its basic assumptions, can elicit no other response than celebration or despair. To that Hobson's choice, Marx still offers the possibility of an alternative.

Marx's position in the Enlightenment tradition is in a sense exactly the reverse of Weber's. Like Weber, he acknowledged both the benefits and costs of progress, and especially of capitalism; but he jettisoned the teleology while preserving the critical and emancipatory vision of the Enlightenment. His critique of political economy and his concept of the mode of production liberated history and social theory from the limiting categories of capitalist ideology. But having departed from the Enlightenment concept of progress only as far as was necessary to break out of its bourgeois teleology, and having replaced teleology with *historical process*, he took up and expanded the Enlightenment programme of human emancipation. While supremely conscious of capitalism's systemic coercions, he ended with a *less* deterministic vision. By offering *history* instead of teleology, he also offered the possibility of change instead of despair or unstinting embrace. By putting a *critique* of political economy in place of an uncritical submission to the assumptions and categories of capitalism, he made it possible to see within it the conditions of its supersession by a more humane society. The result was both a greater appreciation of historical specificity and a more universalistic vision.

This combination may hold some fruitful lessons in the face of an unholy alliance between capitalist triumphalism and socialist

[27] For a discussion of Weber's liberalism and other aspects of his thought in relation to the politics of his time and place, see W. Mommsen, *Max Weber und die deutsche Politik 1890–1920* (Tübingen, 1950).

pessimism, at a time when 'grand narratives' are out of fashion, and when even on the left we are being asked, in the interests of 'difference' and the politics of 'identity', to abandon all univeral projects of human emancipation, while submitting to the irresistible power of capitalism.

PART II

Democracy against capitalism

CHAPTER 6

Labour and democracy, ancient and modern

The Greeks did not invent slavery, but they did in a sense invent free labour. Although chattel slavery grew to unprecedented proportions in classical Greece and Athens in particular, there was nothing novel in the ancient world about unfree labour or the relationship of master and slave. But the free labourer enjoying the status of citizenship in a stratified society, specifically the *peasant citizen*, with the juridical/political freedom this implied and the liberation from various forms of exploitation through direct coercion by landlords or states, was certainly a distinctive formation and one that signalled a unique relationship between appropriating and producing classes.

This unique formation lies at the heart of much else that is distinctive about the Greek polis and especially the Athenian democracy. Hardly a political or cultural development in Athens is not in some way affected by it, from the conflicts between democrats and oligarchs in the transactions of democratic politics to the classics of Greek philosophy. The political and cultural traditions that have come down to us from classical antiquity are, therefore, imbued with the spirit of the labouring citizen, together with the anti-democratic animus which he inspired and which informed the writings of the great philosophers. The status of labour in the modern Western world, in both theory and practice, cannot be fully explained without tracing its history back to Graeco-Roman antiquity, to the distinctive disposition of relations between appropriating and producing classes in the Greek and Roman city-state.

At the same time, if the social and cultural status of labour in the modern West can trace its pedigree back to classical antiquity, we have just as much to learn from the radical break dividing modern capitalism from Athenian democracy in this regard. This is true not only in the obvious sense that chattel slavery, after a renewed and prominent role in the rise of modern capitalism, has been displaced, but also in the sense that free labour, while becoming the dominant form, has lost much of the political and cultural status it enjoyed in Greek democracy.

This argument runs counter not only to conventional wisdom but also to scholarly opinion. The point is not just that there is something deeply counter-intuitive about the proposition that the evolution from ancient slave societies to modern liberal capitalism has also been marked by a decline in the status of labour. There is also the fact that free labour has never been accorded the historical importance typically attributed to slavery in the ancient world. When historians of classical antiquity address themselves at all to the question of labour and its cultural effects, they generally give pride of place to slavery. Slavery, it is often said, was responsible for technological stagnation in ancient Greece and Rome. The association of labour with slavery, this argument runs, produced a general contempt for labour in ancient Greek culture. Slavery in the short term enhanced the stability of the democratic polis by uniting rich and poor citizens, while in the long term it caused the decline of the Roman Empire – whether by its presence (as an obstacle to the development of productive forces) or by its absence (as a decline in the supply of slaves placed intolerable strains on the Roman imperial state). And so on. No such determinative effects are generally ascribed to free labour. In what follows, there will be some attempt to redress the balance and to consider what a different perception of labour in antiquity may tell us about its counterpart in modern capitalism.

THE DIALECTIC OF FREEDOM AND SLAVERY

Few historians would hesitate to identify slavery as an essential feature of the social order in ancient Greece, and Athens in particular. Many might even say that slavery is, in one way or another, *the* essential feature and describe classical Athens as a 'slave economy', a 'slave society', or an example of the 'slave mode of production'. Yet there is little agreement about what exactly it means to characterize Athenian society in this way or about what exactly such a characterization is meant to explain.

Such descriptions would be relatively unproblematic if we knew that the bulk of production in Greece was performed by slaves and that the division between producing and appropriating classes corresponded more or less transparently to the division between a juridically defined community of free men, especially citizens, and a subjected labouring class of slaves. But since it is now commonly accepted that production throughout Greek and Roman history rested at least as much on free labour as on slavery, the role of slavery as the key to ancient history has become a rather more thorny question.[1]

Athens, the case for which evidence is most substantial, poses especially difficult problems. It is both the Greek polis that most unambiguously fits the description of a 'slave society' and, at the same time, the most democratic polis, in which the majority of citizens were people who worked for a living. In this sense, free labour was the backbone of Athenian democracy. It cannot even be said that, in this still essentially agrarian society, agricultural production rested largely on slave labour. The extent of agricultural slavery remains a matter of controversy;[2] but there can be little doubt that smallholders who worked their own land remained at the heart of agricultural production. On large estates, there undoubtedly existed a permanent though not very large stock of farm slaves; but landholdings were generally modest, and even wealthy landowners typically owned several scattered smaller properties rather than large estates. Although little is known about how such smaller holdings were worked, farming them out to tenants or sharecroppers may have been a more practical expedient than the

---

[1] For example, M.I. Finley, describes Greece and Rome as 'slave societies', not because slavery predominated over free labour but because these societies were characterized by 'an institutionalized system of large-scale employment of slave-labour in both the countryside and the cities' (*Ancient Slavery and Modern Ideology* [London, 1980], p. 67). G.E.M de Ste Croix argues that, although 'it would not be technically correct to call the Greek (and Roman) world "a *slave* economy"', because 'the combined production of free peasants and artisans must have exceeded that of unfree agricultural and industrial producers in most places at all times', nevertheless this designation remains appropriate because slavery was, he maintains, the dominant mode of surplus extraction or exploitation (*The Class Struggle in the Ancient Greek World* [London, 1981], p. 133). Perry Anderson, in *Passages from Antiquity to Feudalism* (London, 1974), chooses to retain the Marxist concept, 'slave mode of production', but, again, not on the grounds that slave labour predominated in Greek or Roman production but because it cast its ideological shadow over other forms of production. See also Yvon Garland, *Slavery in Ancient Greece* (Ithaca and London, 1988; revised and expanded edition of *Les esclaves en Grèce* [1982]), especially the Conclusion, for a consideration of such concepts as 'slave mode of production' as applied to ancient Greece.

[2] I discuss the question of agricultural slavery at length in *Peasant-Citizen and Slave: The Foundations of Athenian Democracy* (London, 1988), chap. 2 and appendix i. The question of tenancy is also taken up in that chapter, with a consideration of the scant and ambiguous evidence, in appendix ii.

employment of slaves. At any rate, there were no slave plantations, huge estates worked by slave gangs living in barracks, like the Roman latifundia. Casual wage labour was widely used at the harvest and was probably available at all times in the form of propertyless citizens or smallholders whose own lands (or tenancies) were insufficient to support their families. A great many things we do not know, and very likely never will, about the Attic countryside in classical antiquity, but one thing seems certain: the peasant-farmer remained its most characteristic figure.

Slaves were more important to the urban economy, though large manufactories employing many slaves seem to have been very rare. The citizen craftsman may not have been as prominent a figure as the peasant citizen, but he was certainly not eclipsed by slaves. Slavery did appear in virtually every corner of Athenian life, from the most menial labour to the most skilled, from the mine slaves of Laureion to the Scythian archers who served as a kind of police force; from domestic servants to business agents (one of the richest men in Athens, the banker Pasion, had been a slave of this kind), teachers and the nearest thing to civil servants; from the most servile conditions to the relatively independent and privileged. But there were only two domains which we know with any degree of certainty were more or less monopolized by slave labour – domestic service and the silver mines (though there existed small leaseholders who may have worked the mines on their own). The mines were, to be sure, critically important to the Athenian economy; and a polis in which free men and women, rather than slaves, were employed as servants in the households of their wealthy compatriots would have been a very different place than democratic Athens. Nonetheless, the centrality of free labour in the material foundations of Athenian society demands, at the very least, a nuanced definition of the 'slave society'.[3]

The point here is not to play down the importance of slavery in Athenian society. Chattel slavery was more widespread in Greece – notably in Athens – and Rome than anywhere else in the ancient world, and indeed than anywhere but in a handful of societies at any

---

[3] Such a definition would have to begin, like Ste Croix's defence of the 'slave economy', with the proposition that the essential criterion is not the dominant form of production but the principal form of surplus extraction, the mode of exploitation that created the wealth of the dominant class. There would, however, still remain questions about the extent to which wealth was indeed produced by slaves, as distinct, for example, from free tenants.

time in history.[4] Estimates of the number of slaves in classical Athens have varied greatly among modern scholars: for example, for the late fourth century BC, estimates have ranged from 20,000 as against a free population of 124,000, to 106,000 slaves with a free population of 154,000 (112,000 citizens with families, and 42,000 metics).[5] A more common figure now is something like a 60,000–80,000 maximum in peak periods; but this is still a very substantial number, comprising something like 20–30% of the total population. And even if slaves did not dominate material production, they almost certainly dominated (the albeit relatively limited number of) large enterprises, agricultural and 'industrial'.[6] Slavery on such a scale must remain a critical defining feature of Graeco-Roman antiquity, and it justifies the designation 'slave society'. But no account of ancient history, and especially the history of democratic Athens, is even remotely adequate that does not place free labour on at least an equal footing as an explanatory factor.

The simple truth is that, while various forms of unfree labour have been a common feature in most places at most times, the status enjoyed by free labour in democratic Athens was without known precedent and in many respects has remained unequalled since. The peasant citizen of classic antiquity – in varying degrees a characteristic of both Greek and Roman society but nowhere more fully developed than in the Athenian democracy – represents a truly unique social form. The clarity of slavery as a category of unfree labour distinct from others such as debt bondage or serfdom stands out in sharp relief precisely because the freedom of the peasant had erased the whole spectrum of dependence that has characterized the productive life of most societies throughout most of recorded history. It is not so much that the existence of slavery sharply defined the freedom of the citizen but, on the contrary, that the freedom of the labouring citizen, both in theory and in practice, defined the bondage of slaves.

---

[4] Although slaves have existed in many societies, throughout history there have been only five recorded cases of 'slave societies' in Finley's sense: classical Athens, Roman Italy, the West Indian islands, Brazil and the southern United States. See Finley, *Ancient Slavery*, p. 9, and Keith Hopkins, *Conquerors and Slaves* (Cambridge, 1978), pp. 99–100.

[5] The low figure comes from A.H.M Jones, *Athenian Democracy* (Oxford, 1957), pp. 76–9; the higher one from the article on 'Population (Greek)' in the *Oxford Classical Dictionary*, based, with a few modifications, on A.W. Gomme's classic, *The Population of Athens* (Oxford, 1933).

[6] This is what Finley has in mind when he describes Greece and Rome as slave societies: not that slaves predominated in the economy as a whole but that they constituted the *permanent*

The liberation of Attic peasants from traditional forms of dependence encouraged the growth of slavery by foreclosing other forms of unfree labour. In this sense, democracy and slavery in Athens were inextricably united. But this dialectic of freedom and slavery, which accords a central place to free labour in material production, suggests something different from the simple proposition that Athenian democracy rested on the material foundation of slavery. And if we acknowledge that the freedom of free labour, no less than the bondage of slaves, was an essential, and perhaps the most distinctive, feature of Athenian society, we are obliged to consider the ways in which that feature helps to account for much else that is distinctive about the economic, social, political and cultural life of the democracy.

Giving the labouring citizen his due is no less important to an understanding of slavery than to an appreciation of free labour. Neither one nor the other can be fully understood outside the nexus that unites them. In both Greece and Rome, there was always a direct relation between the extent of slavery and the freedom of the peasantry. Democratic Athens had slaves, Sparta had helots. Oligarchic Thessaly and Crete had what might be called serfs. Outside Roman Italy (and even here the majority of the population outside the city of Rome were probably still peasants even when slavery was at its height), various forms of tenancy and share-cropping always prevailed over slavery. In North Africa and in the eastern Empire, slavery in agriculture was never important. Both in the Hellenistic kingdoms and in the Roman Empire, slavery was always less important in those regions traditionally dominated by some kind of monarchical or tributary state, where peasants lacked the civic status they enjoyed in the polis.

If the exceptional growth of chattel slavery in Athens resulted from the liberation of the Athenian peasantry, so the crisis of slavery in the Roman Empire was accompanied by the increasing dependence of peasants. It is beyond the scope of this essay to determine which is cause and which effect; but, in one way or the other, the key to the transition from slavery to serfdom has as much to do with the status of peasants as with the condition of slaves: either the propertied classes needed to depress the condition of the free poor

workforce 'in all Greek or Roman establishments larger than the family unit' (*Ancient Slavery*, p. 81).

because the supply of slaves had declined and slavery had ceased to be as productive as it once had been; or, as the growth of monarchical and imperial government in Rome produced a gradual decline in the political and military power of poor citizens and imposed on them an increasingly insupportable burden, there occurred a 'structural transformation' in Roman society which made peasants more available for exploitation and thus reduced the demand for slave labour.[7] In either case, slavery recedes as the civic status of the peasantry declines.

When centuries later, chattel slavery again assumed a major role in Western economies, it was inserted into a very different context (with some striking ideological effects on the connection between slavery and racism, which I shall take up in chapter 9). Plantation slavery in the American South, for example, was not part of an agrarian economy dominated by peasant producers but belonged to a large-scale commercial agriculture in an increasingly international system of trade. The main driving force at the core of the capitalist world economy was not the nexus of master and slave, nor landlord and peasant, but capital and labour. Free wage labour was becoming the dominant form in a system of property relations increasingly polarized between absolute property and absolute propertylessness; and, in this polarized system, slaves too ceased to occupy a broad spectrum of economic functions. There was nothing like the banker Pasion or the slave civil servant. Slave labour occupied the most unambiguously menial and servile position in the plantation economy.

RULERS AND PRODUCERS

Historians generally agree that the majority of Athenian citizens laboured for a livelihood. Yet, having placed the labouring citizen alongside the slave in the productive life of the democracy, they have made little effort to explore the consequences of this unique formation, this uniquely free labourer and his unprecedented political status. Where there is any attempt at all to draw connections between the material foundations of Athenian society and its politics or culture (and the dominant tendency is still to detach Greek

[7] For the first argument, see Ste Croix, *Class Struggle*, pp. 453–503; for the second, Finley, *The Ancient Economy* (Berkeley, 1973), pp. 86ff.

political and intellectual history from *any* social roots), it is slavery that takes centre stage as the single most determinative fact.

This neglect is truly extraordinary if we consider just how exceptional the position of free labour was and just how far reaching its consequences. It would be no overstatement to say, for example, that the real distinctiveness of the *polis* itself as a form of state organization lies precisely here, in the union of labour and citizenship and specifically in the *peasant citizen*. The polis certainly belongs to what is commonly, if somewhat imprecisely, called the 'city-state', which the Greeks in broad terms had in common with the Romans, as well as the Phoenicians and Etruscans – that is, the small autonomous state consisting of a town and its surrounding countryside. But that category must be further broken down to identify what is most distinctive about the Greek polis.

In pre-capitalist societies, where peasants were the predominant producing class, appropriation – whether by landlords directly or through the medium of the state – typically took the form of what we might call politically constituted property, that is, appropriation achieved through various mechanisms of juridical and political dependence, by direct coercion – forced labour in the form of debt bondage, serfdom, tributary relations, taxation, corvée, and so on. This was true in the advanced civilizations of the ancient world, where the typical state form was one or another variant of the 'bureaucratic-redistributive' or 'tributary' state in which a ruling body was superimposed upon subject communities of direct producers whose surplus labour was appropriated by the ruling apparatus.[8]

Such forms had existed in Greece before the advent of the polis, in the Bronze Age kingdoms. But in Greece a new form of organization emerged which united landlords and peasants into one civic and military community. A broadly similar pattern was to appear in Rome. The very idea of a *civic community* and *citizenship*, as distinct from a superimposed state apparatus or community of rulers, was distinctively Greek and Roman; and it signalled a wholly new relationship between appropriators and producers. In particular, the *peasant citizen*, a social type specific to the Greek and Roman

---

[8] The first formula is used by Karl Polanyi – for instance, in *The Great Transformation* (Boston: Beacon Press, 1957), pp. 51–2; the 'tributary mode of production' is a concept formulated by Samir Amin in *Unequal Development* (Hassocks, 1976), pp. 13 ff.

city-states – and not even to all Greek states[9] – represented a radical departure from all other known advanced civilizations of the ancient world, including the state-forms that preceded it in Bronze Age Greece.

The Greek polis broke a general pattern in stratified societies of a division between *rulers* and *producers*, and especially the opposition of appropriating states and subject peasant communities. In the civic community, the producer's membership – especially in the Athenian democracy – meant an unprecedented degree of freedom from the traditional modes of exploitation, both in the form of debt bondage or serfdom and in the form of taxation.

In this respect, the democratic polis in particular violated what a Chinese philosopher (in a passage that could, with some philosophical refinements, have been written by Plato) once described as a principle universally recognized as right 'everywhere under Heaven':

Why then should you think ... that someone who is carrying on the government of a kingdom has time also to till the soil? The truth is, that some kinds of business are proper to the great and others to the small. Even supposing each man could unite in himself all the various kinds of skill required in every craft, if he had to make for himself everything that he used, this would merely lead to everyone being completely prostrate with fatigue. True indeed is the saying, 'Some work with their minds, others with their bodies. Those who work with their minds rule, while those who work with their bodies are ruled. Those who are ruled produce food; those who rule are fed.'[10]

It can even be argued that the polis (broadly defined to include the Roman city-state[11]) represented the emergence of a new social dynamic, in the form of *class* relations. This is not to say that the polis was the first form of state in which relations of production between appropriators and producers played a central role. The point is rather that these relations took a radically new form. The civic community represented a direct relationship, with its own logic of process, between landlords and peasants as individuals and as

[9] For example, the helots of Sparta and the serfs of Crete and Thessaly represented the antithesis of the peasant citizen.

[10] Mencius, in Arthur Waley, ed., *Three Ways of Thought in Ancient China* (Garden City, n.d.), p. 140.

[11] For an example of this broad usage, see Finley, *Politics in the Ancient World* (Cambridge, 1983).

classes, separated out from the old relation between rulers and subjects.

The old dichotomous relationship between appropriating state and subject peasant producers was compromised to a certain extent throughout the Graeco-Roman world wherever there existed a civic community uniting landlords and peasants, that is, wherever peasants possessed the status of citizenship. This was true even where, as in Rome, the peasant's civic status was relatively restricted. There were, however, significant differences between the conditions of aristocratic Rome and democratic Athens. In both Athens and Rome, the juridical and political status of the peasantry imposed restrictions on the available means of landlordly appropriation and encouraged the development of alternatives, notably chattel slavery. But in Athenian democracy the peasant regime was more restrictive than in aristocratic Rome and left its imprint much more decisively on the whole of the democracy's political, economic and cultural life, even tailoring the rhythm and objectives of warfare to the requirements of the small farmer and his agricultural calendar.[12] Indeed, the democracy, while encouraging the growth of slavery, at the same time, by inhibiting the concentration of property, limited the ways in which slavery could be utilized, especially in agriculture.

By contrast, although the aristocratic regime in Rome was restricted in various ways by the civic and military status of the peasant, the Roman city-state was dominated by the logic of the landlord. The concentration of property which made possible the intensive use of slaves in agriculture was one important manifestation of this aristocratic dominance. Another was the spectacular drama of imperial expansion (in which the indispensable participation of the peasant soldier made him vulnerable to dispossession at home), a landgrabbing operation on a scale the world had never seen. It was on this aristocratic foundation that city-state gave way to empire, and with it the status of the peasant citizen declined. Neither slave latifundia nor a vast territorial empire, two of Rome's defining characteristics, would have been compatible with the smallholder's regime of democratic Athens.

Nowhere, then, was the typical pattern of division between rulers

---

[12] For an excellent discussion of this point, see Robin Osborne, *Classical Landscape with Figures: The Ancient Greek City and its Countryside* (London, 1987), pp. 13, 138–9, 144.

and producers broken as completely as it was in the Athenian democracy. No explanation of Athenian political and cultural development can be complete that fails to take account of this distinctive formation. Although political conflicts between democrats and oligarchs in Athens never neatly coincided with a division between appropriating and producing classes, a tension remained between citizens who had an interest in restoring an aristocratic monopoly of political status and those who had an interest in resisting it, a division between citizens for whom the state would serve as a means of appropriation and those for whom it served as a protection from exploitation. There remained, in other words, an opposition between those who were interested in restoring the division between rulers and producers and those who were not.

This opposition is nowhere more visible than in the classics of Greek philosophy. To put the point baldly: the division between rulers and producers is the fundamental principle of Plato's philosophy, not just his political thought but his epistemology. It is in his work that we can take the full measure of the status of labour in the Athenian democracy. This is so, however, not in the sense that Plato's visible contempt for labour, and for the moral or political capacities of those who are bound to the material necessities of working for a living, represents a cultural norm. On the contrary, the writings of Plato represent a powerful counter-example, a deliberate negation of the democratic culture.

There is sufficient evidence in other classics of Athenian culture to indicate the presence of an attitude to labour very different from Plato's, one more in keeping with the realities of a democracy in which peasants and artisans enjoyed full rights of citizenship. Indeed, Plato himself provides testimony to that attitude when, for example, in the dialogue *Protagoras*, at the beginning of Protagoras's long speech defending the Athenian practice of allowing shoemakers and smiths to make political judgments (320a ff.), he puts into the sophist's mouth a version of the Promethean myth in which the 'practical arts' are the foundations of civilized life. The hero of Aeschylus's *Prometheus*, the bringer of fire and crafts, is the benefactor of humanity, while in Sophocles's *Antigone*, the Chorus sings a hymn of praise to human arts and labour (350 ff.). And the association of democracy with the freedom of labour is suggested by a speech in Euripides's *Suppliants* (429 ff.), where it is said that among the blessings of a free people is not only the fact that the rule of law gives equal justice to rich and poor alike, or that anyone has the right to speak before the public, but also that the citizen's labour is not wasted, in contrast to despotic states where people labour only to enrich tyrants by their toil. It is no doubt significant, too, that Athens' eponymous deity, the goddess Athena, was patron of the arts and crafts, while nowhere in Greece was there a larger temple devoted to Hephaestus, god of the forge, than the one built in the mid fifth century BC overlooking the Athenian agora. But none of these bits of evidence testify to the status of free labour in the democracy more eloquently than does Plato's reaction against it.[13]

PLATO VERSUS PROTAGORAS ON RULERS AND PRODUCERS

In his dialogue, *Protagoras*, Plato sets the agenda for much of his later philosophical work. Here, he raises questions about virtue, knowledge and the art of politics which will preoccupy him in his later works, most notably in the *Republic*; and the context in which those questions are raised tells us a great deal about the centrality of labour in the political discourse of the democracy. In this dialogue, perhaps for the last time in his work, Plato gives the opposition a reasonably fair hearing, presenting the sophist Protagoras in a more or less sympathetic light as he constructs a defence of the democracy, the only systematic argument for democracy to have survived from antiquity. Plato was to spend the rest of his career implicitly refuting Protagoras's case.

The *Protagoras* has to do with the nature of virtue and whether it can be taught. The question is raised in an explicitly political context, as Socrates sets the terms of the debate:

Now when we meet in the Assembly, then if the State is faced with some building project, I observe that the architects are sent for and consulted about the proposed structure, and when it is a matter of shipbuilding, the naval designers, and so on with everything which the Assembly regards as a subject for learning and teaching. If anyone tries to give advice, whom they

---

[13] Much the same is true of Aristotle, whose ideal polis in the *Politics* denies citizenship to people engaged in labour which supplies the basic goods and services of the polis. Such people are 'conditions' rather than 'parts' of the polis, differing from slaves only in that they perform their menial duties for the community rather than for individuals (1277a–1278a). In my discussion of Greek attitudes toward labour in *Peasant-Citizen and Slave*, pp. 137–62, I argue, among other things, that, if there were ideological barriers to technological development, they had less to do with a contempt for labour derived from its association with slavery than with the independence of small producers and the absence of compulsions to improve labour productivity.

do not consider an expert, however handsome or wealthy or nobly-born he may be, it makes no difference: the members reject him noisily and with contempt, until either he is shouted down and desists, or else he is dragged off or ejected by the police on the orders of the presiding magistrate. That is how they behave over subjects they consider technical. But when it is something to do with the government of the country that is to be debated, the man who gets up to advise them may be a builder or equally well a blacksmith or a shoemaker, merchant or shipowner, rich or poor, of good family or none. No one brings it up against any of these, as against those I have just mentioned, that here is a man who without any technical qualifications, unable to point to anybody as his teacher, is yet trying to give advice. The reason must be that they do not think that this is a subject that can be taught.[14]

In reply to Socrates, Protagoras sets out to demonstrate that 'your countrymen act reasonably in accepting the advice of smith and shoemaker on political matters'.[15] And so the fundamental episte-mological and ethical questions that form the basis of Greek phil-osophy, and indeed of the whole Western philosophical tradition, are situated in an explicitly political context, having to do with the democratic practice of allowing shoemakers and smiths to make political judgments.

Protagoras's argument proceeds, first, by way of an allegory intended to demonstrate that political society, without which men cannot benefit from the arts and skills that are their only distinctive gift from the gods, cannot survive unless the civic virtue that quali-fies people for citizenship is a universal quality. He then goes on to show how virtue can be a universal quality without being innate, a quality that must and can be taught. Everyone who lives in a civilized community, especially a polis, is from birth exposed to the learning process that imparts civic virtue, in the home, in school, through admonition and punishment, and above all through the city's customs and laws, its *nomoi*. Civic virtue is both learned and universal in much the same way as one's mother tongue. The sophist who, like Protagoras himself, claims to teach virtue can only perfect this continuous and universal process, and a man can possess the qualities of good citizenship without the benefit of the sophist's expert instruction.

Protagoras's emphasis on the universality of virtue is, of course, critical to his defence of democracy. But equally important is his

---

[14] *Protagoras*, 319b–d.   [15] *Ibid.*, 324d.

conception of the process by which moral and political knowledge is transmitted. Virtue is certainly taught, but the model of learning is not so much scholarship as *apprenticeship*. Apprenticeship, in so-called 'traditional' societies, is more than a means of learning technical skills. 'It is also', to quote a distinguished historian of eighteenth-century England, 'the mechanism of inter-generational transmission', the means by which people are both initiated into adult skills or particular practical arts and at the same time inducted 'into the social experience and common wisdom of the community'.[16] There is no better way of characterizing the learning process described by Protagoras, the mechanism by which the community of citizens passes on its collective wisdom, its customary practices, values and expectations.

The principle invoked by Socrates against Protagoras – at this stage, still rather tentatively and unsystematically – is that virtue is knowledge. This principle was to become the basis of Plato's attack on democracy, especially in *The Statesman* and *The Republic*. In Plato's hands, it represents the replacement of Protagoras's moral and political apprenticeship with a more exalted conception of virtue as philosophic knowledge, not the conventional assimilation of the community's customs and values but a privileged access to higher universal and absolute truths.

Yet Plato too constructs his definition of political virtue and justice on the analogy of the practical arts. He too draws on the common experience of democratic Athens, appealing to the familiar experience of the labouring citizen by invoking the ethic of craftsmanship, *technē*. Only this time, the emphasis is not on universality or the organic transmission of conventional knowledge from one generation to another, but on *specialization*, expertise and exclusiveness. Just as the best shoes are made by the trained and expert shoemaker, so the art of politics should be practised only by those who specialize in it. No more shoemakers and smiths in the Assembly. The essence of justice in the state is the principle that the cobbler should stick to his last.

Both Protagoras and Plato, then, place the cultural values of *technē*, the practical arts of the labouring citizen, at the heart of their political arguments, though to antithetical purposes. Much of what follows in the whole tradition of Western philosophy proceeds from

[16] E.P. Thompson, *Customs in Common* (London, 1991), p. 7.

this starting point. It is not only Western political philosophy that owes its origins to this conflict over the political role of shoemakers and smiths. For Plato the division between those who rule and those who labour, between those who work with their minds and those who work with their bodies, between those who rule and are fed and those who produce food and are ruled, is not simply the basic principle of politics. The division of labour between rulers and producers, which is the essence of justice in *The Republic*, is also the essence of Plato's theory of knowledge. The radical and hierarchical opposition between the sensible and the intelligible worlds, and between their corresponding forms of cognition – an opposition that has been identified as the most distinctive characteristic of Greek thought and which has set the agenda for Western philosophy ever since[17] – is grounded by Plato in an analogy with the social division of labour which excludes the producer from politics.

THE ECLIPSE OF FREE LABOUR

So great is the imbalance between the historic importance of free labour in ancient Greece and its neglect by modern historiography that something needs to be said about how this imbalance occurred, about how the labouring citizen, for all his historic distinctiveness, has been lost in the shadow of slavery.[18] It is not, again, that historians have failed to acknowledge that the citizen body in democratic Athens consisted in large part of people who laboured for a livelihood. It is rather that this acknowledgement has not been accompanied by a commensurate effort to explore the historic significance of that remarkable fact. As a determinative factor in the movement of history, free labour in the ancient world has been virtually eclipsed by slavery, and not only for the admirable reason that our best instincts have been preoccupied by the horrors of that evil institution.

The eclipse of the labouring citizen in democratic Athens has less to do with the realities of Athenian democracy than with the politics of modern Europe. Before the second half of the eighteenth century, and especially before the American and French Revolutions, there

---

[17] This point is elaborated by Jacques Gernet in 'Social History and the Evolution of Ideas in China and Greece from the Sixth to the Second Century BC', in Jean-Pierre Vernant, *Myth and Society in Ancient Greece* (Sussex, 1980).

[18] This section is based on my book, *Peasant-Citizen and Slave*, chap. 1.

would have been nothing unusual about a characterization of the ancient Athenian democracy as a 'mechanic' commonwealth, a commonwealth in which the aristocracy was subordinated to a 'banausic' multitude of labouring citizens – in contrast, for example, to Sparta, where the citizenry as a whole constituted a kind of nobility, 'such as live upon their own revenues in plenty, without engagement either unto the tilling of their lands or other work for their livelihood'.[19] Characterizations of this kind were part of a long tradition, stretching back to ancient Greece itself and the identification of democracy with the dominance of a 'banausic' *demos*. In these accounts of the democracy, the labouring citizen is still very much alive.

But by the late eighteenth century, a significant shift had occurred. The mechanic multitude had begun to give way to the 'idle mob', supported by the labour of slaves. The explanation of this shift is not that historians had suddenly discovered the extent of chattel slavery in democratic Athens. Earlier writers had been no less aware of it. Montesquieu, for example, if anything greatly overestimated the number of slaves in Athens; and as the author of an influential attack on slavery, he was not inclined to make apologies for its Greek manifestations. Yet none of this prevented him from maintaining that the essence of Athenian democracy – in contrast to Sparta, whose citizens were 'obliged to be idle' – was that its citizens worked for a living.[20] Nor can the appearance of the idle mob be explained by a new preoccupation with the evils of slavery, generated by a heightened democratic consciousness in the Age of Revolution. On the contrary, the idle mob was born primarily in the minds of reactionary anti-democrats.

The principal culprits were, in the first instance, British historians who wrote the first modern narrative and political histories of ancient Greece, with the explicit object of warning their contemporaries against the dangers of democracy. The most important of these was William Mitford, the Tory country gentleman and opponent of parliamentary reform, who wrote an influential history of Greece, published in several volumes between 1784 and 1810. When

---

[19] James Harrington, 'The Commonwealth of Oceana' in J.G.A. Pocock, ed., *The Political Works of James Harrington* (Cambridge, 1977), pp. 259–60. Harrington is here borrowing Machiavelli's definition of the nobility.

[20] Charles de Secondat, Baron de Montesquieu, *The Spirit of the Laws* (New York, 1949), p. 46.

in the course of his work the French Revolution intervened, he interrupted his narrative to explain why the English had been spared this evil; and his explanation had to do with the ways in which England differed from modern France and ancient Athens. England enjoyed an unequalled harmony among 'the several ranks of citizenry', while Greece (and France) lacked any comparable harmonizing mechanism. In particular, 'throughout Greece, the noble and wealthy, served by their slaves, not only as domestics, but as husbandmen and manufacturers, had little connection with the poorer Many, but to command them in oligarchical states, and in the democratical, to fear, flatter, solicit, and either deceive, or be commanded by them. No common interest united the two descriptions of men . . . '.[21] The result was a licentious and turbulent mob, 'citizens without property, without industry, and perhaps without objects for industry', an idle mob sustained by slavery and by public payments, and always eager to plunder the wealth of the rich.[22]

But if Mitford represents a particularly extreme example of anti-democratic rhetoric, the same idle mob makes an appearance in much more sober and scholarly works throughout the following century. In August Böckh's influential economic history, slavery and public payments are again the sources of corruption in the democracy, making the multitude accustomed to 'indolence' and giving them the leisure to participate in politics, 'whereas in countries in which slavery does not exist, the citizens having to labour for their subsistence are less able to employ themselves in the business of governments . . . '. The result was that: 'Even in the noblest races of Greece, among which the Athenians must without doubt be reckoned, depravity and moral corruption were prevalent throughout the whole people.'[23] And even Fustel de Coulanges was to attribute the turbulence of ancient Greece to the absence of economic principles that would have compelled rich and poor to live together on good terms, as they might have done '[i]f, for example, the one had stood in need of the other, – if the wealthy could not have enriched themselves except by calling upon the poor for their labor, and the poor could have found the means of selling their labor to the rich'.[24] As it was, 'The citizen found few employments, little to do; the want

[21] William Mitford, *The History of Greece*, vol. v (London, 1814), pp. 34–5.
[22] *Ibid.*, p. 16.
[23] August Boeckh [Böckh], *The Public Economy of Athens* (1842), pp. 611–14.
[24] Numa Denis Fustel de Coulanges, *The Ancient City* (Garden City, n.d.), p. 337.

of occupation soon rendered him indolent. As he saw only slaves at work, he despised labor'. And so on.

None of these writers was unaware that the Athenian citizens laboured, as farmers and craftsmen. The point was not so much that they did not work but that they did not work *enough* and above all that they did not *serve*. Their independence and the leisure they enjoyed to participate in politics proved the undoing of Greek democracy. For Mitford and Böckh, participation by the multitude was evil in itself. For the more liberal Fustel, it was rather that, in the absence of traditional forms of political control, what was needed was the kind of *economic* discipline afforded in modern society by the material necessity which obliges propertyless labourers to sell their labour for a wage. What was lacking, in other words, was a modern bourgeois state and economy. But, in all these cases, the independence of the labouring citizen was consistently translated into the indolence of the idle mob, and with it came the dominance of slavery.

The effects of this historical revision were enormous, extending far beyond the original anti-democratic motivations of historians like Mitford. The idle mob reached from Hegel's account of the democracy, where the basic condition of democratic politics was that citizens should be freed from necessary labour and 'that what among us is performed by free citizens – the work of daily life – should be done by slaves',[25] to the Marxist inversion of the idle mob in the 'slave mode of production'.

There is, however, a paradox here, because the ideological weight attached to slavery was not expressed in a commensurate scholarly interest in it.[26] The anti-democrats who pushed slaves into prominence by playing on the theme of the idle mob were far less interested in exploring the problem of slavery itself than in denigrating the democratic multitude. On the other side, liberals who invoked the example of ancient Greece in defence of modern political reform were even less anxious to dwell on the embarrassment of slavery, while, in their ambivalence toward democracy, toward the extension of political rights to the working class (as distinct from the improvement of representative institutions and civil liberties), they

---

[25] G.W.F. Hegel, *The Philosophy of History*, tr. J. Sibree (New York, 1912), p. 336.

[26] For a historical sketch of the ideological foundations of modern scholarship on ancient slavery, see Finley, *Ancient Slavery*, pp. 11–66, and Garland, *Slavery*, pp. 1–14. See also Luciano Canfora, *Ideologie del classicismo* (1980), esp. pp. 11–19.

were generally no more keen to emphasize the role of the labouring multitude in Athenian democracy.

The result was a curious vagueness about the political economy of Athens, perhaps even more among liberals than conservatives. George Grote, political reformer and author of a distinguished history of ancient Greece, makes only passing mention of dependent labour and then in relation to the serfs of Thessaly or Crete rather than the slaves of Athens; while Grote's friend, J.S. Mill, was less inclined to focus on the *democratic* features of the Athenian democracy than to praise its *liberal* values, the individuality and variety of Athenian life – in contrast to the illiberal Spartans, whom, in his review of Grote's history for the *Edinburgh Review*, he actually describes as 'those hereditary Tories and Conservatives of Greece'. None of this did much to illuminate the position of either slavery or free labour in classical antiquity.

LABOUR AND THE 'SPIRIT OF CAPITALISM'

It is not surprising that the transition from mechanic multitude to idle mob took place in the eighteenth century (and especially in England, Mitford's encomium to the English constitution notwithstanding). 'The eighteenth century', writes E.P. Thompson,

witnessed a qualitative change in labour relations .... a substantial proportion of the labour force actually became *more* free from discipline in their daily work, more free to choose between employer and between work and leisure, less situated in a position of dependence in their whole way of life, than they had been before or than they were to be in the first decades of the discipline of the factory and of the clock. ...

Working often in their own cottages, owning or hiring their own tools, usually working for small employers, frequently working irregular hours and at more than one job, they had escaped from the social controls of the manorial village and were not yet subject to the discipline of factory labour. ...

Free labour had brought with it a weakening of the old means of social discipline.[27]

The language with which these developments were greeted by the English ruling class is the very language of the idle mob. The labouring poor in England, scorning the 'great law of subordination' and the traditional deference of servant to master, were

---

[27] Thompson, *Customs*, pp. 38–42.

200 Democracy against capitalism

alternately 'clamorous and mutinous', growing 'ripe for all manner of mischief, whether publick Insurrection, or private plunder', and 'saucy, lazy, idle and debauch'd . . . they will Work but two or three Days in the Week'.[28]

The myth of the idle Athenian mob is then the age-old complaint of master against servant, but with the added urgency of a new social order, in which free and propertyless wage labour was becoming the dominant mode of work for the first time in history. In the same process of capitalist development, the concept of labour was undergoing other transformations too. It is often said that the modern world has witnessed the elevation of labour to an unprecedented cultural status which owes much to the 'Protestant Ethic', and the Calvinist idea of the 'calling'. And with or without Max Weber's 'Protestant Ethic', the association of the 'spirit of capitalism' with the glorification of work has become part of conventional wisdom.

Yet while capitalism, with its imperatives of profitability and labour productivity, has certainly brought with it more stringent labour disciplines, the glorification of hard work has been a two-edged sword. The ideology of work has had an ambiguous meaning for workers, justifying their subjection to capitalist disciplines at least as much as it has elevated their cultural status. But perhaps the most important point about the transformation in the cultural status of labour that accompanied the rise of capitalism is the conflation of labour with *productivity*, which we noted in our discussion of Weber. This transformation is, as we saw, already visible in the work of John Locke and his conception of 'improvement'. The virtues of labour no longer unequivocally belong to labourers themselves. They are above all the attributes of *capitalists*, and not because they work themselves but because they utilize their property actively and productively, in contrast to the passive appropriation of the traditional rentier. The 'glorification' of work in the 'spirit of capitalism' has less to do with the rising status of the labourer than with the displacement of rentier property by capital.

The conception of 'labour' as 'improvement' and productivity, qualities that belong less to workers than to the capitalist who puts them to work, lies at the core of 'bourgeois ideology' and is con-

---

[28] Daniel Defoe, *The Great law of Subordination Consider'd; or, the Insolence and Unsufferable Behaviour of Servants in England duly enquir'd into* (1724), quoted in Thompson, *Customs*, p. 37.

stantly reproduced in the language of modern economics, where 'producers' are not workers but capitalists. It bespeaks an economic order where production is subordinated to market imperatives and where the driving mechanism is competition and profit maximization, not the 'extra-economic' coercions of politically constituted property but the purely 'economic' imperatives of the market which demand increasing labour productivity.

The social property relations that set this driving mechanism to work have placed labour in a historically unique position. Subject to economic imperatives that do not depend directly on a subordinate juridical or political status, the propertyless wage labourer in capitalism can enjoy juridical freedom and equality, even full political rights in a system of universal suffrage, without depriving capital of its appropriating power. It is here that we find the greatest difference between the status of labour in ancient Athenian democracy and in modern capitalism.

LABOUR AND DEMOCRACY, ANCIENT AND MODERN

In modern capitalist democracy, socio-economic inequality and exploitation coexist with civic freedom and equality. Primary producers are not juridically dependent or politically disfranchised. In ancient democracy too civic identity was dissociated from socio-economic status, and here too political equality coexisted with class inequality. But there remains a fundamental difference. In capitalist society, primary producers are subject to economic compulsions which are independent of their political status. The power of the capitalist to appropriate the surplus labour of workers is not dependent on a privileged juridical or civic status but on the workers' propertylessness, which obliges them to exchange their labour power for a wage in order to gain access to the means of labour and subsistence. Workers are subject both to the power of capital and to the imperatives of competition and profit maximization. The separation of civic status and class position in capitalist societies thus has two sides: on the one hand, the right of citizenship is not determined by socio-economic position – and in this sense, capitalism can coexist with formal democracy – on the other hand, civic equality does not directly affect class inequality, and formal democracy leaves class exploitation fundamentally intact.

By contrast, in ancient democracy there existed a class of primary producers who were juridically free and politically privileged, and who were at the same time largely free of the necessity to enter the market to secure access to the conditions of labour and subsistence. Their civic freedom was not, like that of the modern wage labourer, offset by the economic compulsions of capitalism. As in capitalism, the right to citizenship was not determined by socio-economic status, but unlike capitalism, relations between classes were directly and profoundly affected by civic status. The most obvious example is the division between citizens and slaves. But citizenship directly determined economic relations in other ways too.

Democratic citizenship in Athens meant that small producers were to a great extent free of the extra-economic exactions to which direct producers in pre-capitalist societies have always been subject. They were free, for example, from the depradations of Hesiod's 'gift-devouring' lords, using jurisdictional powers to milk the peasantry; or from the direct coercion of the Spartan ruling class, exploiting helots by means of what amounted to a military occupation; or from the feudal obligations of the medieval peasant, subject to the military and jurisdictional powers of the lords; or from the taxation of European absolutism, in which public office was a primary instrument of private appropriation; and so on. As long as direct producers remained free of purely 'economic' imperatives, politically constituted property would remain a lucrative resource, as an instrument of private appropriation or, conversely, a protection against exploitation; and in that context, the civic status of the Athenian citizen was a valuable asset which had direct economic implications. Political equality not only coexisted with but substantially modified socio-economic inequality, and democracy was more substantive than 'formal'.

In ancient Athens, citizenship had profound consequences for peasants and craftsmen; and, of course, a change in the juridical status of slaves – and, indeed, women – would have transformed the society entirely. In feudalism, juridical privilege and political rights could not have been redistributed without transforming the prevailing social property relations. Only in capitalism has it become possible to leave the property relations between capital and labour fundamentally intact while permitting the democratization of civic and political rights.

That capitalism could survive democracy, at least in this 'formal' sense, was not, however, always obvious. As the growth of capitalist property relations began to separate property from privilege, and especially while free labour was not yet subject to the new disciplines of industrial capitalism and complete propertylessness, the ruling classes of Europe were deeply preoccupied with the dangers posed by the labouring multitude. For a long time, it seemed that the only solution was the preservation of some kind of division between rulers and producers, between a politically privileged propertied elite and a disfranchised labouring multitude. Nor were political rights, needless to say, freely given when they were finally granted to the working classes, after prolonged and much resisted popular struggles.

In the meantime, a wholly new conception of democracy had pushed aside the ancient Greek idea. The critical moment in this redefinition, which had the effect (and the intention) of *diluting* the meaning of democracy, was the foundation of the United States, which I shall take up in the next chapter. Yet, however much the ruling classes of Europe and America may have feared the extension of political rights to the labouring multitude, it turned out that political rights in capitalist society no longer had the salience of citizenship in ancient democracy. The achievement of formal democracy and universal suffrage certainly represented tremendous historic advances, but it turned out that capitalism offered a new solution to the age-old problem of rulers and producers. It was no longer necessary to embody the division between privilege and labour in a political division between appropriating rulers and labouring subjects, now that democracy could be confined to a formally separate 'political' sphere while the 'economy' followed rules of its own. If the extent of the citizen body could no longer be restricted, the scope of citizenship could now be narrowly contained, even without constitutional limits.

The contrast between the status of labour in ancient democracy and modern capitalism invites some very large questions: in a system where purely 'economic' power has replaced political privilege, what is the meaning of citizenship? What would be required to recover, in a very different context, the salience of citizenship in ancient democracy and the status of the labouring citizen?

CHAPTER 7

The demos versus 'we, the people': from ancient to modern conceptions of citizenship

The ancient concept of democracy grew out of a historical experience which had conferred a unique civic status on subordinate classes, creating in particular that unprecedented formation, the peasant citizen. In all – or at least a great deal – but name, the modern concept belongs to a different historical trajectory, most vividly exemplified in the Anglo-American tradition. The landmarks along the road to the ancient democracy, such as the reforms of Solon and Cleisthenes, represent pivotal moments in the elevation of the *demos* to citizenship. In the other history, originating not in Athenian democracy but in European feudalism and culminating in liberal capitalism, the major milestones, like Magna Carta and 1688, mark the ascent of the propertied classes. In this case, it is not a question of peasants liberating themselves from the political domination of their overlords but lords themselves asserting their independent powers against the claims of monarchy. This is the origin of modern constitutional principles, ideas of limited government, the separation of powers, and so on: principles which have displaced the social implications of 'rule by the *demos*' – such as the balance of power between rich and poor – as the central criterion of democracy. If the peasant-citizen is the most representative figure of the first historical drama, in the second it is the feudal baron and the Whig aristocrat.

If *citizenship* is the constitutive concept of ancient democracy, the founding principle of the other variety is, perhaps, *lordship*. The Athenian citizen claimed to be *masterless*, a servant to no mortal man. He owed no service or deference to any lord, nor did he waste his labour to enrich a tyrant by his toil. The freedom, *eleutheria*, entailed by his citizenship was the freedom of the *demos from* lordship. Magna Carta, in contrast, was a charter not of a masterless *demos* but of masters themselves, asserting feudal privileges and the freedom *of* lordship against both Crown and popular multitude, just as the *liberty* of 1688 represented the privilege of propertied gentlemen, their freedom to dispose of their property and servants at will.

Certainly, the assertion of aristocratic privilege against encroaching monarchies produced the tradition of 'popular sovereignty' from which the modern conception of democracy derives; yet the 'people' in question was not the *demos* but a privileged stratum constituting an exclusive political nation situated in a public realm between the monarch and the multitude. While Athenian democracy had the effect of breaking down the age-old opposition between rulers and producers by turning peasants into citizens, the division between ruling landlords and subject peasants was a constitutive condition of 'popular sovereignty' as it emerged in early modern Europe. On the one hand, the fragmentation of sovereignty and the power of lordship which constituted European feudalism, the check on monarchy and state centralization exercised by these feudal principles, were to be the basis of a new kind of 'limited' state power, the source of what were later to be called democratic principles, such as constitutionalism, representation and civil liberties. On the other hand, the obverse side of feudal lordship was a dependent peasantry, while the 'political nation' which grew out of the community of feudal lords retained its exclusiveness and the political subordination of producing classes.

In England, the exclusive political nation found its embodiment in Parliament, which, as Sir Thomas Smith wrote in the 1560s, 'hath the power of the whole realme both the head and the bodie. For everie Englishman is entended to bee there present, either in person or by procuration and attornies, of what preheminence, state dignitie, or qualitie soever he be, from the Prince (be he King or Queene) to the lowest person of England. And the consent of the Parliament is taken to be everie man's consent.'[1] It is worth noting that a man was deemed to be 'present' in Parliament even if he had no right to vote for his representative. Thomas Smith, like others before and after him, took it for granted that a propertied minority would stand for the population as a whole.

The doctrine of parliamentary supremacy was to operate against popular power even when the political nation was no longer restricted

---

[1] Sir Thomas Smith, *De Republica Anglorum*, ed. Mary Dewar (Cambridge, 1982), p. 79.

to a relatively small community of property holders and when the 'people' was extended to include the 'popular multitude'. In Britain today, for example, politics is the special preserve of a sovereign Parliament. Parliament may be ultimately accountable to its electorate, but the 'people' are not truly *sovereign*. For all intents and purposes, there is no *politics* – or at least no legitimate politics – outside Parliament. Indeed, the more inclusive the 'people' has become, the more the dominant political ideologies – from Conservative to mainstream Labour – have insisted on depoliticizing the world outside Parliament and delegitimating 'extra-parliamentary' politics. Running parallel with this process has been a growing centralization of parliamentary power itself in the executive, producing something very much like cabinet, or even prime ministerial, sovereignty.

There did emerge, in early modern England, a body of political thought – especially in the work of James Harrington, Algernon Sidney and Henry Neville – which, on the face of it, appears to run counter to this dominant parliamentary tradition. This school of political theory, which has come to be known as classical republicanism, had, or seemed to have, as its central organizing principle a concept of citizenship, implying not simply the passive enjoyment of individual rights which we have come to associate with 'liberal democracy' but a community of active citizens in pursuit of a common good. Yet there is one fundamental point on which early modern republicans like James Harrington agreed with their 'liberal' contemporaries: the exclusivity of the political nation.[2] Active citizenship was to be reserved for men of property and must exclude not only women but also those men who lacked, as Harrington put it, the 'wherewithal to live of themselves' – that is, those whose livelihood depended on working for others. This conception of citizenship had at its core a division between propertied elite and labouring multitude. It is not surprising that republicans of this variety, when seeking models in antiquity, chose the aristocratic ('mixed') constitution of Sparta or Rome instead of democratic Athens.

In fact, such a division between propertied elite and labouring multitude may have belonged to the essence of English classical republicanism even more absolutely and irreducibly than to, say, Lockean liberalism. When Harrington set out to construct political principles appropriate to a society where feudal lordship no longer prevailed, he did not altogether jettison the principles of feudalism. It is even possible to say that his conception of citizenship was modelled in certain important respects on feudal principles. On the one hand, there was no longer to be a category of dependent property, a juridical and political division between different forms of landed property, as there had been between feudal lords and their dependants. All landed property was to be juridically and politically privileged. On the other hand, property itself was still defined as a political and military status; it was, in other words, still characterized by the inextricable unity of economic and political/military power which had constituted feudal lordship.

In this, classical republicanism was already an anachronism at the moment of its conception. Landed property in England was already assuming a *capitalist* form, in which economic power was no longer inextricably bound up with juridical, political and military status, and wealth depended increasingly on 'improvement' or the *productive* use of property subject to the imperatives of a competitive market. Here, John Locke's conception of property and agricultural 'improvement' was more in keeping with current realities.[3] And while Locke himself was no democrat, it is arguable that a conception of property such as his was ultimately more amenable to relaxing the restrictions on membership in the political nation.[4] To put it simply, once the economic power of the propertied classes no longer depended upon 'extra-economic' status, on the juridical, political and military powers of lordship, a monopoly on politics was no longer indispensable to the elite. By contrast, within a framework dominated by an essentially pre-capitalist conception of property, with all its juridical and political 'embellishments' (as Marx once called them), the 'formal' equality made possible by the capitalist

---

[3] See Neal Wood, *John Locke and Agrarian Capitalism* (Berkeley and Los Angeles, 1984).

[4] For a powerful critique of attempts to portray Locke as a democrat, see David McNally, 'Locke, Levellers and Liberty: Property and Democracy in the Thought of the First Whigs', *History of Political Thought*, 10(1) (1989), pp. 17–40. I have also argued against such interpretations in 'Locke Against Democracy: Consent, Representation and Suffrage in the *Two Treatises*', *History of Political Thought*, 13(4) (1992), pp. 657–89, and 'Radicalism, Capitalism and Historical Contexts: Not Only a Reply to Richard Ashcraft on John Locke', *History of Political Thought*, 15(3) (1994).

separation of the 'economic' and the 'political' was not even *thinkable* (literally), let alone desirable.

Capitalism, by shifting the locus of power from *lordship* to *property*, made civic status less salient, as the benefits of political privilege gave way to purely 'economic' advantage. This eventually made possible a new form of democracy. Where classical republicanism had solved the problem of propertied elite and labouring multitude by restricting the extent of the citizen body (as Athenian oligarchs would have liked to do), capitalist or liberal democracy would permit the extension of citizenship by restricting its powers (as the Romans did). Where one proposed an active but exclusive citizen body, in which the propertied classes ruled the labouring multitude, the other could – eventually – envisage an inclusive but largely passive citizen body, embracing both elite and multitude, but whose citizenship would be limited in scope.

Capitalism transformed the political sphere in other ways too. The relation between capital and labour presupposes formally free and equal individuals, without prescriptive rights or obligations, juridical privileges or disabilities. The detachment of the individual from corporate institutions and identities began very early in England (it is, for example, reflected in Sir Thomas Smith's definition of a commonwealth as 'a societie or common doing of a multitude of free men collected together and united by common accords and covenauntes among themselves',[5] and in the individualistic psychologism that runs through the tradition of British social thought from Hobbes and Locke to Hume and beyond); and the rise of capitalism was marked by the increasing detachment of the individual (not to mention individual property) from customary, corporate, prescriptive and communal identities and obligations.

The emergence of this isolated individual did, needless to say, have its positive side, the emancipatory implications of which are emphasized by liberal doctrine, with its constitutive concept

---

[5] Smith, *De Republica Anglorum*, p. 57. It is interesting in this connection to compare Smith's definition with that of his contemporary, Jean Bodin, who, in his *Six Books of the Commonwealth*, treats 'families, colleges, or corporate bodies', not individual free men, as the constituent units of the commonwealth, reflecting the realities of France, where corporate institutions and identities continued to play a prominent role in political life.

(myth?) of the sovereign individual. But there was also another side. In a sense, the creation of the sovereign individual was the price paid by the 'labouring multitude' for entry into the political community; or, to be more precise, the historical process which gave rise to capitalism, and to the modern 'free and equal' wage labourer who would eventually join the body of citizens, was the same process in which the peasant was dispossessed and deracinated, detached from both his property and his community, together with its common and customary rights.

Let us consider briefly what this means. The peasant in pre-capitalist societies, unlike the modern wage labourer, remained in possession of property, in this case land, the means of labour and subsistence. This meant that the capacity of landlord or state to appropriate labour from him depended on a superior coercive power, in the form of juridical, political and military status. The principal modes of surplus extraction to which peasants were subject – rent and tax – typically took the form of various kinds of juridical and political dependence: debt-bondage, serfdom, tributary relations, obligations to perform corvée labour, and so on. By the same token, the capacity of peasants to resist or limit their exploitation by landlords and states depended in great measure on the strength of their own political organization, notably the village community. To the extent that peasants were able to achieve a degree of political independence by extending the jurisdiction of the village community – for example, imposing their own local charters or replacing landlord representatives with their own local magistrates – they also extended their economic powers of appropriation and resistance to exploitation. But however strong the village community became from time to time, there generally remained one insurmountable barrier to peasant autonomy: the state. The peasant village almost universally remained as it were outside the state, and subject to its alien power, as the peasant was excluded from the community of citizens.

It is here that Athenian democracy represents a radically unique exception. Only here was the barrier between state and village breached, as the village effectively became the constitutive unit of the state, and peasants became citizens. The Athenian citizen acquired his civic status by virtue of his membership in a deme, a geographical unit generally based on existing villages. The establishment by Cleisthenes of the deme as the constituent unit of the polis was in a critical sense the foundation of the democracy. It created a civic identity abstracted from differences of birth, an identity common to aristocracy and *demos*, symbolized by the adoption by Athenian citizens of a *demotikon*, a deme-name, as distinct from (though in practice never replacing, especially in the case of the aristocracy) the patronymic. But even more fundamentally, Cleisthenes' reforms 'politicised the Attic countryside and rooted political identity there'.[6] They represented, in other words, the incorporation of the village into the state, and the peasant into the civic community. The economic corollary of this political status was an exceptional degree of freedom for the peasant from 'extra-economic' exactions in the form of rent or tax.[7]

The medieval peasant, in contrast, remained firmly excluded from the state and correspondingly more subject to extra-economic surplus extraction. The institutions and solidarities of the village community could afford him some protection against landlords and states (though it could also serve as a medium of lordly control – as, for example, in manorial courts), but the state itself was alien, the exclusive preserve of feudal lords. And as the feudal 'parcellization of sovereignty' gave way to more centralized states, the exclusivity of this political sphere survived in the privileged political nation.[8] Finally, as feudal relations gave way to capitalism, specifically in England, even the mediation of the village community, which had stood between peasant and landlord, was lost. The individual and his property were detached from the community, as production increasingly fell outside communal regulation, whether by manorial courts or village community (the most obvious example of this process is the replacement of the English open-field system by enclosure); customary tenures became economic leaseholds subject to the impersonal competitive pressures of the market; smallholders lost their customary use-rights to common land; increasingly, they were dispossessed, whether by coercive eviction or the economic pressures of competition. Eventually, as landholding became increasingly concentrated, the peasantry gave way to large land-

---

[6] Robin Osborne, *Demos: The Discovery of Classical Attika* (Cambridge, 1985), p. 189.

[7] For more on these points, see my *Peasant-Citizen and Slave: The Foundations of Athenian Democracy*, (London, 1988), pp. 101–7.

[8] For a discussion of the relation between peasants, lords, and the state in medieval and early modern Europe, see Robert Brenner, 'The Agrarian Roots of European Capitalism', in T.H. Aston and C.H.E. Philpin, eds., *The Brenner Debate: Agrarian Class Structure and Economic Development in Pre-Industrial Europe* (Cambridge, 1985), pp. 213–327.

holders, on the one hand, and propertyless wage labourers, on the other. In the end, the 'liberation' of the individual was complete, as capitalism, with its indifference to the 'extra-economic' identities of the labouring multitude, dissipated prescriptive attributes and 'extra-economic' differences in the solvent of the labour market, where individuals become interchangeable units of labour abstracted from any specific personal or social identity.

It is as an aggregate of such isolated individuals, without property and abstracted from communal solidarities, that the 'labouring multitude' finally entered the community of citizens. Of course, the dissolution of traditional prescriptive identities and juridical inequalities represented an advance for these now 'free and equal' individuals; and the acquisition of citizenship conferred upon them new powers, rights, and entitlements. But we cannot take the measure of their gains and losses without remembering that the historical presupposition of their citizenship was the *devaluation* of the political sphere, the new relation between the 'economic' and the 'political' which had reduced the salience of citizenship and transferred some of its formerly exclusive powers to the purely economic domain of private property and the market, where purely economic advantage takes the place of juridical privilege and political monopoly. The devaluation of citizenship entailed by capitalist social relations is an essential attribute of modern democracy. For that reason, the tendency of liberal doctrine to represent the historical developments which produced formal citizenship as nothing other than an enhancement of individual liberty – the freeing of the individual from an arbitrary state, as well as from the constraints of tradition and prescriptive hierarchies, from communal repressions or the demands of civic virtue – is inexcusably one-sided.

Nor can we assess the ideological effects of the modern relation between individual citizen and civic community or *nation*, without considering the degree to which that 'imagined community' is a fiction, a mythical abstraction, in conflict with the experience of the citizen's daily life.[9] The nation can certainly be real enough to inspire individuals to die for their country; but we must consider the extent to which this abstraction is also capable of serving as an ideological device to deny or disguise the more immediate

[9] On the nation as an 'imagined community', see Benedict Anderson, *Imagined Communities* (London, 1983).

experience of individuals, to disaggregate and delegitimate, or at least to depoliticize, the solidarities that stand between the levels of individual and nation, such as those forged in the workplace, the local community, or in a common class experience. When the political nation was privileged and exclusive, the 'commonwealth' in large part corresponded to a real community of interest among the landed aristocracy. In modern democracies, where the civic community unites extremes of social inequality and conflicting interests, the 'common good' shared by citizens must be a much more tenuously abstract notion.

Here, again, the contrast with ancient democracy is striking. Constructed upon the foundation of the deme, the democratic polis was built upon what Aristotle in the *Nicomachean Ethics* called a *natural* community. That this 'real community' had real political implications is suggested by the tangible consequences of peasant citizenship. Nor was the contradiction between civic community and the realities of social life as great in Athenian democracy as in the modern democratic state. Modern liberal democracy has in common with ancient Greek democracy a dissociation of civic identity from socio-economic status which permits the coexistence of formal political equality with class inequality. But this similarity disguises a deeper difference between the two forms of democracy, reflecting radically different relations between 'political' and 'social' or 'economic' planes in the two cases.

In ancient Athenian democracy, as I argued in chapter 6, the right to citizenship was not determined by socio-economic status; but the power of appropriation, and relations between classes, were directly affected by democratic citizenship. In Athens democratic citizenship meant that small producers, and peasants in particular, were to a great extent free of 'extra-economic' exploitation. Their political participation – in the assembly, in the courts, and in the street – limited their economic exploitation. At the same time, unlike workers in capitalism, they were still not subject to the purely 'economic' compulsions of propertylessness. Political and economic freedom were inseparable – the dual freedom of the *demos* in its simultaneous meaning as a political status and a social class, the common people or the poor; while political equality did not simply coexist with, but substantially modified, socio-economic inequality. In this sense, democracy in Athens was not 'formal' but substantive.

In capitalist democracy, the separation between civic status and class position operates in both directions: socio-economic position does not determine the right to citizenship – and that is what is *democratic* in capitalist democracy – but, since the power of the capitalist to appropriate the surplus labour of workers is not dependent on a privileged juridical or civic status, civic equality does not directly affect or significantly modify class inequality – and that is what limits democracy in capitalism. Class relations between capital and labour can survive even with juridical equality and universal suffrage. In that sense, political equality in capitalist democracy not only coexists with socio-economic inequality but leaves it fundamentally intact.

THE AMERICAN REDEFINITION OF DEMOCRACY

Capitalism, then, made it possible to conceive of 'formal democracy', a form of civic equality which could coexist with social inequality and leave economic relations between 'elite' and 'labouring multitude' in place. Needless to say, however, the conceptual *possibility* of 'formal democracy' did not make it a historical actuality. There were to be many long and arduous struggles before the 'people' grew to encompass the labouring multitude, let alone women. It is a curious fact that in the dominant ideologies of Anglo-American political culture these struggles have not achieved the status of principal milestones in the history of democracy. In the canons of English-speaking liberalism, the main road to modern democracy runs through Rome, Magna Carta, the Petition of Right and the Glorious Revolution, not Athens, the Levellers, Diggers and Chartism. Nor is it simply that the historical record belongs to the victors; for if 1688, not Levellers and Diggers, represents the winners, should not history record that democracy was on the losing side?

It is here that the American experience was decisive. English Whiggery could have long remained content to celebrate the forward march of Parliament without proclaiming it a victory for *democracy*. The Americans had no such option. Despite the fact that in the struggle to determine the shape of the new republic it was the anti-democrats who won, even at the moment of foundation the impulse toward mass democracy was already too strong for that victory to be complete. Here, too, the dominant ideology divided governing elite from governed multitude; and the Federalists might have wished, had it been possible, to create an exclusive political nation, an aristocracy of propertied citizens, in which property – and specifically landed property – remained a privileged juridical/political/military status. But economic and political realities in the colonies had already foreclosed that option. Property had irrevocably discarded its extra-economic 'embellishments', in an economy based on commodity exchange and purely 'economic' modes of appropriation, which undermined the neat division between politically privileged property and disenfranchised labouring multitude. And the colonial experience culminating in revolution had created a politically active populace.

The Federalists thus faced the unprecedented task of preserving what they could of the division between mass and elite in the context of an increasingly democratic franchise and an increasingly active citizenry. It is now more generally acknowledged than it was not very long ago that US democracy was deeply flawed in its very foundations by the exclusion of women, the oppression of slaves and a genocidal colonialism in relation to indigenous peoples. What may not be quite so self-evident are the anti-democratic principles contained in the idea of democratic citizenship itself as it was defined by the 'Founding Fathers'. The framers of the Constitution embarked on the first experiment in designing a set of political institutions that would both embody and at the same time curtail popular power, in a context where it was no longer possible to maintain an exclusive citizen body. Where the option of an active but exclusive citizenry was unavailable, it would be necessary to create an inclusive but passive citizen body with limited scope for its political powers.

The Federalist ideal may have been to create an aristocracy combining wealth with republican virtue (an ideal that would inevitably give way to the dominance of wealth alone); but their practical task was to sustain a propertied oligarchy with the electoral support of a popular multitude. This also required the Federalists to produce an ideology, and specifically a redefinition of democracy, which would disguise the ambiguities in their oligarchic project. It was the anti-democratic victors in the USA who gave the modern world its definition of democracy, a definition in which the dilution of popular power is an essential ingredient. If American political institutions have not been imitated everywhere, the American experiment has nonetheless left this universal legacy.[10]

In the previous chapter, I quoted a passage from Plato's *Protagoras* referring to the Athenian practice of letting shoemakers and blacksmiths, rich and poor alike, make political judgments. This passage, which gives expression to the democratic principle of *isegoria*, not just freedom but equality of speech, neatly identifies the essence of Athenian democracy. Here, by contrast, is a quotation from *Federalist* no. 35, by Alexander Hamilton:

The idea of actual representation of all classes of the people, by people of each class, is altogether visionary.... Mechanics and manufacturers will always be inclined, with few exceptions, to give their votes to merchants in preference to persons of their own professions or trades.... they are aware, that however great the confidence they may justly feel in their own good sense, their interests can be more effectually promoted by merchants than by themselves. They are sensible that their habits in life have not been such as to give them those acquired endowments without which, in a deliberative assembly, the greatest natural abilities are for the most part useless.... We must therefore consider merchants as the natural representatives of all these classes of the community.

Some of the most essential differences between ancient and modern democracy are nicely summed up in these two quotations. Alexander Hamilton is spelling out the principles of what he elsewhere calls 'representative democracy', an idea with no historical precedent in the ancient world, an American innovation. And here, shoemakers and blacksmiths are represented by their social superiors. What is at stake in this contrast is *not* simply the conventional distinction between direct and representative democracy. There are other more fundamental differences of principle between the two conceptions of democracy contained in these two quotations.

The concept of *isegoria* is arguably the most distinctive concept associated with Athenian democracy, the one most distant from any analog in modern liberal democracy – including its closest approximation, the modern concept of free speech. Alexander Hamilton was no doubt an advocate of free speech in the modern liberal

[10] For an illuminating discussion of this model and its implications, see Peter Manicas, 'The Foreclosure of Democracy in America', *History of Political Thought*, 9(1) (1988), pp. 137–60. On the Federalists in the context of the debates leading up to and surrounding the Constitution, see Gordon S. Wood, *The Creation of the American Republic, 1776–1787* (New York, 1972).

democratic sense, having to do with protecting the right of citizens to express themselves without interference, especially by the state. But there is in Hamilton's conception no incompatibility between advocating civil liberties, among which the freedom of expression is paramount, and the view that in the political domain the wealthy merchant is the natural representative of the humble craftsman. The man of property will speak politically for the shoemaker or blacksmith. Hamilton does not, of course, propose to silence these demotic voices. Nor does he intend to deprive them of the right to choose their representatives. He is, evidently with some reluctance, obliged to accept a fairly wide and socially inclusive or 'democratic' franchise. But like many *anti*-democrats before him, he makes certain assumptions about representation according to which the labouring multitude, like Sir Thomas Smith's 'lowest person', must find its political voice in its social superiors.

These assumptions also have to be placed in the context of the Federalist view that representation is not a way of implementing but of *avoiding* or at least partially circumventing democracy. Their argument was not that representation is necessary in a large republic, but, on the contrary, that a large republic is desirable so that representation is unavoidable – and the smaller the proportion of representatives to represented, the greater the distance between them, the better. As Madison put it in *Federalist* 10, the effect of representation is 'to refine and enlarge the public views, by passing them through the medium of a chosen body of citizens . . .'. And an extensive republic is clearly preferable to a small one, 'more favorable to the election of proper guardians of the public weal', on the grounds of 'two obvious considerations': that there would be a smaller proportion of representatives to represented, and that each representative would be chosen by a larger electorate. Representation, in other words, is intended to act as a *filter*. In these respects, the Federalist conception of representation – and especially Hamilton's – is the very antithesis of *isegoria*.

We have become so accustomed to the formula, 'representative democracy', that we tend to forget the novelty of the American idea. In its Federalist form, at any rate, it meant that something hitherto perceived as the *antithesis* of democratic self-government was now not only compatible with but constitutive of democracy: not the *exercise* of political power but its *relinquishment*, its *transfer* to others, its *alienation*.

The alienation of political power was so foreign to the Greek conception of democracy that even election could be regarded as an oligarchic practice, which democracies might adopt for certain specific purposes but which did not belong to the essence of the democratic constitution. Thus Aristotle, outlining how a 'mixed' constitution might be constructed out of elements from the main constitutional types, such as oligarchy and democracy, suggests the inclusion of election as an oligarchic feature. It was oligarchic because it tended to favour the *gnorimoi*, the notables, the rich and well born who were less likely to be sympathetic to democracy. Athenians might resort to election in the case of offices requiring a narrowly technical expertise, notably the top financial and military posts (such as the military office of *strategos* to which Pericles was elected); but such offices were hedged about with stringent measures for ensuring accountability, and they were clearly understood as exceptions to the rule that all citizens could be assumed to possess the kind of civic wisdom required for general political functions. The quintessentially democratic method was selection by lot, a practice which, while acknowledging the practical constraints imposed by the size of a state and the number of its citizens, embodies a criterion of selection in principle opposed to the alienation of citizenship and to the assumption that the *demos* is politically incompetent.

The American republic firmly established a definition of democracy in which the transfer of power to 'representatives of the people' constituted not just a necessary concession to size and complexity but rather the very essence of democracy itself. The Americans, then, though they did not invent representation, can be credited with establishing an essential constitutive idea of modern democracy: its identification with the alienation of power. But, again, the critical point here is not simply the substitution of representative for direct democracy. There are undoubtedly many reasons for favouring representation even in the most democratic polity. The issue here is rather the assumptions on which the Federalist conception of representation was based. Not only did the 'Founding Fathers' conceive representation as a means of *distancing* the people from politics, but they advocated it for the same reason that Athenian democrats were suspicious of election: that it favoured the propertied classes. 'Representative democracy', like one of Aristotle's mixtures, is civilized democracy with a touch of oligarchy.

A 'PEOPLE' WITHOUT SOCIAL CONTENT

The Federalist argument, which is predicated on a conception of the 'public weal' as more rather than less distant from the will of the citizens, displays a very particular conception of citizenship which contrasts sharply with the ancient Athenian idea. The modern American conception of citizenship may be more inclusive and universalistic than the Athenian, more indifferent to the particularisms of kinship, blood ties, or ethnicity. In this respect, it is more like ancient Roman citizenship than Athenian. But if US citizenship has more in common with Roman than with Greek civic identity in its universality, its capacity for extension to 'aliens', it may also have something else in common with (not just republican but even imperial) Rome in this respect, namely a greater distance between the 'people' and the sphere of political action, a less immediate connection between citizenship and political participation. US, like Roman, citizenship may be more expansive and inclusive than the democratic citizenship of Athens, but it may also be more *abstract* and more passive.

If it was the intention of the 'Founding Fathers' to create this kind of passive citizenship, or at least to temper the civic activism of the revolutionary culture, it differs from Athenian democracy in another respect. It has been argued that in both the American and the Athenian cases, the emergence of democracy resulted from, among other things, 'a pre-existing democratic culture' outside the political realm, egalitarian habits in 'civil society'.[11] Cleisthenes's act of 'foundation', it is suggested, had the effect of institutionalizing this pre-existing democratic culture. But, if this is so, then the US Constitution is related to its pre-existing democratic culture in a rather different sense.

The founders of the US Constitution were faced not only with a democratic culture but with fairly well-developed democratic institutions; and they were at least as much concerned to *contain* as to entrench the democratic habits which had established themselves in colonial and revolutionary America not only in 'civil society' but even in the political sphere, from town meetings to representative assemblies. They achieved the desired effect in part by widening the

---

[11] See W.R. Connor, 'Festival and Democracy', in Charles Hedrick and Josiah Ober, eds., *Democracy Ancient and Modern* (unpublished, 1994).

distance between civic identity and action in the public space – not only by interposing the filter of representation between the citizen and the political sphere but even by means of a literal, geographic displacement. Where Cleisthenes made the local deme the basis of Athenian citizenship, the Federalists did their best to shift the focal point of politics from the locality to the federal centre.

It says a great deal about the meaning of citizenship and popular sovereignty as conceived by the Founding Fathers that some anti-Federalists attacked the anti-democratic implications of the proposed constitution by rejecting the Constitution's opening formula, 'We, the People ...'.[12] This formula, apparently the most unambiguous appeal to popular sovereignty, seemed to its critics as, on the contrary, a recipe for despotism, for an extensive empire ruled at the centre by an unrepresentative and tyrannical state. For these critics, the more democratic formula, closing the distance between the people and the realm of politics, would have been 'We, the States ...'. The Federalists' invocation of 'the people' was, according to such anti-Federalists, simply a means of vesting true sovereignty in the federal government, giving it the stamp of popular sovereignty while actually by-passing institutions more immediately accountable to the people and converting republican into imperial government.

Americans were later to discover anti-democratic possibilities in the doctrine of 'states' rights' that could not have been foreseen by either early critics or advocates of the Constitution; but to their contemporaries it seemed clear that the Federalists were invoking popular sovereignty in support of an effort to distance the people from politics and to redefine citizenship, shifting the balance away from republican activism to imperial passivity. The 'people' was no longer being defined, like the Athenian *demos*, as an active citizen community but as a disaggregated collection of private individuals whose public aspect was represented by a distant central state. In contrast to the ancient notion of citizenship as *sharing* in a political community, even the concept of individual *rights*, which may be modern democracy's greatest claim to superiority over the ancient variety, bears the connotation of passivity.[13]

The 'people' underwent another major transformation in the

---

[12] For a discussion of this point, see G. Wood, *Creation*, pp. 526–7.

[13] See Martin Ostwald, 'Shares and Rights: "Citizenship" Greek and American Style', in Hedrick and Ober, eds., *Democracy*.

hands of the Federalists which again sets their conception of democracy far apart from the democratic principles embodied in the idea of *isegoria*. The very possibility of reconciling Hamilton's particular conception of representation with the idea of democracy required a major innovation, which remains part of our definition of democracy today. The concept of 'representative democracy' itself would have been difficult enough for Athenians to absorb, but I can imagine conceptions of representation based on more democratic assumptions than Hamilton's (not least, that of Tom Paine). What is more important here is the fact that Hamilton's conception required the complete evacuation of any social content from the concept of democracy and a political conception of the 'people' in which social connotations were suppressed.

Consider, by way of contrast, Aristotle's classic definition of democracy as a constitution in which 'the free-born and poor control the government – being at the same time a majority' (*Politics* 1290b), as distinct from oligarchy, in which 'the rich and better-born control the government – being at the same time a minority'. The social criteria – poverty in one case, wealth and high birth in the other – play a central role in these definitions. In fact, they outweigh the numerical criterion. Aristotle emphasizes that the true difference between democracy and oligarchy is the difference between poverty and wealth (1279b), so that a polis would be democratic even in the unlikely event that its poor rulers were at the same time a minority.

In his account of the ideal polis, Aristotle proposes a more specific social distinction which may be even more decisive than the division between rich and poor (*Politics* 1328a–1329a). In the polis, he suggests, as in every other natural compound, there is a difference between those elements that are integral parts and those that are necessary conditions. The latter merely serve the former and cannot be regarded as organic parts of the whole. In the polis, the 'conditions' are people who labour to supply the community's necessities, whether free men or slaves, while the 'parts' are men of property. The category of 'necessary' people – who cannot be organic 'parts', or citizens, of the ideal polis – includes *banausoi*, those engaged in 'base and mechanic' arts and trades, as well as others – including small farmers – who must labour for a livelihood and lack the leisure (and freedom of spirit?) to 'produce goodness' and to engage in politics. This, then, may be the critical dividing line between oligarchs and democrats: whether 'necessary' people should be included in the citizen body.

The social distinctions drawn by Greek anti-democrats – between conditions and parts of the polis, or 'necessary' and good or worthy people, *kaloi kagathoi* or *chrestoi* – also defined the anti-democratic conception of freedom, as against the democratic constitutional ideal of liberty, *eleutheria*. Critics of democracy might oppose *eleutheria* altogether, by identifying it with licence and social disorder; but this was just one of the strategies adopted by oligarchs and philosophical opponents of democracy. Another one was to redefine *eleutheria* so that it excluded labourers, craftsmen or traders who were *not* slaves. Aristotle in the *Rhetoric* (1367a), for example, defines the *eleutheros* as a gentleman who does not live for someone else's sake or at someone else's beck and call because he does not practise a sordid or menial craft – which is why, he maintains, long hair in Sparta is a symbol of nobility, the mark of a free man, since (Aristotle rather quaintly observes) it is difficult to do menial labour when one's hair is long. And what he has to say in the *Politics* about the ideal state, among other things, suggests that this distinction – not the distinction between free men and slaves but that between gentlemen and *banausoi*, as well as other 'necessary' people – should have not only social but political and constitutional implications. Here, all those supplying the community's basic needs – farmers, craftsmen, shopkeepers – cannot be citizens at all.

It hardly needs adding that this kind of distinction between freedom and servility is even more emphatic in Plato, for whom bondage to material necessity is an irreducible disqualification for practising the art of politics. In the *Statesman* (289c ff.), for example, anyone supplying necessary goods and services, any practitioner of the 'contributory' arts, is basically servile and unfit for the political art – for example, agricultural labour should even be done by foreign slaves. So, for both Plato and Aristotle, the distinction between freedom and servility, *douleia*, would then correspond not just to the juridical difference between free men and slaves but to the difference between those who are free from the necessity of labour and those who are obliged to work for a living.

That this conception of *eleutheria* was not so distant from at least some conventional usages is suggested by M.I. Finley's definition, that 'the free man was one who neither lived under the constraint of, nor was employed for the benefit of, another; who lived preferably

on his ancestral plot of land, with its shrines and ancestral tombs'.[14]
But if this was indeed the conventional usage, there would have been
some significant differences between how the ordinary Athenian
citizen understood its implications and the meaning attached to it
by Plato or Aristotle. For these opponents of democracy, even the
independent craftsman or small farmer, for example, could not be
said to be free in this sense, to the extent that his livelihood
depended on providing – and selling – necessary goods and services
to others. I doubt that the Athenian craftsman or peasant citizen
would have been prepared to accept this extended definition of
douleia, however metaphorical. But the main point is that it would
not, for the democrat, be the relevant one in defining citizenship,
while for Plato and Aristotle, at least ideally it would. Even in
Aristotle's best practicable polis, there is some question about the
citizenship of craftsmen, let alone hired labourers.

This is not to say that Aristotle's definition of democracy was the
conventional one. The very concept of *demokratia* itself may originally have been an anti-democratic coinage;[15] and it was also
anti-democrats who were likely to define democracy as rule by the
demos in its *social* meaning, the lower classes or the poor. A moderate
democrat like Pericles defined the Athenian constitution not as a
form of class rule but simply as a government by the many instead of
the few. Nevertheless, it was critical to his definition that rank was
no criterion for public honours and poverty no bar to office. For
Pericles no less than for Aristotle, a polis ruled by a political
community that did not include the *demos* in its social meaning
would not have qualified as a democracy.[16]

Pericles may not, like Aristotle, have defined democracy as rule
by the poor; but it was rule by the many *including* the poor. More
than that, it was a democracy precisely *because* the political community included the poor. In fact, the conflation of meanings in which
the *demos* denoted both the lower classes and the political community as a whole is suggestive of a democratic culture. It is as if the
Roman category *plebs*, with all its social connotations, had replaced
the category *populus* – and even this does not fully convey the
democratic implications of the Greek usage, since *plebs*, unlike *demos*,
could not be identified with the poor or the masses.

[14] M.I. Finley, *Ancient Slavery and Modern Ideology* (London, 1980), p. 90.
[15] See Paul Cartledge, 'Comparatively Equal', in Hedrick and Ober, eds., *Democracy*.
[16] Thucydides, *The Peloponnesian War* II. 37.

In the Greek context the political definition of the *demos* itself had a social meaning because it was deliberately set against the exclusion of the lower classes, shoemakers and blacksmiths, from politics. It was an assertion of democracy against non-democratic definitions of the polis and citizenship. By contrast, when the Federalists invoked the 'people' as a political category, it was not for the purpose of asserting the rights of 'mechanics' against those who would exclude them from the public sphere. On the contrary, there is ample evidence, not least in explicit pronouncements by Federalist leaders, that their purpose – and the purpose of many provisions in the Constitution – was to dilute the power of the popular multitude, most particularly in defence of property.[17] Here, the 'people' were being invoked in support of *less* against *more* democratic principles.

In Federalist usage the 'people' was, as in Greek, an inclusive, political category; but here, the point of the political definition was not to stress the political equality of social non-equals. It had more to do with enhancing the power of the federal government; and, if the criterion of social class was to have no political relevance, it was not only in the sense that poverty or undistinguished rank was to be no formal bar to public office but more especially in the sense that the balance of class power would in no way represent a criterion of democracy. There would, in effect, be no incompatibility between democracy and rule by the rich. It is in this sense that social criteria continue to be politically irrelevant today; and the modern definition of democracy is hardly less compatible with rule by the rich than it was for Alexander Hamilton.

There was a structural foundation underlying these differences in the relation between political and social meanings of the 'people' as conceived respectively in Athens and post-revolutionary America. The Federalists, whatever their inclinations, no longer had the option, available to ruling classes elsewhere, of defining the 'people' narrowly, as synonymous with an exclusive political nation. The political experience of the colonies and the Revolution precluded it (though, of course, women and slaves were by definition excluded from the political nation). But another possibility existed for Americans which had not existed for the Greeks: to displace democracy to a purely political sphere, distinct and separate from 'civil

---

[17] Hamilton's views are fairly unambiguous, but even the more 'Jeffersonian' Madison felt the need to dilute the powers of the popular multitude for the protection of property. See, for example, G. Wood, *Creation*, pp. 221, 410–11, 503–4.

society' or the 'economy'. In Athens, there was no such clear division between 'state' and 'civil society', no distinct and autonomous 'economy', not even a conception of the state as distinct from the community of citizens – no state of 'Athens' or 'Attica', only 'the Athenians'.

Political and economic powers and rights, in other words, were not as easily separated in Athens as in the US, where property was already achieving a purely 'economic' definition, detached from juridical privilege or political power, and where the 'economy' was acquiring a life of its own. Large segments of human experience and activity, and many varieties of oppression and indignity, were left untouched by political equality. If citizenship was taking precedence over other more particularistic social identities, it was at the same time becoming in many ways inconsequential.

The possibility of a democracy devoid of social content – and the absence of any such possibility in ancient Greece – has, again, to do with the vast differences in social property relations between ancient Greece and modern capitalism. I have suggested that the social structure of capitalism changes the meaning of citizenship, so that the universality of political rights – in particular, universal adult suffrage – leaves property relations and the power of appropriation intact in a way that was never true before. It is capitalism that makes possible a form of democracy in which formal equality of political rights has a minimal effect on inequalities or relations of domination and exploitation in other spheres. These developments were sufficiently advanced in late eighteenth-century America to make possible a redefinition of democracy devoid of social content, the invention of 'formal democracy', the suppression of social criteria in the definition of democracy and in the conception of liberty associated with it. It was therefore possible for the Federalists to lay claim to the language of democracy while emphatically dissociating themselves from rule by the *demos* in its original Greek meaning. For the first time, 'democracy' could mean something entirely different from what it meant for the Greeks.

For the Federalists in particular, ancient democracy was a model explicitly to be avoided – mob rule, the tyranny of the majority, and so on. But what made this such an interesting conceptual problem was that, in the conditions of post-revolutionary America, they had to reject the ancient democracy not in the name of an opposing political ideal, not in the name of oligarchy, but in the name of democracy itself. The colonial and revolutionary experience had already made it impossible just to reject democracy outright, as ruling and propertied classes had been doing unashamedly for centuries and as they would continue to do for some time elsewhere. Political realities in the US were already forcing people to do what has now become conventional and universal, when all good political things are 'democratic' and everything we dislike in politics is undemocratic: everyone had to claim to be a democrat. The problem then was to construct a conception of democracy which would, by definition, exclude the ancient model.

The Constitutional debates represent a unique historical moment, with no parallel that I know of, in which there is a visible transition from the traditional indictment of democracy to the modern rhetorical naturalization of democracy for all political purposes, including those that would have been regarded as *anti*-democratic according to the old definition. Here we can even watch the process of redefinition as it happens. The Federalists alternate between sharply contrasting democracy to the republican form of government they advocate and calling that very same republican form a 'representative democracy'. This ideological transformation takes place not only in the sphere of political theory but in the symbolism of the new republic. Just consider the significance of the appeal to *Roman* symbols – the Roman pseudonyms adopted by the Federalists, the name of the Senate, and so on. And consider the Roman eagle as an American icon. Not Athens but Rome. Not Pericles but Cicero as role model. Not the rule of the *demos* but SPQR, the 'mixed constitution' of the Senate and the Roman people, the *populus* or *demos* with rights of citizenship but governed by an aristocracy.

FROM DEMOCRACY TO LIBERALISM

As late as the last quarter of the eighteenth century, at least until the American redefinition, the predominant meaning of 'democracy', in the vocabulary of both advocates and detractors, was essentially the meaning intended by the Greeks who invented the word: rule by the *demos*, the 'people', in its dual meaning as a civic status and a social category. This accounts for the widespread and unapologetic denigration of democracy by the dominant classes. Thereafter, it underwent a transformation which allowed its erstwhile enemies to embrace it, indeed often to make it the highest expression of praise in their political vocabulary. The American redefinition was decisive; but it was not the end of the process, and it would take more than another century to complete. In 'representative democracy' rule by the people remained the principal criterion of democracy, even if *rule* was filtered through representation tinged with oligarchy, and the *people* was evacuated of its social content. In the following century, the concept of democracy was to distance itself even further from its ancient and literal meaning.

In the United States and Europe, the essential question of the social composition and inclusiveness of the 'people' who had the right to choose their representatives had not yet been resolved, and it continued to be a fiercely contested terrain until well into the twentieth century. It took a long time, for example, for the Americans to improve upon the ancient Greek exclusion of women and slaves, and the labouring classes cannot be said to have won full inclusion until the last property qualifications were abolished (and even then, there remained a wealth of devices for excluding the poor, and especially blacks). But already in the second half of the nineteenth century, it had become sufficiently clear that the issue was being decided in favour of 'mass democracy'; and the ideological advantages of redefining democracy became increasingly obvious as the era of mass mobilization – and mass electoral politics – progressed.

The imperatives and constraints imposed on the ruling classes of Europe by an inevitably growing democratization have been very effectively described by Eric Hobsbawm:

Unfortunately for the historian, these problems [posed for governments and ruling classes by mass mobilization] disappear from the scene of open political discussion in Europe, as the growing democratization made it impossible to debate them publicly with any degree of frankness. What candidate wanted to tell his voters that he considered them too stupid and ignorant to know what was best in politics, and that their demands were as absurd as they were dangerous to the future of the country? What statesman, surrounded by reporters carrying his words to the remotest corner tavern, would actually say what he meant? ... Bismarck had probably never addressed other than an elite audience. Gladstone introduced mass electioneering to Britain (and perhaps to Europe) in the campaign of 1879. No longer would the expected implications of democracy be discussed, except by political outsiders, with the frankness and realism of the debates which had surrounded the British Reform Act of 1867. ...

The age of democratization thus turned into the era of public political hypocrisy, or rather duplicity, and hence also into that of political satire.[18]

In earlier times, democracy had meant what it said, yet its critics showed no hesitation in denouncing the stupidity, ignorance, and unreliability of the 'common herd'. Adam Ferguson was speaking in the eighteenth century for a long and unembarrassed tradition of anti-democrats when he asked, 'How can he who has confined his views to his own subsistence or preservation, be intrusted with the conduct of nations? Such men, when admitted to deliberate on matters of state, bring to its councils confusion and tumult, or servility and corruption; and seldom suffer it to repose from ruinous factions, or the effects of resolutions ill formed and ill conducted.'[19]

This kind of transparency was no longer possible in the late nineteenth century. Just as the ruling classes sought various ways to limit mass democracy in practice, they adopted ideological strategies to place limits on democracy in theory. And just as revolutionary theories were 'domesticated' – for example, by French, American, and even English ruling classes[20] – so too they appropriated and naturalized democracy, assimilating its meaning to whatever political goods their particular interests could tolerate. The reconceptualization of democracy belongs, it might be said, to the new climate of political hypocrisy and duplicity.

In an age of mass mobilization, then, the concept of democracy was subjected to new ideological pressures from dominant classes, demanding not only the alienation of 'democratic' power but a clear dissociation of 'democracy' from the '*demos*' – or at least a decisive shift away from popular power as the principal criterion of democratic values. The effect was to shift the focus of 'democracy' away from the active exercise of popular power to the passive enjoyment of constitutional and procedural safeguards and rights, and away from the collective power of subordinate classes to the privacy and isolation of the individual citizen. More and more, the concept of 'democracy' came to be identified with *liberalism*.[21]

---

[18] Eric Hobsbawm, *The Age of Empire: 1875–1914* (London, 1987), pp. 87–8.

[19] Adam Ferguson, *An Essay on the History of Civil Society*, ed. Duncan Forbes (Edinburgh, 1978), p. 187.

[20] Hobsbawm, *Age of Empire*, pp. 93–4.

[21] The meaning of the word 'liberalism' is notoriously elusive and variable. I am using it here to refer to a body of commonly related principles having to do with 'limited' government,

The moment of this transvaluation is difficult to isolate, associated as it was with protracted and arduous political and ideological struggles. But hints can be found in the unresolved tensions and contradictions in the theory and practice of nineteenth-century liberalism, torn between a distaste for mass democracy and a recognition of its inevitability, perhaps even its necessity and justice, or at any rate the advantages of mass mobilization in promoting programmes of reform and the wisdom of domesticating the 'many-headed hydra', the turbulent multitude, by drawing it into the civic community.

John Stuart Mill is perhaps only the most extreme example of the contradictions that constituted nineteenth-century liberalism. On the one hand, he showed a strong distaste for the 'levelling' tendencies and 'collective mediocrity' of mass democracy (nowhere more than in the *locus classicus* of modern liberalism, his essay 'On Liberty'), his Platonism, his elitism, his imperialist conviction that colonial peoples would benefit from a period of tutelage under the rule of their colonial masters; and on the other hand, his advocacy of the rights of women, of universal suffrage (which could be made compatible with a kind of *class* tutelage by maintaining weighted voting, as he proposes in *Considerations on Representative Government*); and he even flirted with socialist ideas (always on the condition that capitalism be preserved until 'better minds' had lifted the multitude out of its need for 'coarse stimuli', the motivations of material gain and subjection to the lower appetites). Mill never resolved this systematic ambivalence toward democracy, but we can perhaps find some hint of a possible resolution in a rather curious place, in his judgment on the original democracy of ancient Athens.

What is striking about Mill's judgment is his identification of Athenian democracy with its encouragement of variety and individuality, in contrast to the narrow and stultifying conservatism of the Spartans – whom Mill, as we have seen, even called the Tories of Greece. This characterization of ancient Athens contrasts sharply, of course, with Mill's account of modern democracy and the threat he perceives in it to individuality and excellence. The very different assessment of democracy in its ancient form was, however, made possible only by a conspicuous evasiveness about the one literally

civil liberties, toleration, the protection of a sphere of privacy against intrusion by the state, together with an emphasis on individuality, diversity and pluralism.

democratic feature of Athenian democracy, its extension of citizenship to labouring, 'base' and 'mechanic' classes. While Mill advocated a (qualified) extension of the suffrage to the 'multitude', he evinced a notable lack of enthusiasm for rule by the *demos* and was not inclined to dwell on its role in the ancient democracy. Far better to invoke the *liberal* values of classical Athens.

And so we come to 'liberal democracy'. The familiarity of this formula may disguise everything that is historically and ideologically problematic in this distinctively modern coupling, and it could do with some critical unpacking. There is more to this formula than the expansion of 'liberalism' to 'liberal democracy' – that is, the addition of democratic principles like universal suffrage to the pre-democratic values of constitutionalism and 'limited government'. Rather more difficult questions are raised by the *contraction* of democracy to liberalism. There is a long-standing convention that political progress or 'modernization' has taken the form of a movement from monarchy to 'limited' or constitutional government to democracy, and more particularly from absolutism to 'liberalism' to 'liberal democracy'. In a sense, the process I am describing here reverses the conventional sequence: democracy has been overtaken by liberalism.

There was no 'liberalism' – no constitutionalism, limited government, 'individual rights' and 'civil liberties' – in classical antiquity. Ancient democracy, where the 'state' had no separate existence as a corporate entity apart from the community of citizens, produced no clear conception of a separation between 'state' and 'civil society' and no set of ideas or institutions to check the power of the state or to protect 'civil society' and the individual citizen from its intrusions. 'Liberalism' had as its fundamental pre-condition the development of a centralized state separate from and superior to other, more particularistic jurisdictions.

But, although 'liberalism' is a modern coinage which presupposes the 'modern' state (at least early modern absolutism), its central conceptions of liberty and constitutional limits have an earlier provenance. Liberal conceptions of limited or constitutional government, and of inviolable liberties asserted against the state, have their origins, in the late medieval and early modern periods, in the assertion of independent powers of *lordship* by European aristocracies against encroachment by centralizing monarchies. These conceptions, in other words, at the outset represented an attempt to safeguard feudal liberties, powers and privileges. They were not democratic in their intent or in their consequences, representing backward-looking claims to a piece of the old parcellized sovereignty of feudalism, not a looking forward to a more modern democratic political order. And the association of these ideas with lordship persisted for a long time, well beyond the demise of feudalism.

There is no doubt that these essentially feudal principles were later appropriated for more democratic purposes by more 'modern' or progressive forces. Since the seventeenth century, they have been expanded from the privileges of lordship to more universal civil liberties and human rights; and they have been enriched by the values of religious and intellectual toleration. But the original principles of liberalism are derived from a system of social relations very different from the one to which they have been adapted. They were not conceived to deal with the wholly new disposition of social power that emerged with modern capitalism. This inherent limitation (about which more in a moment) is compounded by the fact that the idea of liberalism has been made to serve much larger purposes than its basic principles were ever intended to do. Liberalism has entered modern political discourse not only as a set of ideas and institutions designed to limit state power but also as a *substitute* for democracy.

The original, aristocratic idea of constitutional checks on monarchical power had no associations with the idea of democracy. Its identification with 'democracy' was a much later development, which had more to do with an assertion of ruling class powers *against* the people. The unquestionable benefits of this 'liberal' idea should not obscure the fact that its *substitution* for democracy was a *counter-revolutionary* project – or at least a means of containing revolutions already underway, stopping them short of exceeding acceptable boundaries.

The first significant encounter between democracy and constitutionalism may have occurred in the English Civil War. Here, a revolutionary popular army of an unprecedented kind had been mobilized by Oliver Cromwell. But when army radicals demanded the franchise and asked what they had fought for in the revolution if they were to be denied the right to vote, the right to be governed only by their own consent, the army grandees led by Cromwell and his son-in-law Ireton responded by saying that these people had gained quite enough already. They had won the right to be governed by a constitutional, parliamentary government and not by the arbitrary rule of one man.

It never occurred to Cromwell to claim that what he was proposing was *democracy*. On the contrary, he was deliberately offering a substitute. He might have said that political authority in some mysterious though largely notional sense was ultimately 'derived' from the people (an idea of medieval origin), but he would have understood that *democracy* was something else. Like his contemporaries in general, he would have understood the idea of democracy in more or less its ancient, and literal, meaning. His successors in the settlement of 1688 were in even less doubt that parliamentary government (or 'constitutional monarchy') was meant to be an oligarchy.

The opposition of democracy and constitutionalism may have been resolved by the later democratization of parliamentary government; but this process was not unambiguous. It was not simply a matter of adapting constitutional to democratic principles. There was also an assimilation of democracy to constitutionalism. The framers of the US Constitution, while still obliged to accommodate themselves to the ancient definition, took a significant step away from it and toward oligarchic constitutionalism, seeking to appropriate the name of democracy for something not so very distant from Cromwell's anti-democratic republicanism. Here too the intention was to hold the Revolution within acceptable limits – though in the conditions of revolutionary America, the Federalists did not, like Cromwell, have the option of limiting the franchise to a small minority and were obliged to find other ways of distancing the 'people' from power, ensuring that political rights would be largely passive and limited in scope.

Today we have become thoroughly accustomed to defining democracy less (if at all) in terms of rule by the *demos* or popular power than in terms of civil liberties, freedom of speech, of the press and assembly, toleration, the protection of a sphere of privacy, the defence of the individual and/or 'civil society' against the state, and so on. So, for example, 'The Glorious Revolution', said Margaret Thatcher, opening Parliament's tricentenary celebration of that ambiguous event in 1988, 'established the enduring qualities of democracy – tolerance, respect for the law, for the impartial administration of justice'.

These are all admirable qualities. It would have been a good thing if the Settlement of 1688 had indeed established them, as it would have been a distinct improvement on Thatcher's regime if her government had indeed been committed to them. But they have little specifically to do with *democracy*. Conspicuously absent from this catalogue of democratic characteristics is the very quality that gives democracy its specific and literal meaning: rule by the *demos*. It remained for the left wing of the Labour Party, in the person of Tony Benn, to point out in his own response to these parliamentary festivities that there was little democracy in a 'revolution' which did nothing to promote popular power, as it excluded women and propertyless people, while firmly consolidating the rule of the dominant class – indeed, if anything establishing a regime even *less* democratic in the literal sense than the preceding one.[22]

The very possibility of identifying the Glorious Revolution as a defining moment in the history of 'democracy' bespeaks a very particular ideological disposition (by no means confined to Thatcherite Tories). The rewriting of history which has forged a new pedigree for the concept of democracy – traceable not to ancient democracy but to medieval lordship – has pushed any other history to the sidelines of political discourse. The alternative tradition which emerged in early modern Europe – the egalitarian, demotic and democratic tradition – has been effectively suppressed, as oligarchic Rome, Magna Carta and the Glorious Revolution have taken precedence over democratic Athens, the Levellers, Diggers and Chartists, while in the US, the Federalist solution has pushed aside the story of its more democratic competitors. Democ-

---

[22] The 'tolerance' of the 1688 Settlement was, of course, strictly limited, excluding Catholics from the monarchy, and indeed all non-Anglicans from public office and the established universities. As for 'respect for the law', it was unambiguously the law of the dominant propertied class, embodied in a Parliament which, especially in the eighteenth century, embarked on a spree of self-interested legislation, multiplying the number of capital crimes to protect private property, undertaking a series of Parliamentary enclosures, and so on. The 'impartial administration of justice' is a quaint way of describing the justice of the gentry as administered by the landed class itself, notably in the persons of Justices of the Peace. But then this unqualified praise for the Glorious Revolution came from a Prime Minister who presided over the most sustained attack on both popular power *and* civil liberties in Britain since the advent of universal suffrage – in the form of security laws, destruction of local authorities, profoundly restrictive trade union legislation, etc.

If anything, 1688 represented a regression of democratic power, not only relative to the more radical period of the English Civil War, but in some respects even in comparison to the restored monarchy. In fact, the franchise was more restricted in the eighteenth century than it had been for much of the seventeenth.

racy, in its original and literal meaning, has been on the losing side.
Even democratic socialist movements which kept the other tradition
alive have increasingly come to accept the liberal domestication of
democracy.

The oligarchs of 1688, defending the rights of Parliament against the
Crown, made their 'revolution' in the name of liberty. They were
asserting their right, their freedom to dispose of their property – and
their servants – at will against interference from the king. The
property they were defending was already substantially capitalist,
but the liberty they invoked to protect it, in a usage virtually
synonymous with *privilege*, was rooted in pre-capitalist lordship.

This takes us to the heart of the contradictions in 'liberal democracy'. What makes the story of modern democracy particularly
interesting and problematic is that, at the very moment that the
history of democracy was being conflated with the history of *lordship*,
lordship itself had already been displaced as the main form of
domination. It had been replaced not only by a centralized state but
by a new form of private property, in which purely economic power
was separated out from juridical status and privilege. Lordship and
extra-economic modes of exploitation had, in other words, been
replaced by capitalist property. Ideas of freedom rooted in traditional privilege may have remained for a time well suited to the
interests of the propertied classes, and today they may even serve
more democratic purposes in transactions between citizen and state;
but they are not designed as a check against the new forms of power
created by capitalism.

Liberties that meant a great deal to early modern aristocracies,
and whose extension to the multitude *then* would have completely
transformed society, cannot mean the same thing now – not least
because the so-called economy has acquired a life of its own, completely outside the ambit of citizenship, political freedom, or democratic accountability. The essence of modern 'democracy' is not so
much that it has *abolished* privilege, or alternatively that it has
extended traditional privileges to the multitude, but rather that it has
borrowed a conception of freedom designed for a world where
privilege was the relevant category and applied it to a world where
privilege is not the problem. In a world where juridical or political

status is not the primary determinant of our life chances, where our activities and experiences lie largely outside the reach of our legal or political identities, freedom defined in these terms leaves too much out of account.

There is here a paradox. Liberalism is a modern idea based on pre-modern, pre-capitalist forms of power. At the same time, if the basic principles of liberalism pre-date capitalism, what makes it possible to identify *democracy* with liberalism is capitalism itself. The idea of 'liberal democracy' became thinkable – and I mean literally thinkable – only with the emergence of capitalist social property relations. Capitalism made possible the *redefinition* of democracy, its reduction to liberalism. On the one hand, there was now a separate political sphere, in which 'extra-economic' – political, juridical or military – status had no direct implications for economic power, the power of appropriation, exploitation and distribution. On the other hand, there now existed an economic sphere with its own power relations not dependent on juridical or political privilege.

So the very conditions that make liberal democracy possible also narrowly limit the scope of democratic accountability. Liberal democracy leaves untouched the whole new sphere of domination and coercion created by capitalism, its relocation of substantial powers from the state to civil society, to private property and the compulsions of the market. It leaves untouched vast areas of our daily lives – in the workplace, in the distribution of labour and resources – which are not subject to democratic accountability but are governed by the powers of property and the 'laws' of the market, the imperatives of profit maximization. This would remain true even in the unlikely event that our 'formal democracy' were perfected so that wealth and economic power no longer meant the gross inequality of access to state power which now characterizes the reality, if not the ideal, of modern capitalist democracy.

The characteristic way in which liberal democracy deals with this new sphere of power is not to check but to liberate it. In fact, liberalism does not even recognize it as a sphere of power or coercion at all. This, of course, is especially true of the market, which tends to be conceived as an opportunity, not a compulsion. The market is conceived as a sphere of freedom, choice, even by those who see the need to regulate it. Any limits that may be necessary to correct the harmful effects of this freedom are perceived as just that, limits. As with most kinds of freedom, there may have to be certain restrictions or regulations imposed on it to maintain social order; but it is still a kind of freedom. In other words, in the conceptual framework of liberal democracy, we cannot really talk, or even *think*, about freedom *from* the market. We cannot think of freedom from the market as a kind of empowerment, a liberation from compulsion, an emancipation from coercion and domination.

What about the current tendency to *identify* democracy with the 'free market'? What about this new definition, according to which the 'new democracies' of eastern Europe are 'democratic' in proportion to their progress in 'marketization', President Yeltsin's accretion of power to the presidency is 'democratic' because it is conducted in the name of 'privatization' and 'the market', or General Pinochet was more 'democratic' than a freely elected Salvador Allende? Does this usage represent a subversion or distortion of liberal democracy?

The balance has certainly been tilted too far, but it is not completely inconsistent with the fundamental principles of liberal democracy. The very condition that makes it possible to define democracy as we do in modern liberal capitalist societies is the separation and enclosure of the economic sphere and its invulnerability to democratic power. Protecting that invulnerability has even become an essential criterion of democracy. This definition allows us to invoke democracy *against* the empowerment of the people in the economic sphere. It even makes it possible to invoke democracy in defence of a *curtailment* of democratic rights in other parts of 'civil society' or even in the political domain, if that is what is needed to protect property and the market against democratic power.

The sphere of economic power in capitalism has expanded far beyond the capacities of 'democracy' to cope with it; and liberal democracy, whether as a set of institutions or a system of ideas, is not designed to extend its reach into that domain. If we are confronting the 'end of History', it may not be in the sense that liberal democracy has triumphed but rather in the sense that it has very nearly reached its limits. There is much good in liberalism that needs to be preserved, protected and improved, not only in parts of the world where it scarcely exists but even in capitalist democracies where it is still imperfect and often under threat. Yet the scope for further historical development may belong to the *other* tradition of democracy, the tradition overshadowed by liberal democracy, the idea of democracy in its literal meaning as popular power.

Although we have found new ways of protecting 'civil society'

from the 'state', and the 'private' from intrusions by the 'public', we
have yet to find new, modern ways to match the depth of freedom
and democracy enjoyed by the Athenian citizen in other respects. In
The Persians (242), Aeschylus has a chorus of Persian elders tell us
that to be an Athenian citizen is to be masterless, a servant to no
mortal man. Or recall the speech in Euripides' *The Suppliants* (429
ff.), describing a free polis as one in which the rule of law allows
equal justice to rich and poor, strong and weak alike, where anyone
who has something useful to say has the right to speak before the
public – that is, where there is *isegoria* – but also where the free
citizen does not labour just in order to enrich a tyrant by his toil.
There is something here which is completely absent from, and even
antithetical to, the later European concept of liberty. It is the
freedom of the *demos from* masters, not the freedom of the masters
themselves. It is not the oligarch's *eleutheria*, in which freedom *from*
labour is the ideal qualification for citizenship, but the *eleutheria* of
the labouring *demos* and the freedom *of* labour.

In practice, Athenian democracy was certainly exclusive, so
much so that it may seem odd to call it a democracy at all. The
majority of the population – women, slaves, and resident aliens
(metics) – did not enjoy the privileges of citizenship. But the necessity of working for a living and even the lack of property were not
grounds for exclusion from full political rights. In this respect,
Athens exceeded the criteria of all but the most visionary democrats
for many centuries thereafter.

Nor is it self-evident that even the most democratic polity today
confers on its propertyless and working classes powers equal to those
enjoyed by 'banausic' citizens in Athens. Modern democracy has
become more inclusive, finally abolishing slavery and granting
citizenship to women as well as to working men. It has also gained
much from the absorption of 'liberal' principles, respect for civil
liberties and 'human rights'. But the progress of modern democracy
has been far from unambiguous, for as political rights have become
less exclusive, they have also lost much of their power.

We are, then, left with more questions than answers. How might
citizenship, in modern conditions and with an inclusive citizen
body, regain the salience it once had? What would it mean, in a
modern capitalist democracy, not only to preserve the gains of
liberalism, civil liberties and the protection of 'civil society', nor
even just to invent more democratic conceptions of representation

and new modes of local autonomy, but also to recover powers lost to the 'economy'? What would it take to recover democracy from the formal separation of the 'political' and the 'economic', when political privilege has been replaced by economic coercion, exerted not just by capitalist property directly but also through the medium of the market? If capitalism has replaced political privilege with the powers of economic coercion, what would it mean to extend citizenship – and this means not just a greater equality of 'opportunity', or the passive entitlements of welfare provision, but democratic accountability or active self-government – into the economic sphere?

Is it possible to conceive of a form of democratic citizenship that reaches into the domain sealed off by modern capitalism? Could capitalism survive such an extension of democracy? Is capitalism compatible with democracy in its literal sense? If its current malaise proves still more protracted, will it even remain compatible with liberalism? Can capitalism still rely on its capacity to deliver material prosperity, and will it triumph together with liberal democracy, or will its survival in hard times increasingly depend on a curtailment of democratic rights?

Is liberal democracy, in theory and practice, adequate to deal even with the conditions of modern capitalism, let alone whatever may lie outside or beyond it? Does liberal democracy look like the end of History because it has surpassed all conceivable alternatives, or because it has exhausted its own capacities, while concealing other possibilities? Has it really overcome all rivals or simply obscured them temporarily from view?

The task that liberalism sets for itself is, and will always remain, indispensable. As long as there are states, there will be a need to check their power and to safeguard independent powers and organizations outside the state. For that matter, any kind of social power needs to be hedged around with protections for freedom of association, communication, diversity of opinion, an inviolable private sphere, and so on. On these scores, any future democracy will continue to have lessons to learn from the liberal tradition in theory and in practice. But liberalism – even as an ideal, let alone as a deeply flawed actuality – is not equipped to cope with the realities of power in a capitalist society, and even less to encompass a more inclusive kind of democracy than now exists.

CHAPTER 8

Civil society and the politics of identity

At a time when a critique of capitalism is more urgent than ever, the dominant theoretical trends on the left are busy conceptualizing away the very idea of capitalism. The 'post-modern' world, we are told, is a pastiche of fragments and 'difference'. The systemic unity of capitalism, its 'objective structures' and totalizing imperatives, have given way (if they ever existed) to a bricolage of multiple social realities, a pluralistic structure so diverse and flexible that it can be rearranged by discursive construction. The traditional capitalist economy has been replaced by a 'post-Fordist' fragmentation, where every fragment opens up a space for emancipatory struggles. The constitutive class relations of capitalism represent only one personal 'identity' among many others, no longer 'privileged' by its historic centrality. And so on.

However diverse the methods of conceptually dissolving capitalism – including everything from the theory of post-Fordism to post-modern 'cultural studies' and the 'politics of identity' – they often share one especially serviceable concept: 'civil society'. After a long and somewhat tortuous history, after a series of milestones in the works of Hegel, Marx and Gramsci, this versatile idea has become an all-purpose catchword for the left, embracing a wide range of emancipatory aspirations, as well – it must be said – as a whole set of excuses for political retreat. However constructive this idea may be in defending human liberties against state oppression, or in marking out a terrain of social practices, institutions and relations neglected by the 'old' Marxist left, 'civil society' is now in danger of becoming an alibi for capitalism.

THE IDEA OF CIVIL SOCIETY: A BRIEF HISTORICAL SKETCH

There has been a long intellectual tradition in the West, even reaching back to classical antiquity, which has in various ways delineated a terrain of human association, some notion of 'society', distinct from the body politic and with moral claims independent of, and sometimes opposed to, the state's authority. Whatever other factors have been at work in producing such concepts, their evolution has been from the beginning bound up with the development of private property as a distinct and autonomous locus of social power. For example, although the ancient Romans, like the Greeks, still tended to identify the state with the community of citizens, the 'Roman people', they did produce some major advances in the conceptual separation of state and 'society', especially in the Roman Law which distinguished between public and private spheres and gave private property a legal status and clarity it had never enjoyed before.[1]

In that sense, although the modern concept of 'civil society' is associated with the specific property relations of capitalism, it is a variation on an old theme. Nevertheless, the variation is a critical one; and any attempt to dilute the specificity of this 'civil society', to obscure its differentiation from earlier conceptions of 'society', risks disguising the particularity of capitalism itself as a distinct social form with its own characteristic social relations, its own modes of appropriation and exploitation, its own rules of reproduction, its own systemic imperatives.[2]

The very particular modern conception of 'civil society' – a conception that appeared systematically for the first time in the eighteenth century – is something quite distinct from earlier notions of 'society': civil society represents a separate sphere of human relations and activity, differentiated from the state but neither public nor private or perhaps both at once, embodying not only a whole range of social interactions apart from the private sphere of the household and the public sphere of the state, but more specifically a network of distinctively economic relations, the sphere of the market place, the arena of production, distribution and exchange. A necessary but not sufficient pre-condition for this conception of civil society was the modern idea of the state as an abstract entity with its own corporate identity, which evolved with the rise of European

[1] For an argument that the Romans, specifically in the person of Cicero, had a concept of 'society', see Neal Wood, *Cicero's Social and Political Thought* (Berkeley and Los Angeles, 1988) esp. pp. 136–42.

[2] Much of John Keane's argument in *Democracy and Civil Society* (London, 1988) is, for example, predicated on a criticism of Marxism for its identification of 'civil society' with capitalism, which he opposes by invoking the long tradition of conceptions of 'society' in the West, reaching much further back than the advent of capitalism.

absolutism; but the full conceptual differentiation of 'civil society' required the emergence of an autonomous 'economy', separated out from the unity of the 'political' and 'economic' which still characterized the absolutist state.

Paradoxically – or perhaps not so paradoxically – the early usages of the term 'civil society' in the birthplace of capitalism, in early modern England, far from establishing an opposition between civil society and the state, conflated the two. In sixteenth and seventeenth century English political thought, 'civil society' was typically synonymous with the 'commonwealth' or 'political society'. This conflation of state and 'society' represented the subordination of the state to the community of private-property holders (as against both monarch and 'multitude') which constituted the political nation. It reflected a unique political dispensation, in which the dominant class depended for its wealth and power increasingly on purely 'economic' modes of appropriation, instead of on directly coercive 'extra-economic' modes of accumulation by political and military means, like feudal rent taking or absolutist taxation and office holding as primary instruments of private appropriation.

But if English usage tended to blur the distinction between state and civil society, it was English conditions – the very same system of property relations and capitalist appropriation, but now more advanced and with a more highly developed market mechanism – that made possible the modern conceptual opposition between the two. When Hegel constructed his conceptual dichotomy, Napoleon was his inspiration for the 'modern' state; but it was primarily the capitalist economy of England – through the medium of classical political economists like Smith and Steuart – that provided the model of 'civil society' (with certain distinctively Hegelian corrections and improvements).

Hegel's identification of 'civil' with 'bourgeois' society was more than just a fluke of the German language. The phenomenon which he designated by the term *bürgerliche Gesellschaft* was a historically specific social form. Although this 'civil society' did not refer exclusively to purely 'economic' institutions (it was, for example, supplemented by Hegel's modern adaptation of medieval corporate principles), the modern 'economy' was its essential condition. For Hegel, the possibility of preserving both individual freedom and the 'universality' of the state, instead of subordinating one to the other as earlier societies had done, rested on the emergence of a new class

and a whole new sphere of social existence: a distinct and autonomous 'economy'. It was in this new sphere that private and public,
particular and universal, could meet through the interaction of
private interests, on a terrain that was neither household nor state
but a mediation between the two.

Marx, of course, transformed Hegel's distinction between the
state and civil society by denying the universality of the state and
insisting that the state expressed the particularities of 'civil society'
and its class relations, a discovery that compelled him to devote his
life's work to exploring the anatomy of 'civil society' in the form of a
critique of political economy. The conceptual differentiation of state
and civil society was thus a pre-condition to Marx's analysis of
capitalism, but the effect of that analysis was to deprive the Hegelian
distinction of its rationale. The state–civil society dualism more or
less disappeared from the mainstream of political discourse.

It required Gramsci's reformulation to revive the concept of civil
society as a central organizing principle of socialist theory. The
object of this new formulation was to acknowledge both the complexity of political power in the parliamentary or constitutional
states of the West, in contrast to more openly coercive autocracies,
and the difficulty of supplanting a system of class domination in
which class power has no clearly visible point of concentration in the
state but is diffused throughout society and its cultural practices.
Gramsci thus appropriated the concept of civil society to mark out
the terrain of a new kind of struggle which would take the battle
against capitalism not only to its economic foundations but to its
cultural and ideological roots in everyday life.

THE NEW CULT OF CIVIL SOCIETY

Gramsci's conception of 'civil society' was unambiguously intended
as a weapon against capitalism, not an accommodation to it. Despite
the appeal to his authority which has become a staple of contemporary social theories of the left, the concept in its current usage no
longer has this unequivocally anti-capitalist intent. It has now
acquired a whole new set of meanings and consequences, some very
positive for the emancipatory projects of the left, others far less so.
The two contrary impulses can be summed up in this way: the new
concept of 'civil society' signals that the left has learned the lessons of
liberalism about the dangers of state oppression, but we seem to be

forgetting the lessons we once learned from the socialist tradition about the oppressions of civil society. On the one hand, the advocates of civil society are strengthening our defence of non-state institutions and relations against the power of the state; on the other hand, they are tending to weaken our resistance to the coercions of capitalism.

The concept of 'civil society' is being mobilized to serve so many varied purposes that it is impossible to isolate a single school of thought associated with it; but some common themes have emerged. 'Civil society' is generally intended to identify an arena of (at least potential) freedom outside the state, a space for autonomy, voluntary association and plurality or even conflict, guaranteed by the kind of 'formal democracy' that has evolved in the West. The concept is also meant to reduce the capitalist system (or the 'economy') to one of many spheres in the plural and heterogeneous complexity of modern society. The concept of 'civil society' can achieve this effect in one of two principal ways. It can be made to designate that multiplicity itself as against the coercions of both state and capitalist economy; or, more commonly, it can encompass the 'economy' within a larger sphere of multiple non-state institutions and relations.[3] In either case, the emphasis is on the plurality of social relations and practices among which the capitalist economy takes its place as one of many.

The principal current usages proceed from the distinction between civil society and state. 'Civil society' is defined by the advocates of this distinction in terms of a few simple oppositions: for example, 'the state (and its military, policing, legal, administrative, productive, and cultural organs) and the non-state (market-regulated, privately controlled or voluntarily organized) realm of civil society';[4] or 'political' versus 'social' power, 'public' versus 'private' law, 'state-sanctioned (dis)information and propaganda' versus 'freely circulated public opinion'.[5] In this definition, 'civil society' encompasses a very wide range of institutions and relations, from households, trade unions, voluntary associations, hospitals,

---

[3] Something like the first conception can, for example, be extracted from Jean L. Cohen, *Class and Civil Society: The Limits of Marxian Critical Theory* (Amherst, 1982). The second view is elaborated by John Keane in *Democracy and Civil Society*. (For his criticism of Cohen's conception, see p. 86n.).

[4] John Keane, ed., *Civil Society and the State* (London, 1988) p. 1.

[5] *Ibid.*, p. 2.

churches, to the market, capitalist enterprises, indeed the whole capitalist economy. The significant antitheses are simply state and non-state, or perhaps political and social.

This dichotomy apparently corresponds to the opposition between coercion, as embodied in the state, and freedom or voluntary action, which belongs in principle, if not necessarily in practice, to civil society. Civil society may be in various ways and degrees submerged or eclipsed by the state, and different political systems or whole 'historical regions' may vary according to the degree of 'autonomy' which they accord to the non-state sphere. It is a special characteristic of the West, for example, that it has given rise to a uniquely well-developed separation of state and civil society, and hence a particularly advanced form of political freedom.

The advocates of this state–civil society distinction generally ascribe to it two principal benefits. First, it focuses our attention on the dangers of state oppression and on the need to set proper limits on the actions of the state, by organizing and reinforcing the pressures against it within society. In other words, it revives the liberal concern with the limitation and legitimation of political power, and especially the control of such power by freedom of association and autonomous organization within society, too often neglected by the left in theory and practice. Second, the concept of civil society recognizes and celebrates difference and diversity. Its advocates make pluralism a primary good, in contrast, it is claimed, to Marxism, which is, they say, essentially monistic, reductionist, economistic.[6] This new pluralism invites us to appreciate a whole range of institutions and relations neglected by traditional socialism in its preoccupation with the economy and class.

The impetus to the revival of this conceptual dichotomy has come from several directions. The strongest impulse undoubtedly came from Eastern Europe, where 'civil society' was a major weapon in the ideological arsenal of opposition forces against state oppression. Here, the issues were fairly clear: the state – including both its political and economic apparatuses of domination – could be more or less unambiguously set against a (potentially) free space outside the state. The civil society/state antithesis could, for example, be said to

---

[6] Norman Geras debunks such myths about Marxism in 'Seven Types of Obliquy: Travesties of Marxism', in *Socialist Register* (1990).

correspond neatly to the opposition of Solidarity to Party and State.[7]

The crisis of the Communist states has, needless to say, also left a deep impression on the Western left, converging with other influences: the limitations of social democracy, with its unbounded faith in the state as the agent of social improvement, as well as the emergence of emancipatory struggles by social movements not based on class, with a sensitivity to dimensions of human experience all too often neglected by the traditional socialist left. These heightened sensitivities to the dangers posed by the state and to the complexities of human experience have been associated with a wide range of activisms, taking in everything from feminism, ecology and peace, to constitutional reform. Each of these projects has often drawn upon the concept of civil society.

No socialist can doubt the value of these new sensitivities, but there must be serious misgivings about this particular method of focusing our attention on them. We are being asked to pay a heavy price for the all-embracing concept of 'civil society'. This conceptual portmanteau, which indiscriminately lumps together everything from households and voluntary associations to the economic system of capitalism, confuses and disguises as much as it reveals. In Eastern Europe, it can be made to apprehend everything from the defence of political rights and cultural freedoms to the marketization of post-Communist economies and the restoration of capitalism. 'Civil society' can serve as a code word or cover for capitalism, and the market can be lumped together with other less ambiguous goods, like political and intellectual liberties, as an unequivocally desirable goal.

But if the dangers of this conceptual strategy and of assigning the market to the free space of 'civil society' appear to pale before the enormity of Stalinist oppression in the East, problems of an altogether different order arise in the West, where a fully developed capitalism does actually exist and where state oppression is not an immediate and massive evil which overwhelms all other social ills. Since in this case 'civil society' is made to encompass a whole layer of social reality that did not exist in Communist societies, the impli-

[7] For the application of 'civil society' to events in Poland, see Andrew Arato, 'Civil Society Against the State: Poland 1980–81', *Telos*, 47 (1981) and 'Empire versus Civil Society: Poland 1981–82', *Telos*, 50 (1982).

cations of its usage are in some important respects even more problematic.

Here, the danger lies in the fact that the totalizing logic and the coercive power of capitalism become invisible, when the whole social system of capitalism is reduced to one set of institutions and relations among many others, on a conceptual par with households or voluntary associations. Such a reduction is, in fact, the principal distinctive feature of 'civil society' in its new incarnation. Its effect is to conceptualize away the problem of capitalism, by disaggregating society into fragments, with no overarching power structure, no totalizing unity, no systemic coercions – in other words, no capitalist system, with its expansionary drive and its capacity to penetrate every aspect of social life.

It is a typical strategy of the 'civil society' argument – indeed, its *raison d'être* – to attack Marxist 'reductionism' or 'economism'. Marxism, it is said, reduces civil society to the 'mode of production', the capitalist economy. 'The importance of other institutions of civil society – such as households, churches, scientific and literary associations, prisons and hospitals – is devalued'.[8]

Whether or not Marxists have habitually paid too little attention to these 'other' institutions, the weakness of this juxtaposition (the capitalist economy and 'other institutions' like hospitals?) should be immediately apparent. It must surely be possible even for non-Marxists to acknowledge, for example, the very simple truth that in the West hospitals are situated within a capitalist economy which has profoundly affected the organization of health care and the nature of medical institutions. But is it possible to conceive of an analogous proposition about the effects of hospitals on capitalism? Does this observation about 'other institutions' mean that Marx did not value households and hospitals, or is it rather that he did not attribute to them the same historically determinative force? Is there no basis for distinguishing among these various 'institutions' on all sorts of quantitative and qualitative grounds, from size and scope to social power and historical efficacy? Typically, the current usage of 'civil society' evades questions like this. It also has the effect of confusing the moral claims of 'other' institutions with their determinative power, or rather of dismissing altogether the essentially empirical question of historical and social determinations.

[8] Keane, *Democracy and Civil Society*, p. 32.

There is another version of the argument which, instead of simply evading the systemic totality of capitalism, explicitly denies it. The very existence of other modes of domination than class relations, other principles of stratification than class inequality, other social struggles than class struggle, is taken to demonstrate that capitalism, whose constitutive relation is class, is not a totalizing system. The Marxist preoccupation with 'economic' relations and class at the expense of other social relations and identities is understood to demonstrate that the attempt to 'totalize all society from the stand-point of one sphere, the economy or the mode of production', is misconceived for the simple reason that other 'spheres' self-evidently exist.[9]

This argument is circular and question begging. To deny the totalizing logic of capitalism, it is not enough merely to indicate the plurality of social identities and relations. The class relation that constitutes capitalism is not, after all, just a personal identity, nor even just a principle of 'stratification' or inequality. It is not only a specific system of power relations but also the constitutive relation of a distinctive social process, the dynamic of accumulation and the self-expansion of capital. Of course it can be easily – self-evidently – shown that class is not the only principle of 'stratification', the only form of inequality and domination. But this tells us virtually nothing about the totalizing logic of capitalism.

To deny the totalizing logic of capitalism, it would have to be convincingly demonstrated that these other spheres and identities do not come – or not in any significant way – within the determina-tive force of capitalism, its system of social property relations, its expansionary imperatives, its drive for accumulation, its commodifi-cation of all social life, its creation of the market as a necessity, a compulsive mechanism of competition and self-sustaining 'growth', and so on. But 'civil society' arguments (or, indeed, 'post-Marxist' arguments in general) do not typically take the form of historically and empirically refuting the determinative effects of capitalist rela-tions. Instead (when they do not take the simple circular form: capitalism is not a totalizing system because spheres other than the economy exist) they tend to proceed as abstract philosophical argu-ments, as internal critiques of Marxist theory, or, most commonly, as

---

[9] Cohen, *Class and Civil Society*, p. 192.

moral prescriptions about the dangers of devaluing 'other' spheres of human experience.

In one form or another, capitalism is cut down to the size and weight of 'other' singular and specific institutions and disappears into a conceptual night where all cats are grey. The strategy of dissolving capitalism into an unstructured and undifferentiated plurality of social institutions and relations cannot help but weaken both the analytic and the normative force of 'civil society', its capacity to deal with the limitation and legitimation of power, as well as its usefulness in guiding emancipatory projects. The current theories occlude 'civil society' in its distinctive sense as a social form specific to capitalism, a systemic totality within which all 'other' institutions are situated and all social forces must find their way, a specific and unprecedented sphere of social power, which poses wholly new problems of legitimation and control, problems not addressed by traditional theories of the state nor by contemporary liberalism.

CAPITALISM, 'FORMAL DEMOCRACY', AND THE SPECIFICITY OF THE WEST

One of the principal charges levelled against Marxism by the advocates of 'civil society' is that it endangers democratic freedoms by identifying Western 'formal democracy' – the legal and political forms that guarantee a free space for 'civil society' – with capitalism: 'civil' equals 'bourgeois' society. The danger, they claim, is that we might be tempted to throw out the baby with the bath water, to reject liberal democracy together with capitalism.[10] We should instead, they argue, acknowledge the benefits of formal democracy, while expanding its principles of individual freedom and equality by dissociating them from capitalism in order to deny that capitalism is the sole or best means of advancing these principles.

It must be said that criticism of contemporary Western Marxism on these grounds must disregard the bulk of Marxist political theory since the sixties, and especially since the theory of the state was revived by the 'Miliband-Poulantzas' debate. Certainly civil liberties were a major preoccupation of both the principals in that

[10] See, for example, *ibid.*, p. 49; Keane, *Democracy and Civil Society*, p. 59; Agnes Heller, 'On Formal Democracy', in Keane, *Civil Society and the State*, p. 132.

controversy, and of many others who have followed in their train. Even the contention that 'classical' Marxism – in the person of Marx or Engels – was too indifferent to civil liberties is open to question. But without reducing this discussion to a merely textual debate about the Marxist ('classical' or contemporary) attitude to 'bourgeois' liberties, let us accept that all socialists, Marxist or otherwise, must uphold civil liberties (now commonly, if somewhat vaguely, called 'human rights'), principles of legality, freedom of speech and association, and the protection of a 'non-state' sphere against incursions by the state. We must acknowledge that some institutional protections of this kind are necessary conditions of any democracy, even though we may not accept the identification of democracy with, or its confinement to, the formal safeguards of 'liberalism', and even if we may believe that 'liberal' protections will have to take a different institutional form in socialist democracy than under capitalism.[11]

Difficulties nevertheless remain in the 'civil society' argument. There are other ways (indeed the principal ways in Marxist theory) of associating 'formal democracy' with capitalism than by rejecting the one with the other. We can recognize the historical and structural connections without denying the value of civil liberties. An understanding of these connections does not compel us to devalue civil liberties, but nor does it oblige us to accept capitalism as the sole or best means of maintaining individual autonomy; and it leaves us perfectly free also to acknowledge that capitalism, while in certain historical conditions conducive to 'formal democracy', can easily do without it – as it has done more than once in recent history. At any rate, not to see the connections, or to mistake their character, limits our understanding of both democracy and capitalism.

The historical and structural connection between formal democracy and capitalism can certainly be formulated with reference to the separation of the state from civil society. Much depends, however, on how we interpret that separation and the historical process that brought it about. There is a view of history, and a concomitant interpretation of the state–civil society separation, which cannot see the evolution of capitalism as anything but progressive. It is a view of history commonly associated with liberalism

---

[11] I have discussed these points at greater length in my *The Retreat from Class: A New 'True' Socialism* (London, 1986) chap. 10.

or 'bourgeois' ideology, but one that seems increasingly to underlie conceptions of democracy on the left.

The historical presuppositions underlying the advocacy of 'civil society' are seldom explicitly spelled out. There is, however, a particularly useful and sophisticated account by a Hungarian scholar, published in English translation in a volume devoted to reviving 'civil society' (East and West), which may serve as a model of the relevant historical interpretation. In an attempt to characterize three different 'historical regions of Europe' – Western and Eastern Europe and something in between – Jenö Szücs (following Istvan Bibo) offers the following account of the 'Western' model, in 'a search for the deepest roots of a "democratic way of organizing society"'.[12] The most distinctive 'characteristic of the West is the structural – and theoretical – separation of "society" from the "state"', a unique development which lies at the heart of Western democracy, while its corresponding absence in the East accounts for an evolution from autocracy to totalitarianism.[13] The roots of this development, according to Szücs, lie in Western feudalism.

The uniqueness of Western history lay, according to this argument, in 'an entirely unusual "take-off" in the rise of civilizations. This take-off took place amidst disintegration instead of integration, and amidst declining civilization, re-agrarianization and mounting political anarchy'.[14] This fragmentation and disintegration were the preconditions of the separation of 'society' and 'state'. In the high civilizations of the East, where no such separation took place, the political function continued to be exercised 'downwards from above'.

In the process of feudal 'fragmentation' in the West, the old political relations of states and subjects were replaced by new social ties, of a contractual nature, between lords and vassals. This substitution of social–contractual relations for political relations had among its major consequences a new principle of human dignity, freedom and the 'honour' of the individual. And the territorial disintegration into small units each with its own customary law produced a decentralization of law which could resist '"descending" mechanisms of exercising power'.[15] When sovereignty was later reconstructed by the Western monarchies, the new state

[12] Jenö Szücs, 'Three Historical Regions of Europe', in Keane, *Civil Society and the State*, p. 294.
[13] *Ibid.*, p. 295.   [14] *Ibid.*, p. 296.   [15] *Ibid.*, p. 302.

was essentially constituted 'vertically from below'.[16] It was a 'unity in plurality' that made 'freedoms' the 'internal organizing principles' of Western social structure 'and led to something which drew the line so sharply between the medieval West and many other civilizations: the birth of "society" as an autonomous entity'.[17]

There is much in this argument that is truly illuminating, but equally instructive is the bias in its angle of vision. Here, in fact, are all the staples of liberal history: the progress of civilization (at least in the West) as an unambiguous ascent of individual 'freedom' and 'dignity' (if there is a critical difference between Szücs's account and the traditional liberal view, it is that the latter is more frank about the identification of individuality with private property); the prime focus on the tension between individual or 'society' and the state as the moving force of history; even – and perhaps especially – the tendency to associate the advance of civilization, and democracy itself, with milestones in the ascent of the propertied classes. Although there was nothing democratic about the medieval West, Szücs concedes, this is where the 'deepest roots' of democracy are to be found. Although Szücs does not say it in so many words, it appears that the 'constitutive idea' of modern democracy was *lordship*.

Suppose we look at the same sequence of events from a different angle. Seen from another vantage point, the same 'fragmentation', the same replacement of political relations by social and contractual bonds, the same 'parcellization' of sovereignty, the same 'autonomy of society', even while their uniqueness and importance in the trajectory of Western development are acknowledged, can have very different consequences for our appreciation of 'civil society' and the development of Western democracy.

The divergence of the 'West' from the 'Eastern' pattern of state formation began, of course, much earlier than medieval feudalism. It could be traced as far back as early Greek antiquity, but for our purposes a critical benchmark can be identified in ancient Rome. This divergence, it needs to be stressed, had to do not only with political forms but above all with modes of appropriation – and here developments in the Roman system of private property were decisive. (It is a curious but 'symptomatic' feature of Szücs's argument that modes of appropriation and exploitation do not figure cen-

[16] *Ibid.*, p. 304.   [17] *Ibid.*, p. 306.

trally, if at all, in his differentiation of the three historical regions of Europe – which may also explain his insistence on a radical break between antiquity and feudalism. At the very least, the survival of Roman law, the quintessential symbol of the Roman property regime, should have signalled to Szücs some fundamental continuity between the Western 'autonomy' of civil society and the Roman system of appropriation.)

Rome represents a striking contrast to other 'high' civilizations – both in the ancient world and centuries later – where access to great wealth, to the surplus labour of others on a large scale, was typically achieved through the medium of the state (for example, late Imperial China, which had a highly developed system of private property but where great wealth and power resided not in land so much as in the state, in the bureaucratic hierarchy whose pinnacle was the court and imperial officialdom). Rome was distinctive in its emphasis on private property, on the acquisition of massive land holdings, as a means of appropriation. The Roman aristocracy had an insatiable appetite for land which created unprecedented concentrations of wealth and a predatory imperial power unrivalled by any other ancient empire in its hunger not simply for tribute but for territory. And it was Rome which extended its regime of private property throughout a vast and diverse empire, governed without a massive bureaucracy but instead through a 'municipal' system which effectively constituted a federation of local aristocracies. The result was a very specific combination of a strong imperial state and a dominant propertied class autonomous from it, a strong state which at the same time encouraged, instead of impeding, the autonomous development of private property. It was Rome, in short, that firmly and self-consciously established private property as an autonomous locus of social power, detached from, while supported by, the state.

The 'fragmentation' of feudalism must be seen in this light, as rooted in the privatization of power already inherent in the Roman property system and in the Empire's fragmented 'municipal' administration. When the tensions between the Roman imperial state and the autonomous power of private property were finally resolved by the disintegration of the central state, the autonomous power of property remained. The old political relations of rulers and subjects were gradually dissolved into the 'social' relations between lords and vassals, and more particularly, lords and peasants. In the institution of lordship, political and economic powers were united as they had been where the state was a major source of private wealth; but this time, that unity existed in a fragmented and privatized form.

Seen from this perspective, the development of the West can hardly be viewed as simply the rise of individuality, the rule of law, the progress of freedom or power from 'below'; and the autonomy of 'civil society' acquires a different meaning. The very developments described by Szücs in these terms are also, and at the same time, the evolution of new forms of exploitation and domination (the constitutive 'power from below' is, after all, the power of lordship), new relations of personal dependence and bondage, the privatization of surplus extraction and the transfer of ancient oppressions from the state to 'society' – that is, a transfer of power relations and domination from the state to private property. This new division of labour between state and 'society' also laid a foundation (as a necessary though not sufficient condition) for the increasing separation of private appropriation from public responsibilities which came to fruition in capitalism.

Capitalism then represents the culmination of a long development, but it also constitutes a qualitative break (which occurred 'spontaneously' only in the particular historical conditions of England). Not only is it characterized by a transformation of social power, a new division of labour between state and private property or class, but it also marks the creation of a completely new form of coercion, the market – the market not simply as a sphere of opportunity, freedom and choice, but as a compulsion, a necessity, a social discipline, capable of subjecting all human activities and relationships to its requirements.

'CIVIL SOCIETY' AND THE DEVALUATION OF DEMOCRACY

It is not, then, enough to say that democracy can be expanded by detaching the principles of 'formal democracy' from any association with capitalism. Nor is it enough to say that capitalist democracy is incomplete, one stage in an unambiguously progressive development which must be perfected by socialism and advanced beyond the limitations of 'formal democracy'. The point is rather that the association of capitalism with 'formal democracy' represents a contradictory unity of advance and retreat, both an enhancement and a devaluation of democracy. 'Formal democracy' certainly is an improvement on political forms lacking civil liberties, the rule of law and the principle of representation. But it is also, equally and at the same time, a subtraction from the substance of the democratic idea, and one which is historically and structurally associated with capitalism.[18]

I have already elaborated on some of these themes in previous chapters. Here, it is enough to note a certain paradox in the insistence that we should not allow our conception of human emancipation to be constrained by the identification of 'formal democracy' with capitalism. If we think of human emancipation as little more than an extension of liberal democracy, then we may in the end be persuaded to believe that capitalism is after all its surest guarantee.

The separation of the state and civil society in the West has

---

[18] The defence of formal democracy is sometimes explicitly accompanied by an attack on 'substantive' democracy. Agnes Heller, in 'On Formal Democracy', writes: 'The statement of Aristotle, a highly realistic analyst, that all democracies are immediately transformed into anarchy, the latter into tyranny, was a statement of fact, not an aristocratic slandering by an anti-democrat. The Roman republic was not for a moment democratic. And I should like to add to all that that even if the degradation of modern democracies into tyrannies is far from being excluded (we were witness to it in the cases of German and Italian Fascism), the endurance of modern democracies is due precisely to their formal character' (p. 130). Let us take each sentence in turn. The denunciation of ancient democracy as the inevitable forerunner of anarchy and tyranny (which is, incidentally, more typical of Plato or Polybius than Aristotle) is, precisely, an anti-democratic slander. For one thing, it bears no relation to real historical sequences, causal or even chronological. Athenian democracy brought an end to the institution of tyranny, and went on to survive nearly two centuries, only to be defeated not by anarchy but by a superior military power. During those centuries, of course, Athens produced an astonishingly fruitful and influential culture which survived its defeat and also laid the foundation for Western conceptions of citizenship and the rule of law. The Roman republic was indeed 'not for a moment democratic', and the most notable result of its aristocratic regime was the demise of the republic and its replacement by autocratic imperial rule. (That undemocratic Republic was, incidentally, a major inspiration for what Heller calls a 'constitutive' document of modern democracy, the US Constitution.) To say that the 'degradation of modern democracies into tyrannies is far from being excluded' seems a bit coy in conjunction with a (parenthetical) reference to Fascism – not to mention the history of war and imperialism which has been inextricably associated with the regime of 'formal democracy'. As for endurance, it is surely worth mentioning that there does not yet exist a 'formal democracy' whose life span equals, let alone exceeds, the duration of the Athenian democracy. No European 'democracy', by Heller's criteria, is even a century old (in Britain, for example, plural voting survived until 1948); and the American republic, which she credits with the 'constitutive idea' of formal democracy, took a long time to improve on the Athenian exclusion of women and slaves, while free working men – full citizens in the Athenian democracy – cannot be said to have gained full admission even to 'formal' citizenship until the last state property qualifications were removed in the nineteenth century (not to mention the variety of stratagems to discourage voting by the poor in general and blacks in particular, which have not been exhausted to this day). Thus, at best (and for white men only), an endurance record of perhaps one century and a half exists for modern 'formal democracies'.

certainly given rise to new forms of freedom and equality, but it has also created new modes of domination and coercion. One way of characterizing the specificity of 'civil society' as a particular social form unique to the modern world – the particular historical conditions that made possible the modern distinction between state and civil society – is to say that it constituted a new form of social power, in which many coercive functions that once belonged to the state were relocated in the 'private' sphere, in private property, class exploitation, and market imperatives. It is, in a sense, this 'privatization' of public power that has created the historically novel realm of 'civil society'.

'Civil society' constitutes not only a wholly new relation between 'public' and 'private' but more precisely a wholly new 'private' realm, with a distinctive 'public' presence and oppressions of its own, a unique structure of power and domination, and a ruthless systemic logic. It represents a particular network of social relations which does not simply stand in opposition to the coercive, 'policing' and 'administrative' functions of the state but represents the *relocation* of these functions, or at least some significant part of them. It entails a new division of labour between the 'public' sphere of the state and the 'private' sphere of capitalist property and the imperatives of the market, in which appropriation, exploitation and domination are detached from public authority and social responsibility – while these new private powers rely on the state to sustain them, by means of a more thoroughly concentrated power of enforcement than has ever existed before.

'Civil society' has given private property and its possessors a command over people and their daily lives, a power enforced by the state but accountable to no one, which many an old tyrannical state would have envied. Even those activities and experiences that fall outside the immediate command structure of the capitalist enterprise, or outside the very great political power of capital, are regulated by the dictates of the market, the necessities of competition and profitability. Even when the market is not, as it commonly is in advanced capitalist societies, merely an instrument of power for giant conglomerates and multi-national corporations, it is still a coercive force, capable of subjecting all human values, activities and relationships to its imperatives. No ancient despot could have hoped to penetrate the personal lives of his subjects – their life chances, choices, preferences, opinions and relationships – in the same comprehensive and minute detail, not only in the workplace but in every corner of their lives. And the market has created new instruments of power to be manipulated not only by multi-national capital but by advanced capitalist states, which can act to impose draconian 'market disciplines' on other economies while often sheltering their own domestic capital. Coercion, in other words, has been not just a disorder of 'civil society' but one of its constitutive principles. For that matter, the coercive functions of the state have in large part been occupied with the enforcement of domination in civil society.

This historical reality tends to undermine the neat distinctions required by current theories which ask us to treat civil society as, at least in principle, the sphere of freedom and voluntary action, the antithesis of the irreducibly coercive principle which intrinsically belongs to the state. It is certainly true that in capitalist society, with its separation of 'political' and 'economic' spheres, or the state and civil society, coercive public power is centralized and concentrated to a greater degree than ever before, but this simply means that one of the principal functions of 'public' coercion by the state is to sustain 'private' power in civil society.

One of the most obvious examples of the distorted vision produced by the simple dichotomy between the state as the site of coercion and 'civil society' as a free space is the extent to which civil liberties like freedom of expression or the press in capitalist societies are measured not by the breadth of opinion and debate available in the media but the extent to which the media are private property and capital is free to profit from them. The press is 'free' when it is private, however much it may 'manufacture consent'.

The current theories of civil society do, of course, acknowledge that civil society is not a realm of perfect freedom or democracy. It is, for example, marred by oppression in the family, in gender relations, in the workplace, by racist attitudes, homophobia, and so on. In fact, at least in advanced capitalist societies, such oppressions have become the main focus of struggle, as 'politics' in the old-fashioned sense, having to do with state power, parties and opposition to them, has become increasingly unfashionable. Yet these oppressions are treated not as constitutive of civil society but as dysfunctions in it. In principle, coercion belongs to the state while civil society is where freedom is rooted; and human emancipation, according to these arguments, consists in the autonomy of civil society, its expansion and enrichment, its liberation from the state, and its protection by formal democracy. What tends to disappear from view, again, is the relations of exploitation and domination which irreducibly constitute civil society, not just as some alien and correctible disorder but as its very essence, the particular structure of domination and coercion that is specific to capitalism as a systemic totality – and which also determines the coercive functions of the state.

THE NEW PLURALISM AND THE POLITICS OF IDENTITY

The rediscovery of liberalism in the revival of civil society thus has two sides. It is admirable in its intention of making the left more sensitive to civil liberties and the dangers of state oppression. But the cult of civil society also tends to reproduce the mystifications of liberalism, disguising the coercions of civil society and obscuring the ways in which state oppression itself is rooted in the exploitative and coercive relations of civil society. What, then, of its dedication to pluralism? How does the concept of civil society fare in dealing with the diversity of social relations and 'identities'?

It is here that the cult of civil society, its representation of civil society as the sphere of difference and diversity, speaks most directly to the dominant preoccupations of the new new left. If anything unites the various 'new revisionisms' – from the most abstruse 'post-Marxist' and 'post-modernist' theories to the activisms of the 'new social movements' – it is an emphasis on diversity, 'difference', pluralism. The new pluralism goes beyond the traditional liberal recognition of diverse interests and the toleration (in principle) of diverse opinions in three major ways: 1) its conception of diversity probes beneath the externalities of 'interest' to the psychic depths of 'subjectivity' or 'identity' and extends beyond political 'behaviour' or 'opinion' to the totality of 'life styles'; 2) it no longer assumes that some universal and undifferentiated principles of right can accommodate all diverse identities and life styles (women, for example, require different rights from men in order to be free and equal); 3) the new pluralism rests on a view that the essential characteristic, the historical differentia specifica, of the contemporary world – or, more specifically, the contemporary capitalist world – is not the totalizing, homogenizing drive of capitalism but the unique heterogeneity of 'post-modern' society, its unprecedented degree of diversity, even fragmentation, requiring new, more complex pluralistic principles.

The arguments run something like this: contemporary society is characterized by an increasing fragmentation, a diversification of social relations and experiences, a plurality of life styles, a multiplication of personal identities. In other words, we are living in a 'post-modern' world, a world in which diversity and difference have dissolved all the old certainties and all the old universalities. (Here, some post-Marxist theories offer an alternative to the concept of civil society by insisting that it is no longer possible to speak of society at all, because that concept suggests a closed and unified totality.[19]) Old solidarities – and this, of course, means especially class solidarities – have broken down, and social movements based on other identities and against other oppressions have proliferated, having to do with gender, race, ethnicity, sexuality, and so on. At the same time, these developments have vastly extended the scope of individual choice, in consumption patterns and life styles. This is what some people have called a tremendous expansion of 'civil society'.[20] The left, the argument goes, needs to acknowledge these developments and build on them. It needs to construct a politics based on this diversity and difference. It needs both to celebrate difference and to recognize the plurality of oppressions or forms of domination, the multiplicity of emancipatory struggles. The left needs to respond to this multiplicity of social relations with complex concepts of equality, which acknowledge people's different needs and experiences.[21]

There are variations on these themes, but, in broad outline, this is a fair summary of what has become a substantial current on the left. The general direction in which it is pushing us is to give up the idea of socialism and replace it with – or at least subsume it under – what is supposed to be a more inclusive category, democracy, a concept that does not 'privilege' class, as traditional socialism does, but treats all oppressions equally. Now as a very general statement of principle, there are some admirable things here. No socialist can doubt

[19] This is, for example, the view of Ernesto Laclau and Chantal Mouffe in *Hegemony and Socialist Strategy* (London, 1985).
[20] See, for example, Stuart Hall in *Marxism Today*, October 1988.
[21] The notion of complex equality is primarily the work of Michael Walzer, *Spheres of Justice: A Defence of Pluralism and Equality* (London, 1983). See also Keane, *Democracy and Civil Society*, p. 12.

the importance of diversity, or the multiplicity of oppressions that need to be abolished. And democracy is – or ought to be – what socialism is about. But it is not at all clear that the new pluralism – or what has come to be called the 'politics of identity' – gets us much beyond a statement of general principles and good intentions.

The limits of the new pluralism can be tested by exploring the implications of its constitutive principle, the concept of 'identity'. This concept claims the virtue that, unlike 'reductionist' or 'essentialist' notions such as class, it can encompass – equally and without prejudice or privilege – everything from gender to class, from ethnicity or race to sexual preference. The 'politics of identity', then, purports to be both more fine-tuned in its sensitivity to the complexity of human experience and more inclusive in its emancipatory sweep than the old politics of socialism.

What, then, if anything, is lost by seeing the world through the prism of this all-embracing concept (or any analogous one)? The new pluralism aspires to a democratic community which acknowledges all kinds of difference, of gender, culture, sexuality, which encourages and celebrates these differences, but without allowing them to become relations of domination and oppression. Its ideal democratic community unites diverse human beings, all free and equal, without suppressing their differences or denying their special needs. But the 'politics of identity' reveals its limitations, both theoretical and political, the moment we try to situate *class* differences within its democratic vision.

Is it possible to imagine class differences without exploitation and domination? The 'difference' that constitutes class as an 'identity' *is*, by definition, a relationship of inequality and power, in a way that sexual or cultural 'difference' need not be. A truly democratic society can celebrate diversities of life styles, culture, or sexual preference; but in what sense would it be 'democratic' to celebrate *class* differences? If a conception of freedom or equality adapted to sexual or cultural differences is intended to extend the reach of human liberation, can the same be said of a conception of freedom or equality that accommodates *class* differences? There are no doubt many serious weaknesses in the concept of 'identity' as applied to social *relations*, and this applies not only to class; but if emancipation and democracy require celebration of 'identity' in one case and suppression in another, that is surely enough to suggest that some important differences are being concealed in a catch-all category which is meant to cover very diverse social phenomena like class, gender, sexuality or ethnicity. At the very least, class equality means something different and requires different conditions from sexual or racial equality. In particular, the abolition of class inequality would by definition mean the end of capitalism. But is the same necessarily true about the abolition of sexual or racial inequality? Sexual and racial equality, as I shall argue in the next chapter, are not in principle incompatible with capitalism. The disappearance of class inequalities, on the other hand, is by definition incompatible with capitalism. At the same time, although class exploitation is constitutive of capitalism as sexual or racial inequality are not, capitalism subjects all social relations to its requirements. It can co-opt and reinforce inequalities and oppressions that it did not create and adapt them to the interests of class exploitation.

The old liberal concept of formal legal and political equality, or some notion of so-called 'equality of opportunity', is, of course, capable of accommodating class inequalities – and for that reason, it presents no fundamental challenge to capitalism and its system of class relations. It is, in fact, a specific feature of capitalism that a particular kind of universal equality is possible which does not extend to class relations – that is, precisely, a formal equality, having to do with political and legal principles and procedures rather than with the disposition of social or class power. Formal equality in this sense would have been impossible in pre-capitalist societies where appropriation and exploitation were inextricably bound up with juridical, political and military power.

For these very reasons, the old conception of formal equality satisfies the most fundamental criterion of the new pluralism, namely that it gives no privileged status to class. It may even have radical implications for gender or race, because in respect to these differences, no capitalist society has yet reached the limits even of the restricted kind of equality that capitalism allows. Nor is it clear that the new pluralism has found a better way of dealing with diverse inequalities in a capitalist society, something that goes consistently beyond the old liberal accommodation with capitalism.

Efforts have been made to construct new 'complex' or 'pluralist' conceptions of equality which acknowledge diverse oppressions without 'privileging' class. These differ from the liberal-democratic idea in that they explicitly challenge the *universality* of traditional liberalism, its application of uniform standards of freedom and

equality which are blind to differences of identity and social condition. Acknowledging the complexities of social experience, these
new conceptions of equality are meant to apply different criteria to
different circumstances and relations. In this respect, pluralist
notions claim certain advantages over more universalistic principles,
even if they may lose some of the benefits of universal standards.[22] It
might be objected here that the dissociation of the new pluralism,
from any universal values may permit it to serve as an excuse for
suppressing the *old* pluralist principles of civil liberty, free speech and
toleration, and that we are in danger now of coming full circle, as
respect for diversity turns into its opposite. Yet even if we leave that
objection aside, and whatever advantages 'complex' or 'pluralist'
conceptions of equality may claim over traditional liberalism, they
have left intact the liberal accommodation with capitalism, if only
by evading the issue; for at the very heart of the new pluralism is a
failure to confront (and often an explicit denial of) the overarching
totality of capitalism as a social system, which is constituted by class
exploitation but which shapes *all* 'identities' and social relations.

The capitalist system, its totalizing unity, has effectively been
conceptualized away by diffuse conceptions of civil society and by
the submersion of class in catch-all categories like 'identity' which
disaggregate the social world into particular and separate realities.
The social relations of capitalism have been dissolved into an
unstructured and fragmented plurality of identities and differences.
Questions about historical causality or political efficacy can be
evaded, and there is no need to ask how various identities are
situated in the prevailing social structure because the very existence
of the social structure has been conceptualized away altogether.

In these respects, the new pluralism has much in common with
another old pluralism, the one that used to prevail in conventional
political science – pluralism not simply as an ethical principle of
toleration but as a theory about the distribution of social power. The
concept of 'identity' has replaced 'interest groups', and these two
pluralisms may differ in that the old acknowledges an inclusive
political totality – like the 'political system', the nation, or the body
of citizens – while the new insists on the irreducibility of fragmentation and 'difference'. But both deny the importance of class in

[22] For a discussion of both the advantages and disadvantages in Walzer's conception of
complex equality, see Michael Rustin, *For a Pluralist Socialism* (London, 1985) pp.70–95.

capitalist democracies, or at least submerge it in a multiplicity of 'interests' or 'identities'. Both have the effect of denying the systemic unity of capitalism, or its very existence as a social system. Both insist on the heterogeneity of capitalist society, while losing sight of its increasingly global power of homogenization. The new pluralism claims a unique sensitivity to the complexities of power and diverse oppressions; but like the old variety, it has the effect of making invisible the power relations that constitute capitalism, the dominant structure of coercion which reaches into every corner of our lives, public and private. In their failure to acknowledge that various identities or interest groups are differently situated in relation to that dominant structure, both pluralisms recognize not so much *difference* as simple *plurality*.

This latest denial of capitalism's systemic and totalizing logic is, paradoxically, a reflection of the very thing it seeks to deny. The current preoccupation with 'post-modern' diversity and fragmentation undoubtedly expresses a reality in contemporary capitalism, but it is a reality seen through the distorting lens of ideology. It represents the ultimate 'commodity fetishism', the triumph of 'consumer society', in which the diversity of 'life styles', measured in the sheer quantity of commodities and varied patterns of consumption, disguises the underlying systemic unity, the imperatives which create that diversity itself while at the same time imposing a deeper and more global homogeneity.

What is alarming about these theoretical developments is not that they violate some doctrinaire Marxist prejudice concerning the privileged status of class. The problem is that theories which do not differentiate – and, yes, 'privilege', if that means ascribing causal or explanatory priorities – among various social institutions and 'identities' cannot deal critically with capitalism at all. Capitalism, as a specific social form, simply disappears from view, buried under a welter of fragments and 'difference'.

And whither capitalism, so goes the socialist idea. Socialism is the specific alternative to capitalism. Without capitalism, we have no need of socialism; we can make do with very diffuse and indeterminate concepts of democracy which are not specifically opposed to any identifiable system of social relations, in fact do not even recognize any such system. Nothing remains but a fragmented plurality of oppressions and emancipatory struggles. What claims to be a more inclusive project than traditional socialism is actually less so. Instead of the universalist aspirations of socialism and the integrative politics of the struggle against class exploitation, we have a plurality of essentially disconnected particular struggles, which ends in a submission to capitalism.

It is possible that the new pluralism is indeed leaning toward the acceptance of capitalism, at least as the best social order we are likely to get. The collapse of Communism has undoubtedly done more than anything else to encourage the spread of this view. But in the left's responses to these developments, it is often difficult to distinguish between a panglossian optimism and the deepest despair. On the one hand, it has become increasingly common to argue that, however pervasive capitalism may be, its old rigid structures have more or less disintegrated, or become so permeable, opened up so many large spaces, that people are free to construct their own social realities in unprecedented ways. This is precisely what some people mean when they talk about the vast expansion of civil society in modern ('post-Fordist'?) capitalism. On the other hand, and sometimes in the same breath, we hear a counsel of despair: whatever the evils of a triumphant capitalism, there is little hope for any challenge to it beyond the most local and particular resistances.

This may not be the moment for optimism, but a critical confrontation with capitalism is, at the very least, a useful start. We may then be obliged to differentiate not less but much more radically among various kinds of inequality and oppression than even the new pluralism allows. We can, for example, acknowledge that, while all oppressions may have equal moral claims, class exploitation has a different historical status, a more strategic location at the heart of capitalism; and class struggle may have a more universal reach, a greater potential for advancing not only class emancipation but other emancipatory struggles too.

Capitalism is constituted by class exploitation, but capitalism is more than just a system of class oppression. It is a ruthless totalizing process which shapes our lives in every conceivable aspect, and everywhere, not just in the relative opulence of the capitalist North. Among other things, and even leaving aside the direct power wielded by capitalist wealth both in the economy and in the political sphere, it subjects all social life to the abstract requirements of the market, through the commodification of life in all its aspects, determining the allocation of labour, leisure, resources, patterns of production, consumption and the disposition of time. This makes a mockery of all our aspirations to autonomy, freedom of choice, and democratic self-government.

Socialism is the antithesis of capitalism; and the replacement of socialism by an indeterminate concept of democracy, or the dilution of diverse and different social relations into catch-all categories like 'identity' or 'difference', or loose conceptions of 'civil society', represents a surrender to capitalism and its ideological mystifications. By all means let us have diversity, difference, and pluralism; but not an undifferentiated and unstructured pluralism. What is needed is a pluralism that does indeed acknowledge diversity and difference, not merely plurality or multiplicity. This means a pluralism that recognizes the systemic unity of capitalism and can distinguish the constitutive relations of capitalism from other inequalities and oppressions. The socialist project should be enriched by the resources and insights of the (now not so new) 'new social movements', not impoverished by resorting to them as an excuse for disintegrating the resistance to capitalism. We should not confuse respect for the plurality of human experience and social struggles with a complete dissolution of historical causality, where there is nothing but diversity, difference and contingency, no unifying structures, no logic of process, no capitalism and therefore no negation of it, no universal project of human emancipation.

CHAPTER 9

Capitalism and human emancipation: race, gender and democracy

Speaking to American students at the height of student activism in the 1960s, Isaac Deutscher delivered a not altogether welcome message: 'You are effervescently active on the margin of social life, and the workers are passive right at the core of it. That is the tragedy of our society. If you do not deal with this contrast, you will be defeated'.[1] That warning may be no less apposite today than it was then. There are strong and promising emancipatory impulses at work today, but they may not be active at the core of social life, in the heart of capitalist society.

It is no longer taken for granted on the left that the decisive battle for human emancipation will take place on the 'economic' terrain, the home ground of class struggle. For a great many people the emphasis has shifted to struggles for what I shall call *extra-economic* goods – gender-emancipation, racial equality, peace, ecological health, democratic citizenship. Every socialist ought to be committed to these goals in themselves – in fact, the socialist project of *class* emancipation always has been, or should have been, a means to the larger end of human emancipation. But these commitments do not settle crucial questions about agencies and modalities of struggle, and they certainly do not settle the question of class politics.

A great deal still needs to be said about the conditions for the achievement of these extra-economic goods. In particular, if our starting point is *capitalism*, then we need to know exactly what kind of starting point this is. What limits are imposed, and what possibilities created, by the capitalist regime, by its material order and its configuration of social power? What kinds of oppression does

[1] Isaac Deutscher, 'Marxism and the New Left', in *Marxism in Our Times* (London, 1972), p. 74. This chapter is based, with some modifications, on my Isaac Deutscher Memorial Lecture, delivered on 23 November 1987.

capitalism require, and what kinds of emancipation can it tolerate? In particular, what use does capitalism have for extra-economic goods, what encouragement does it give them and what resistance does it put up to their attainment? I want to make a start on answering these questions, and as the argument develops I shall try to throw them into relief by making some comparisons with pre-capitalist societies.

CAPITALISM AND 'EXTRA-ECONOMIC' GOODS

Let me begin by saying that certain extra-economic goods are simply not compatible with capitalism, and I do not intend to talk about them. I am convinced, for example, that capitalism cannot deliver world peace. It seems to me axiomatic that the expansionary, competitive and exploitative logic of capitalist accumulation in the context of the nation-state system must, in the longer or shorter term, be destabilizing, and that capitalism – and at the moment its most aggressive and adventurist organizing force, the government of the United States – is and will for the foreseeable future remain the greatest threat to world peace.[2]

Nor do I think that capitalism can avoid ecological devastation. It may be able to accommodate some degree of ecological care, especially when the technology of environmental protection is itself profitably marketable. But the essential irrationality of the drive for capital accumulation, which subordinates everything to the requirements of the self-expansion of capital and so-called growth, is unavoidably hostile to ecological balance. If destruction of the environment in the Communist world resulted from gross neglect, massive inefficiency, and a reckless urge to catch up with Western industrial development in the shortest possible time, in the capitalist

---

[2] This observation may seem less plausible now than it did when I first made it, before American militarism had been overshadowed by the collapse of Communism, the apparent acceptance by US governments that the Cold War is over, and dramatic outbreaks of so-called ethnic violence, notably in the former Yugoslavia. I contemplated taking out or somehow modifying this bald statement about the destabilizing effects of capitalism and American aggression, or saying something about the new forms of militarism associated with the role of the US as the sole super-power and guardian of the 'new world order'. But nothing that has happened in the last few years changes the fact that there has hardly been a major regional conflict anywhere since World War II that has not been initiated, aggravated or prolonged by US intervention, open or clandestine; and it is far too soon to say that this pattern of adventurism has been finally repudiated – never mind new forms of military intervention such as Desert Storm.

West a far more wide-ranging ecological vandalism is not an index of failure but a token of success, the inevitable by-product of a system whose constitutive principle is the subordination of all human values to the imperatives of accumulation and the require-ments of profitability.

It has to be added, though, that the issues of peace and ecology are not very well suited to generating strong anti-capitalist forces. In a sense, the problem is their very *universality*. They do not constitute social forces because they simply have no specific social identity – or at least they have none except at the point where they intersect with class relations, as in the case of ecological issues raised by the poisoning of workers in the workplace, or the tendency to concen-trate pollution and waste in working-class neighbourhoods rather than in privileged suburbs. But, in the final analysis, it is no more in the interests of the capitalist than of the worker to be wiped out by a nuclear bomb or dissolved in acid rain. We might as well say that given the dangers of capitalism, no rational person should support it; but this, needless to say, is not how things work.

The situation with race and gender is almost the reverse. Anti-racism and anti-sexism do have specific social identities, and they can generate strong social forces. But it is not so clear that racial or gender equality are antagonistic to capitalism, or that capitalism cannot tolerate them as it cannot deliver world peace or respect the environment. Each of these extra-economic goods, then, has its own specific relation to capitalism.

The first point about capitalism is that it is uniquely indifferent to the social identities of the people it exploits. This is a classic case of good news and bad news. First, the good news – more or less. Unlike previous modes of production, capitalist exploitation is not inextric-ably linked with extra-economic, juridical or political identities, inequalities or differences. The extraction of surplus value from wage labourers takes place in a relationship between formally free and equal individuals and does not presuppose differences in juridi-cal or political status. In fact, there is a positive tendency in capital-ism to *undermine* such differences, and even to dilute identities like gender or race, as capital strives to absorb people into the labour market and to reduce them to interchangeable units of labour abstracted from any specific identity.

On the other hand, capitalism is very flexible in its ability to make use of, as well as to discard, particular social oppressions. Part of the bad news is that capitalism is likely to co-opt whatever extra-economic oppressions are historically and culturally available in any given setting. Such cultural legacies can, for example, promote the ideological hegemony of capitalism by disguising its inherent tendency to create underclasses. When the least privileged sectors of the working class coincide with extra-economic identities like gender or race, as they so often do, it may appear that the blame for the existence of these sectors lies with causes other than the necessary logic of the capitalist system.

It is not, of course, a matter of some capitalist conspiracy to deceive. For one thing, racism and sexism function so well in capitalist society partly because they can actually work to the advantage of certain sectors of the working class in the competitive conditions of the labour market. The point, though, is that if capital derives advantages from racism or sexism, it is not because of any structural tendency in capitalism toward racial inequality or gender oppression, but on the contrary because they disguise the structural realities of the capitalist system and because they divide the working class. At any rate, capitalist exploitation can in principle be conducted without any consideration for colour, race, creed, gender, any dependence upon extra-economic inequality or difference; and more than that, the development of capitalism has created ideological pressures *against* such inequalities and differences to a degree with no precedent in pre-capitalist societies.

RACE AND GENDER

Here we immediately come up against some contradictions. Consider the example of race. Despite the structural indifference of capitalism to extra-economic identities (or in some sense because of it), its history has been marked by probably the most virulent racisms ever known. The widespread and deep-rooted racism directed against blacks in the West, for example, is often attributed to the cultural legacy of colonialism and slavery which accompanied the expansion of capitalism. But on second thought, while this explanation is certainly convincing up to a point, by itself it is not enough.

Take the extreme case of slavery. A comparison with the only other known historical examples of slavery on such a scale will illustrate that there is nothing automatic about the association of

slavery with such virulent racism, and may suggest that there is
something specific to capitalism in this ideological effect. In ancient
Greece and Rome, despite the almost universal acceptance of
slavery, the idea that it was justified by natural inequalities among
human beings was not the dominant view. The one notable exception, Aristotle's conception of natural slavery, never gained currency. The more common view seems to have been that slavery was
a convention, though a universal one, which was justifiable simply
on the grounds of its usefulness. In fact, it was even conceded that
this useful institution was *contrary to nature*. Such a view appears not
only in Greek philosophy but was even recognized in Roman law. It
has even been suggested that slavery was the only case in Roman
law where there was an acknowledged conflict between the *ius
gentium*, the conventional law of nations, and the *ius naturale*, the law
of nature.[3]

This is significant not because it led to the abolition of slavery,
which it certainly did not, nor does it in any way mitigate the
horrors of ancient slavery. It is worth noting because it suggests that,
in contrast to modern slavery, there seemed to be no pressing need to
find a justification for this evil institution in the natural, biological
inferiority of certain races. Ethnic conflicts are probably as old as
civilization; and defences of slavery based, for example, on biblical
stories about tainted inheritance have had a long history. There
have also been theories of climatic determinism, from Aristotle to
Bodin; but the determinants here are environmental rather than
racial. Modern racism is something different, a more viciously
systematic conception of inherent and natural inferiority, which
emerged in the late seventeenth or early eighteenth century and
culminated in the nineteenth century when it acquired the pseudo-
scientific reinforcement of *biological* theories of race, and continued
to serve as an ideological support for colonial oppression even after
the abolition of slavery.

It is tempting to ask, then, what it was about capitalism that
created this ideological need, this need for what amounts to a theory

[3] For example, the Roman jurist Florentinus wrote that 'Slavery is an institution of the *ius
gentium* whereby someone is subject to the *dominium* of another contrary to nature.' See M.I.
Finley, 'Was Greek civilization Based on Slave Labour?' and 'Between Slavery and
Freedom', in *Economy and Society in Ancient Greece* (London, 1981), pp. 104, 113, 130. For an
emphatic rejection of the view that Christianity introduced 'an entirely new and better
attitude towards slavery', see G.E.M. de Ste Croix, *The Class Struggle in the Ancient Greek
World* (London, 1981), p. 419.

of natural, not just conventional, slavery. And at least part of the answer must lie in a paradox. While colonial oppression and slavery were growing in the outposts of capitalism, the workforce at home was increasingly proletarianized; and the expansion of wage labour, the contractual relation between formally free and equal individuals, carried with it an ideology of formal equality and freedom. In fact, this ideology, which on the juridical and political planes denies the fundamental inequality and unfreedom of the capitalist economic relation, has always been a vital element in the hegemony of capitalism.

In a sense, then, it was precisely the structural pressure *against* extra-economic difference which made it necessary to justify slavery by excluding slaves from the human race, making them non-persons standing outside the normal universe of freedom and equality. It is perhaps because capitalism recognizes no extra-economic differences among human beings that people had to be rendered less than human in order to accommodate the slavery and colonialism which were so useful to capital at that historical moment. In Greece and Rome, it was enough to identify people as outsiders on the grounds that they were not *citizens*, or that they were not Greeks (the Romans, as we have seen, had a rather less exclusive conception of citizenship). In capitalism, the criterion for excommunication seems to be exclusion from the main body of the human race.

Or consider the case of gender oppression. The contradictions here are not quite so glaring. If capitalism has been associated with a racism more virulent than ever before, I for one would find wholly unconvincing any claim that capitalism has produced more extreme forms of gender oppression than existed in pre-capitalist societies. But here too there is a paradoxical combination of structural indifference to, indeed pressure against, this extra-economic inequality, and a kind of systemic opportunism which allows capitalism to make use of it.

Typically, capitalism in advanced Western capitalist countries uses gender oppression in two kinds of ways: the first it shares with other extra-economic identities, like race or even age, and it is to some extent interchangeable with them as a means of constituting underclasses and providing ideological cover. The second use is specific to gender: it serves as a way of organizing social reproduction in what is thought (maybe incorrectly) to be the least

270 Democracy against capitalism

expensive way.[4] With the existing organization of gender relations, the costs to capital of reproducing labour power can be kept down – or so it has generally been thought – by keeping the costs of child bearing and child rearing in the private sphere of the family. But we have to recognize that, from the point of view of capital, this particular social cost is no different from any other. From the point of view of capital, maternity leaves or day-care centres are not qualitatively different from, say, old-age pensions or unemployment insurance, in that they all involve an undesirable cost.[5] Capital is in general hostile to any such costs – though it has never been able to survive without at least some of them; but the point is that in this respect it is no more incapable of tolerating gender equality than of accepting the National Health Service or social security.

Although capitalism can and does make ideological and economic use of gender oppression, then, this oppression has no privileged status in the structure of capitalism. Capitalism could survive the eradication of all oppressions specific to women as women – while it would not, by definition, survive the eradication of class exploitation. This does not mean that capitalism has made the liberation of women necessary or inevitable. But it does mean that there is no specific structural necessity for, nor even a strong systemic disposition to, gender oppression in capitalism. I shall have some things to say later about how capitalism differs in this respect from precapitalist societies.

I have cited these examples to illustrate two major points: that capitalism does have a structural tendency away from extra-economic inequalities, but that this is a two-edged sword. The strategic implications are that struggles conceived in purely extra-economic terms – as purely against racism or gender oppression, for example – are not in themselves fatally dangerous to capitalism, that they could succeed without dismantling the capitalist system, but that, at the same time, they are probably unlikely to succeed if they remain detached from an anti-capitalist struggle.

---

[4] I have qualified this statement because I am told that there has been important work suggesting that state-funded child-care may be *less* expensive to capital.

[5] There is evidence that a growing burden is being placed on *age*, as distinct from sex or race, at least in the sense that structural youth unemployment combined with growing threats to social security and old-age pensions bear the brunt of capitalist decline. Which of these extra-economic identities will be made to carry the heaviest burden is largely a *political* question which has little to do with the structural disposition of capitalism to choose one rather than another form of extra-economic oppression.

CAPITALISM AND THE DEVALUATION OF POLITICAL GOODS

The ambiguities of capitalism are particularly evident, as we have seen, in its relationship with democratic citizenship. Here, I want to explore the ambiguities of capitalist democracy as they relate to the question of 'extra-economic' goods in general and the position of women in particular.

It has always been a major question for socialism what strategic importance should be attached to the fact that capitalism has made possible an unprecedented extension of citizenship. Almost from the beginning there has existed a socialist tradition which assumes that the formal juridical and political equality of capitalism, in combination with its economic inequality and unfreedom, will set up a dynamic contradiction, a motivating force for a socialist transformation. A basic premise of social democracy, for example, has been that the limited freedom and equality of capitalism will produce overpowering impulses toward complete emancipation. There now exists a strong new tendency to think of socialism as an extension of citizenship rights, or – and this is increasingly common – to think of 'radical democracy' as a *substitute* for socialism. As *democracy* has become the catchword of various progressive struggles, the one unifying theme among the various emancipatory projects of the left, it has begun to stand for all extra-economic goods together.

The idea of regarding socialism as an expansion of democracy can be very fruitful, but I am not at all impressed by the new theoretical trappings of the very old socialist illusion that the ideological impulses of capitalist freedom and equality have created irresistible pressures to transform society at every level. The effects of capitalist democracy have been much more ambiguous than that, and this conception of social transformation is just a sleight of hand which invites us to imagine, if not a smooth transition from capitalist democracy to socialist (or 'radical') democracy, then a substantial realization of democratic aspirations within the interstices of capitalism.

The first requirement here is to have no illusions about the meaning and effects of democracy in capitalism. This means understanding not only the *limits* of capitalist democracy, the fact that even a democratic capitalist state will be constrained by the demands of capital accumulation, and the fact that liberal democracy leaves capitalist exploitation essentially intact, but more particularly the *devaluation* of democracy discussed in our earlier comparisons between ancient and modern democracy.

The critical point is that the status of political goods is in large part determined by their particular location in the system of social property relations. Here again, the contrast with pre-capitalist societies of various kinds is instructive. I have suggested in previous chapters that in pre-capitalist societies, where peasants were the predominant exploited class and exploitation typically took the form of extra-economic, political, juridical, military domination, the prevailing property relations placed a special premium on juridical privilege and political rights. So just as medieval lordship inseparably united political and economic power, so too peasant resistance to economic exploitation could take the form of demanding a share in the privileged juridical and political status of their overlords – as, for example, in the famous English peasant revolt in 1381, provoked by the attempt to impose a poll tax, in which the rebel leader Wat Tyler formulated peasant grievances as a demand for the equal distribution of lordship among all men. This, however, would have meant the end of feudalism. In contrast to capitalism, the salience of political rights imposed an absolute limit on their distribution.

For peasants economic power against exploitation depended to a great extent on the scope of jurisdiction permitted to their own political community, the village, as against the powers of landlord and state. By definition, any extension of the village community's jurisdiction encroached upon and circumscribed the landlord's powers of exploitation. Some powers, however, were more important than others. In contrast to capitalism, the pre-capitalist landlord or the surplus-extracting state did not depend on controlling the process of production as much as on coercive powers of surplus extraction. The pre-capitalist peasant, who retained possession of the means of production, generally remained in control of production, both individually and collectively through his village community. It was a characteristic of feudalism, as of other pre-capitalist forms, that the act of appropriation was generally much more clearly separate from the process of production than it is in capitalism. The peasant produced, the landlord then extracted rent, or the state appropriated tax; or else the peasant produced one day on his own plot and for his own household needs, and on another day on the landlord's demesne, or in some kind of service for the state. So the appropriative powers of landlord or state could be preserved even with a considerable degree of independence for peasants in organizing production, so long as the jurisdiction of the peasant community did not cross the line to control of the juridical and political mechanisms of surplus extraction.

Peasant communities have from time to time pressed hard against those barriers, achieving a substantial degree of independence in their local political institutions, setting up their own local magistrates in place of landlord representatives, imposing their own local charters, and so on. And to the extent that they have achieved this degree of *political* independence, they have also limited their *economic* exploitation. But, as I suggested in chapter 7, the barrier between village and state has generally defeated attempts to overcome the subjection of the peasant; and Athenian democracy may be the one case where that final barrier was breached and where the village community did not remain outside the state, and subject to it, as something alien.[6]

I have argued that by far the most revolutionary aspect of ancient Athenian democracy was the unique, and never equalled, position of the peasant as *citizen*, and with it the position of the village in its relation to the state.[7] In sharp contrast to other peasant societies, the village was the constituent unit of the Athenian state, through which the peasant became a citizen. This represented not just a constitutional innovation but a radical transformation of the peasantry, unrivalled in the ancient world, or indeed anywhere else at any time. If the peasant is, as Eric Wolf has said, a rural cultivator whose surpluses in the form of rent and tax are transferred to someone who 'exercises an effective superior power, or domain, over him',[8] then

[6] On the village community as outside the state and subject to it as an alien power, see Teodor Shanin, 'Peasantry as a Political Factor' and Eric Wolf, 'On Peasant Rebellions', in T. Shanin, ed. *Peasants and Peasant Societies* (Harmondsworth, 1971), especially pp. 244 and 272.

[7] This is a contentious point which is difficult to make clear in this limited space. The well-known evils of Athenian democracy, the institution of slavery and the position of women, cannot help but overshadow any other more attractive features; and it undoubtedly seems perverse to argue, as I do, that the essential characteristic of Athenian democracy, indeed perhaps its most distinctive one, is the extent to which it *excluded* dependence from the sphere of production – that is, the extent to which the material base of Athenian society was free and independent labour. I have explained some of this in chapter 6, and there is a more detailed exposition in my book, *Peasant Citizen and Slave: The Foundations of Athenian Democracy* (London, 1988), where I discuss slavery at length and also deal with the position of women in Athens. I am not asking people to discount or underestimate the importance of slavery or the status of women but simply to consider the unique position of the Athenian peasantry.

[8] Eric Wolf, *Peasants* (Englewood Cliffs, NJ, 1966), pp. 9–10.

what characterized the Athenian smallholder was an unprecedented – and later unequalled – independence from this kind of 'domain', and hence an unusual degree of freedom from rent and tax. The creation of the peasant citizen meant the liberation of peasants from all forms of tributary relationship which had characterized the Greek peasantry before, and continued to characterize peasantries elsewhere. Democratic citizenship here had political and economic implications at the same time.

We saw in chapter 6 how radically the ancient democracy differed from other advanced civilizations of the ancient world, in the Near East and Asia, as well as Bronze Age Greece, in respect to the relation between rulers and producers, how sharply the democratic polis diverged from the widespread pattern of appropriating states and subject villages of peasant producers, and from the rule 'universally recognized everywhere under Heaven', that 'those who work with their minds rule, while those who work with their bodies are ruled'.[9] It was no accident that, when anti-democratic Greek philosophers like Plato and Aristotle depicted their ideal states, they very consciously and explicitly reinstated the principle of division between rulers and producers, a principle whose violation they clearly regarded as essential to Athenian democracy.

In fact, the surplus-appropriating state acting in what Robert Brenner has called 'class-like' ways, was probably more a rule than an exception in advanced pre-capitalist societies.[10] We cannot understand, say, French absolutism without recognizing the role of the state as a means of private appropriation, with its vast apparatus of lucrative offices and its extraction of taxes from the peasantry, a proprietary resource for those who possessed a piece of it. For that matter, we cannot understand an upheaval like the French Revolution without recognizing that a major issue in it was access to this lucrative resource.[11]

If these very diverse cases have in common a unity of political and economic power which gives political rights a special value, the devaluation of political goods in capitalism rests on the separation

[9] See above, p. 189, for the full quotation from Mencius.
[10] Robert Brenner, 'Agrarian Class Structure and Economic Development in Pre-Industrial Europe', in T.H. Aston and C.H.E. Philpin, eds., *The Brenner Debate: Agrarian Class Structure and Economic Development in Pre-Industrial Europe* (Cambridge, 1985), pp. 55–7.
[11] On this point, see the ground-breaking study by George Comninel, *Rethinking the French Revolution: Marxism and the Revisionist Challenge* (London, 1987), especially pp. 196–203.

of the economic and the political. The status of political goods is bound to be diminished by the autonomy of the economic sphere, the independence of capitalist exploitation from direct coercive power, the separation of appropriation from the performance of public functions, the existence of a separate purely 'political' sphere distinct from the 'economy', which makes possible for the first time a 'democracy' that is only 'political', without the economic and social implications attached to ancient Greek democracy.

To put the point differently, the separation of the political and the economic in capitalism means the separation of communal life from the organization of production. For instance, there is nothing comparable to the communal regulation of production exercised by the village community in many peasant economies. And political life in capitalism is separated from the organization of exploitation. At the same time, capitalism also brings production and appropriation together in an inseparable unity. The act of appropriation in capitalism, the extraction of surplus value, is inseparable from the process of production; and both these processes have been detached from the political sphere and, so to speak, privatized.

All this has implications for the conditions of resistance. There is, for example, no parallel in capitalism to the function of the village commune as a form of peasant class organization in the struggle against lordly exploitation, that is, a form of class organization that is inseparably economic and political at once. In capitalism, a great deal can happen in politics and community organization at every level without fundamentally affecting the exploitative powers of capital or fundamentally changing the decisive balance of social power. Struggles in these arenas remain vitally important, but they have to be organized and conducted in the full recognition that capitalism has a remarkable capacity to distance democratic politics from the decisive centres of social power and to insulate the power of appropriation and exploitation from democratic accountability.

To sum up: In pre-capitalist societies, extra-economic powers had a special importance because the economic power of appropriation was inseparable from them. One might speak here of a scarcity of extra-economic goods because they were too valuable to be widely distributed. We might, then, characterize the situation of extra-economic goods in *capitalism* by saying that it has overcome that scarcity. It has made possible a far wider distribution of extra-economic goods, and specifically the goods associated with citizenship, than was ever possible before. But it has overcome scarcity by devaluing the currency.

THE POSITION OF WOMEN

What I have said about the devaluation of political rights applies, of course, to everyone, men and women alike; but it has some interesting consequences for women in particular, or rather for gender relations, which go well beyond purely political questions. First, there is the obvious fact that women under capitalism have achieved political rights undreamed of in earlier societies; and I think it is safe to say that the general tendency toward at least formal equality has created pressures in favour of women's emancipation with no historical precedent. This achievement was not, needless to say, won without a considerable struggle; but the very idea that political emancipation was something women could aspire to and struggle for was fairly late in its appearance on the historical agenda. In part, this development can be put down to the general devaluation of political goods which has made it possible for dominant groups to be less discriminating about their distribution. But in this case, there is much more at stake than formal rights of citizenship.

Let us return to our pre-capitalist examples. We have focussed our attention on the typical combination of peasant production and extra-economic exploitation. Now we can consider what this meant for the position of women. Here it is important to keep in mind that where peasants have been the primary producers and sources of surplus, as they typically have been in pre-capitalist societies, it is not just the peasant himself but the peasant *household* that has constituted the basic unit of production, as well as – and this point needs to be stressed – the basic unit of exploitation. The labour appropriated by landlords and states from the peasantry has been family labour, and it has taken the form not only of productive rent- or tax-producing services performed collectively by the peasant family, or other kinds of labour services both private and public, but also domestic labour in the master's household and, of course, the reproduction of the labour-force itself, the bearing and rearing of children, the future labourers, servants and soldiers in the fields, households and armies of the dominant classes. The division of labour within the peasant family, then, has been deeply and inextricably linked to the demands placed upon the household unit by its role in the process of exploitation. Whatever may have been the historical reasons for particular sexual divisions of labour within the household, in class societies they have always been distorted by hierarchical, coercive and antagonistic production relations between the household and forces outside it.

It is particularly important to remember that pre-capitalist peasants generally kept control of the production process, while landlords increased their surpluses not so much by directing production as by employing and enhancing their powers of surplus *extraction*, that is to say, their jurisdictional, political and military powers. Apart from the general implications of this fact for the distribution of political rights, it also had implications for gender relations within the peasant household. The critical point can be summed up by saying that wherever there is exploitation there has to be hierarchy and coercive discipline, and that in this case they are concentrated in the household and become inseparable from the day-to-day relations of the family. There can be no clear separation here between family relationships and the organization of the workplace of the kind that has developed under capitalism.

It has been said that the peasant's 'dilemma' is that he is both an economic agent and the head of a household, and the peasant household is 'both an economic unit and a home'. On the one hand, the household must meet its own demands as a unit of consumption and as a set of affective relationships, and also the demands of the peasant community of which it is a part; on the other hand, from the point of view of the exploiter, the peasant household is, as Eric Wolf has put it, 'a source of labour and goods with which to increase his fund of power'.[12] One consequence of this contradictory unity seems to be that the household reproduces the hierarchical and coercive relations between exploiter and exploited. As the organizer of production, the head of the household in a sense acts as the agent of his own exploiter.

It is possible, of course, to say that there is no absolute necessity for that hierarchical structure to take the form of male dominance, though it has generally, if not universally, done so. But apart from any other factors that may encourage this particular form of hierarchy – such as differences in physical strength, or the reproductive functions that occupy the woman's energies and time – there is a

[12] Wolf, *Peasants*, pp. 12–17.

disposition to male dominance inherent in the relation between the pre-capitalist peasant household and the world of landlords and the state.

Again, that relation is inseparably economic and political at once. Since the exploitative powers confronting the peasant household are typically 'extra-economic' – that is, juridical, political and military – they are inescapably linked to the one social function that has been most universally a male monopoly, armed violence. In other words, the organization of society in general, and specifically the nature of the ruling class, places a special premium on male dominance. The power and prestige attached to the male role in the society at large and in the dominant ideology of the ruling class have typically had the effect of reinforcing the authority of the male both in political and ceremonial functions within the peasant community and inside the household. If inside the household the head is the agent of landlord and state, outside it he is also the household's political representative, in the encounter with the male-dominated extra-economic powers of landlords and state. So the extra-economic, political coercive character of pre-capitalist exploitation tends to reinforce any other dispositions to male dominance within the peasant household.

Incidentally, one significant test of these propositions might be to imagine a dependent family of producers in which the male has no such political role outside the household, or where the surrounding social relations are not of this extra-economic kind. The closest approximation is perhaps the slave family of the American South, a group of people completely deracinated, cut off from their communal roots, without juridical and political standing, and inserted into a capitalist economy. And it turns out that one of the distinctive characteristics of the American slave family, even in the midst of a society where male dominance remained very tenacious, was the unusual authority of the woman.

At any rate, in capitalism the organization of production and exploitation is generally not so closely connected with the organization of the household, nor is the power of exploitation directly extra-economic, political or military. Although capitalism has an unprecedented drive for accumulation, it fills this need mainly by increasing labour productivity rather than by means of directly coercive surplus extraction. Of course the compulsion to maximize productivity and profitability, and the resulting antagonism of interest between capital and labour, create a need for a hierarchical and highly disciplined organization of production; but capitalism does not concentrate these antagonisms, this hierarchical and co-ercive organization, in the household. They have a separate locale in the workplace. Even where the home is more closely tied to the workplace, as, say, in the small family farm, the capitalist market creates relations of its own with the outside world which differ from and supersede the old relations with the peasant community and the political, juridical and military powers of pre-capitalist landlords and states. These new relations have typically had the effect of weakening patriarchal principles.

The major factors disposing feudalism to male domination are missing here – that is, the unity between the organization of pro-duction and exploitation and the organization of the family, the extra-economic relation between exploiters and exploited, and so on. Where feudalism operated through a relation between lord or state and the household, mediated through the male, capital strives for direct and unmediated relations with *individuals*, male or female, who from the point of view of capital take on the identity of abstract labour. Men who are interested in maintaining old patterns of male domination have been forced to defend them *against* the dissolving effects of capitalism – for instance, against the effects of growing numbers of women leaving the household to enter the wage-labour force.

CAPITALISM AND THE CONTRACTION OF THE EXTRA-ECONOMIC DOMAIN

These, then, are the various consequences of capitalism's separation of economic exploitation from extra-economic power and identities. There remains something more to be said about its ideological effects. It has become commonplace among 'post-Marxist' theorists and their successors to say not only that capitalist democracy has produced powerful ideological impulses toward every kind of freedom and equality, but also that the 'economy' has a limited importance in people's experience, that the autonomy of politics and the openness of social identities are the essence of our current situation in the capitalist West. Let us look at the features of capitalism to which these propositions apparently refer.

Paradoxically, yet again, the very features that have devalued extra-economic goods in capitalist societies have given the appearance of *enhancing* the extra-economic domain and widening its scope. This appearance has been taken for reality by capitalist ideologues who assure us that liberal capitalism is the last word in freedom and democracy (not to mention the end of History), and it now appears that people on the left are, for better or worse, accepting it too. On the face of it, capitalism seems to leave very large free spaces outside the economy. Production is enclosed in specialized institutions, factories and offices. The working day is sharply marked off from non-working hours. Exploitation is not formally associated with juridical or political disabilities. There seems to be a wide range of social relations that lie outside the framework of production and exploitation and create a variety of social identities not immediately connected to the 'economy'. Social identities seem much more 'open' in this sense. So the separateness of the economy may appear to give a wider scope, a freer hand to the world outside it.

But, in fact, the economy of capitalism has encroached upon and narrowed the extra-economic domain. Capital has gained private control over matters that were once in the public domain, while giving up social and political responsibilities to a formally separate state. Even all those areas of social life that lie outside the immediate spheres of production and appropriation, and outside the direct control of the capitalist, are subjected to the imperatives of the market and the commodification of extra-economic goods. There is hardly an aspect of life in capitalist society that is not deeply determined by the logic of the market.

If politics in capitalism has a specific autonomy, there is an important sense in which that autonomy is weaker, not stronger, than the autonomy of pre-capitalist politics. Because the separation of the economic and the political has also meant the transfer of formerly political functions to the separated economic sphere, politics and the state are if anything more, rather than less, constrained by specifically economic imperatives and the demands of appropriating classes. Here we may recall our earlier examples of pre-capitalist states which were free from dominant classes to the extent that they were themselves 'class-like', competing with other class appropriators for the same peasant-produced surpluses.

It used to be a truism for the left that social life in capitalism is uniquely subordinate to and shaped by the imperatives of the 'economy', but the latest trends in social theory on the left seem to have abandoned this simple insight. In fact, it is not too much to say that they have been taken in by the mystifying appearances of capitalism, by the one-sided illusion that capitalism has uniquely liberated and enriched the extra-economic sphere. If the autonomy of politics, the openness of social identities, and the wide distribution of extra-economic goods are part of the truth, they are indeed only part of it, and a small and contradictory part at that.

It has to be said, nevertheless, that there is nothing surprising about the tendency to see only part of the picture. It is one of capitalism's most notable characteristics, this capacity to hide its face behind a mask of ideological mystifications. What is more surprising, when one comes to think of it, is that a convention has developed according to which capitalism is supposed to be un-usually *transparent* in its relations of economic exploitation and domination. We are often told by social scientists that, unlike pre-capitalist modes of production, in capitalism relations of class are sharply delineated, no longer masked by non-economic cate-gories like status-differences or other non-economic principles of stratification. Economic relations stand out in sharp relief, as the economy is no longer embedded in non-economic social relations. It is only now, if ever, they say, that it has become possible to speak of *class* consciousness.

Even those who deny the importance of class in capitalist society – as only one of many 'identities' – may still subscribe to this view. They can agree about the distinctness of the economic sphere in capitalism and about the clarity of class as a distinctly economic category, and then they can go on to treat its separateness as an *isolation* and relegate it to an insular periphery, on the grounds that, while people may belong to classes, class identities are of limited or even marginal importance in the experience of human beings. People have other identities which have nothing to do with class and are equally or more determinative.

Again, there is a grain of truth in some of this, but again it is only part of a contradictory truth, so partial as to be a gross distortion. Of course people have social identities other than class, and of course these shape their experience in powerful ways. But this simple truism will not advance our understanding very far, and it certainly will not tell us much about how these identities should figure in the construction of a socialist politics – or indeed *any* emancipatory programme – as long as we remain vague about what these identities mean, not only what they reveal about people's experience but also what they conceal.

Far too little attention has been given to capitalism's unprecedented capacity to mask exploitation and class – or rather, there is a growing failure to acknowledge that this mask is precisely a mask. Capitalist exploitation, far from being more transparent than other forms, is more opaque than any other, as Marx pointed out, masked by the obscurity of the relation between capital and labour in which the unpaid portion of labour is completely disguised in the exchange of labour power for a wage, where the capitalist pays the worker in contrast, for example, to the peasant who pays rent to a lord. This is the most elemental false appearance at the heart of capitalist relations, but it is only one of many. There is also the familiar 'fetishism of commodities' which gives relations among people the appearance of relations among things, as the market mediates the most basic of human transactions; there is the political mystification that civic equality means that there is no dominant class in capitalism; and so on.

All this is familiar enough, but it needs to be emphasized that capitalist exploitation and unfreedom are in many ways less, not more, transparent than pre-capitalist domination. The exploitation of the medieval peasant, for example, was made more rather than less visible by feudalism's juridical acknowledgment of his dependence. In contrast, the juridical equality, contractual freedom, and citizenship of the worker in a capitalist democracy are likely to obscure the underlying relations of economic inequality, unfreedom and exploitation. In other words, the very separation of the economic from the extra-economic which is supposed to unmask the realities of class in capitalism is, on the contrary, what mystifies capitalist class relations.

The effect of capitalism may be to deny the importance of class at the very moment, and by the same means, that it purifies class of extra-economic residues. If the effect of capitalism is to create a purely economic category of class, it also creates the appearance that class is *only* an economic category, and that there is a very large world beyond the 'economy' where the writ of class no longer runs. To treat this appearance as if it were the unmasked and ultimate reality is certainly no advance in the analysis of capitalism. It mistakes a problem for a solution, and an obstacle for an opportunity. It is less illuminating than the most uncritical pre-Marxist political economy; and to build a political strategy on a retention of this mystification instead of an effort to overcome it must surely be self-defeating.

What, then, does all this mean for extra-economic goods in capitalist society and in the socialist project? Let me sum up: capitalism's structural indifference to the social identities of the people it exploits makes it uniquely capable of discarding extra-economic inequalities and oppressions. This means that while capitalism cannot guarantee emancipation from, say, gender or racial oppression, neither can the achievement of these emancipations guarantee the eradication of capitalism. At the same time, this same indifference to extra-economic identities makes capitalism particularly effective and flexible in using them as ideological cover. Where in pre-capitalist societies extra-economic identities were likely to highlight relations of exploitation, in capitalism they typically serve to obscure the principal mode of oppression specific to it. And while capitalism makes possible an unprecedented redistribution of extra-economic goods, it does so by devaluing them.

What about socialism then? Socialism may not by itself guarantee the full achievement of extra-economic goods. It may not by itself guarantee the destruction of historical and cultural patterns of women's oppression or racism. But it will do at least two important things in this regard, apart from abolishing those forms of oppression that men and women, black and white, share as members of an exploited class. First, it will eliminate the ideological and economic needs that under capitalism can still be served by gender and racial oppressions. Socialism will be the first social form since the advent of class society whose reproduction as a social system is endangered rather than enhanced by relations and ideologies of domination and oppression. And second, it will permit the revaluation of extra-economic goods whose value has been debased by the capitalist economy. The democracy that socialism offers is one that is based on a reintegration of the 'economy' into the political life of the community, which begins with its subordination to the democratic self-determination of the producers themselves.

Conclusion

Most socialists have long given up predicting the imminent demise of capitalism. While the 'business cycle' continues to be punctuated by regular crises, we have grown accustomed to the system's flexibility and its capacity to find new channels for expansion. We may now, however, be encountering something new with which the left has so far failed to come to grips. The protracted crisis in advanced capitalist economies, which even mainstream economists are describing as 'structural', may not signal a terminal decline; but it may indicate that these economies have for the foreseeable future exhausted their capacity to survive without depressing the living and working conditions of their own populations – let alone those of the less-developed countries which they continue to exploit, as sources of cheap labour and the bearers of debt. Yet while there has been no shortage of jeremiads, and not only from the left, about the current condition of capitalism, in theory and practice its implications have still to be absorbed.

Let me first sketch the context. There is surely no need here to say much about the catalogue of decline which is the daily fare of the news media in every Western country. The advanced capitalist economies have been in a deep and prolonged recession, while the collapse of Communism has exposed the fissures and contradictions within the capitalist world which had been papered over and disguised by the Cold War. The stronger European economies are experiencing what for them are new forms of long-term structural unemployment, and the unification of Germany has dramatically aggravated the weaknesses that were already beginning to appear before in Europe's most successful economy. Japan has begun to suffer the ills to which its economic 'miracle' has long seemed immune (never mind the burdensome conditions of life and work that have always sustained it). Meanwhile, we are assured that in the US and elsewhere the recalcitrant recession has at last been reversed; but economists have been even more than usually selective in their reading of economic 'indicators' in order to demonstrate a 'turn-around' in the economy while setting aside the evidence that mass unemployment or underemployment, poverty, homelessness, racism and violent crime seem to be permanent fixtures in the world's richest countries. The somewhat lower rates of unemployment in the US have been achieved at the cost of growth in low-wage jobs and a large class of working poor. Nor has the Western world's growing ecological consciousness been able to make any significant inroads in capitalism's structural imperative to degrade the environment. All this is happening while traditional political formations, right and left, are suffering varying degrees of crisis, in some cases, as most spectacularly in Italy, to the point of virtual collapse.

It will come as news to no one that, in this litany of economic ills, by far the most telling sign is the structural long-term unemployment – together with changes in the pattern of work toward casualization and short-term contractual labour – which has defied fluctuations in all other economic indicators, running counter even to the most basic economic conventions about the connection between growth and employment.[1] But if this is old news, the prevailing terms of debate on these issues in Europe and North America suggest that someone may be missing the point.

MARKETS, 'FLEXIBLE' AND 'SOCIAL'

The latest code word in the economic debate (if debate it can be called) is 'flexibility': advanced capitalist economies, we are told, must deregulate the labour market, weaken the social 'safety net' and probably lift restrictions on environmental pollution in order to compete with Third World capitalisms by allowing the terms and conditions of work to sink toward the level of their less-developed competitors. Not only welfare provision but decent pay and working conditions and even environmental protection are, it seems, obstacles to competitiveness, profitability and growth.

---

[1] As I write, it is estimated that 40 per cent of the Canadian workforce is either unemployed or in insecure part-time or contractual employment. In the US, between 20 and 30 per cent are employed part time or on limited contract, quite apart from the large and growing

This by itself may not be so new, at least on the far right, but there appears to be a new willingness to be explicit about the need to depress the condition of workers in the interest of 'flexible' labour markets and a new inclination to include among the enemies of flexibility even rights and protections that all but the most rabid neo-conservatives might once have left intact. There may also be a new leftward drift of this demand for 'flexibility'. It is not just that Western European conservatives, among whose ranks the British not so long ago seemed isolated in their opposition to the feeble regulations of the Social Chapter, are now speaking the language of flexibility as they awaken to the new realities of long-term unemployment. Even among European parties of the left, it is no longer clear that this is forbidden territory.

If there is any alternative to 'flexibility' in this debate, it is, according to some (notably the British Labour Party), the creation of a highly skilled workforce which will attract capital away from low-wage economies. Training and education are, according to this view, the principal cure for economic ills. But there is perhaps no surer sign of desperation than this faith in a solution which is so weakly supported by evidence. In a context of mass unemployment, the logic of a theory that places the supply of skilled workers before the demand is at best illusive. Is it reasonable to suppose that jobs that do not exist for structural reasons will suddenly be created to absorb a newly skilled workforce? In any case, is it really so clear that the majority of jobs (apart from typically undervalued secretarial work) even in the most advanced 'high-tech' industries require elaborate training, or even skills that cannot be acquired on the job?[2]

More fundamentally, the evidence suggests that capital is, to put it conservatively, no more likely to gravitate toward a highly skilled workforce than to a cheap one. Indeed, the current rise of unemployment in Germany, the very model of a well-trained economy, should be enough to cast doubt on the training solution; and here, precisely in high-tech industry, there are signs of an inclination to relocate plants away from Europe to Asia, away from a skilled but 'inflexible' workforce to locations with lower labour

numbers in low-paid full-time work. On changing patterns of work, especially in the US, see Philip Mattera, *Prosperity Lost* (Reading, Mass., 1990).

[2] On education in today's economy, see Mark Blaug, *The Economic Value of Education: Studies in the Economics of Education* (Aldershot, 1992).

costs, including pension and health contributions, and a 'culture' less resistant to long and unsocial working hours, round-the-clock operation, and generally poor working conditions.[3]

If the training solution is inadequate, are there any other options offered by the left? As right-wing convictions are spreading leftward, displacing even milder forms of neo-Keynesianism, the whole spectrum of debate may be shifting so that loyalty to the Keynesian welfare state may seem an increasingly revolutionary position – and, indeed, there are now people on the farther left who have staked out this ground as their own. Socialism is replaced with 'social citizenship', the enhancement of 'social rights' within capitalism, as the highest (feasible) emancipatory aspiration.

But what if social citizenship is *less* feasible than socialism? What if the right is right? What if the welfare state is no longer a safe haven for the left? What if we have to concede that the welfare state and labour regulation are now incompatible not only with the rationality of short-term profit but even with long-term competitiveness and growth? What if the future of Western capitalism really does depend on lowering the standard of living and work? What if the disparity between the level of productive forces and their contribution to the improvement of living conditions is growing rather than diminishing? What if we cannot dismiss the rantings of the right and it really is true (now if not before) that workers' rights, social citizenship, democratic power and even a decent quality of life for the mass of the population are indeed incompatible with profit, and that capitalism in its most developed forms can no longer deliver both profit or 'growth' and improving conditions of labour and life, never mind social justice? Is this not the message secreted in the discourse of 'flexibility', and should we not be drawing some lessons from the fact that this sombre judgment on our economic system is no longer a preserve of the left?

Instead, we seem to be observing a strange reversal of roles. Now it is the right-wing ideologues of capitalism who are, in effect, preaching its limitations, while the left is finding new reasons for faith in its adaptability. Underlying this curious inversion there may be another odd displacement: if Marxism laid bare the ruthless

[3] See the *Financial Times* ('Cost constraints prompt a continental shift'), 25 August 1992, for the emblematic case of LSI Logic, a US semi-conductor maker, first attracted to Germany by a highly skilled workforce and generous tax incentives, which decided to close its German plant and move to the Far East.

social logic of the capitalist market disguised by classical political
economy, that logic is now being revealed in the financial pages of
the bourgeois press and by economists of 'flexibility', while many on
the formerly Marxist left have been converted to belief in the 'social'
market, a capitalist market with a human face.

Let me put my own position plainly. I think the right is generally
right about the social costs of capitalist profitability. The language
of 'flexibility' is certainly registering important structural changes in
the world economy that make the old interventionist correctives
ineffective. Capitalism with a human face may now require more
state intervention than socialism would, perhaps even more extensive state planning than imagined by the most orthodox Commun-
ists, this time on a vast international scale.[4] This is not to deny that
the left should defend the welfare state or environmental regulation
with all its power, nor that education is an unambiguous good which
should be pursued for reasons that have nothing to do with profit-
maximization. Welfare provision, environmental protection and
education must remain central to short- and long-term programmes
of the left. The point is simply to acknowledge the limits of capitalism. I find it difficult to understand how the market can be an
economic 'discipline', a driving mechanism and a regulator of the
economy, without sooner or later producing the very consequences
that the exponents of flexibility have in mind and that the advocates
of the social market promise to correct.

It is one thing to talk about the adoption of certain 'market'
mechanisms as instruments of circulation and exchange. It is quite
another to call upon the market as an economic regulator, the
guarantor of a 'rational' economy. I shall not explicate that distinction here, except to say that the 'rational' economy guaranteed by
market disciplines, together with the price mechanism on which
they depend, is based on one irreducible requirement, the commodification of labour power and its subjection to the same imperatives of

---

[4] See, for example, Robert Heilbroner's remarks on the changes that now make Keynesian
solutions less feasible. While insisting that we still have something to learn from the 'spirit' of
Keynes's economic theory, Heilbroner argues that 'the persisting unemployment of today,
both in its origins and implications, appears unlike the ailment that Keynes thought could
be remedied by "a somewhat comprehensive socialization of investment"'. Among the
structural differences are 'inflationary pressures unknown in Keynes's day', and 'the
international interpenetration of markets' which 'threatens to dilute the beneficial effect of
any bold recovery program. It points to the need for an international coordination of
economic efforts – a goal that lies, alas, well beyond our grasp.' 'Acts of an Apostle', *New
York Review of Books*, 3 March 1994, p. 9.

competition that determine the movements of other economic 'factors'.[5] This means that, quite apart from the direct effects on workers, there is an irreducible contradiction between the regulatory functions of the market and its capacity for 'socialization'.

I spoke earlier, especially in chapters 4 and 5, about the failure of historians to recognize the distinction between societies with markets and trade, which have existed throughout recorded history, and the specificity of capitalism, where 'the market' is not an opportunity but an imperative. The difference lies in the degree to which the producers' access to the means of production is market dependent. The imperatives of competition, profit maximization and accumulation were set in train, for example, the moment English tenant farmers were denied non-market access to land, subject not only to the requirement of selling their products on the market but also to a market in leases which, in the specific conditions of English property relations, compelled them to produce profitably simply in order to maintain access to the land itself; and those imperatives were reinforced as the pressures of competition accelerated the process of division between a class of large proprietors and a completely propertyless class of labourers obliged to sell their labour power for a wage. The widespread view of capitalist development as an expansion of markets (whether that view takes the form of the old 'commercialization' model, with its closing and opening trade routes, or the more complex demographic argument) is based on a conflation of these very different kinds of 'market'; and the same failure to acknowledge the historical specificity of capitalism and the distinction between market *opportunities* and market *imperatives* seems to me to underlie the current belief in the endless possibilities of a socialized market.

DEMOCRACY AS AN ECONOMIC MECHANISM

If the right is right about the market as an economic regulator, it seems to me that the main long-term theoretical task for the left is to think about alternative mechanisms for regulating social production. The old choice between the market and centralized

---

[5] I refer readers to the work of my friend, colleague and former student, David McNally, who has spelled out the implications of the market as regulator with admirable lucidity in *Against the Market: Political Economy, Market Socialism and the Marxist Critique* (London, 1993), especially chapter 6.

planning is barren. Both in their various ways have been driven by the imperatives of accumulation – in one case imposed by the demands of competition and profit maximization internal to the system, in the other by the requirements of accelerated industrial development. Neither has involved the reappropriation of the means of production by the producers, neither has been motivated by the interests of the workers whose surplus labour is appropriated nor indeed by the interests of the people as a whole; and in neither case has production been susceptible to democratic accountability. Nor does the social market or even 'market socialism' provide an alternative, since, with or without a human face, market imperatives remain the driving mechanism. In today's world economy, as the social market begins to look more utopian, less feasible, even a contradiction in terms, it may now be more rather than less realistic to think about radical alternatives.

I have suggested throughout this book that the capitalist market is a *political* as well as an economic space, a terrain not simply of freedom and choice but of domination and coercion. I now want to suggest that *democracy* needs to be reconceived not simply as a political category but as an economic one. What I mean is not simply 'economic democracy' as a greater equality of distribution. I have in mind democracy as an economic regulator, the *driving mechanism* of the economy.

Here Marx's free association of direct producers (which does not, even in Marx's terms, include only manual workers or people directly involved in material production[6]) is a good place to start. It stands to reason that the likeliest place to begin the search for a new economic mechanism is at the very base of the economy, in the organization of labour itself. But the issue is not simply the internal organization of enterprises; and even the reappropriation of the means of production by the producers, while a necessary condition, would not be sufficient, as long as possession remains market dependent and subject to the old imperatives. The freedom of the

[6] A good starting point for understanding Marx's concept of the producing class is his concept of the 'collective labourer', which in capitalist societies includes a wide variety of workers, both blue and white collar, situated at various points in the process of creating and realizing the surplus value appropriated by capital. (For a discussion of this point, see Peter Meiksins, 'Beyond the Boundary Question', *New Left Review* 157, pp. 101–20.) This is the class whose self-emancipation would constitute socialism; but, of course, with the abolition of capitalist exploitation, the nature of the 'producers' would no longer be defined by their contribution to the production of capital.

free association implies not only democratic organization but emancipation from 'economic' coercions of this kind.

Establishing a democratic organization of direct producers, as distinct from the present hierarchical structure of the capitalist enterprise, is in some respects the easy part. Up to a point, even capitalist firms can accommodate alternative organizations – such as the 'team concept'. There is, to be sure, nothing especially democratic about the team concept as it actually operates in capitalist enterprises; but even with the most democratically organized 'teams', such enterprises would be governed not by the self-determined objectives of those who work in them but by imperatives imposed upon them from without, not even by the needs and desires of the majority of citizens, but by the interests of employers and the coercions imposed by the capitalist market itself: the imperatives of competition, productivity, and profit maximization. And, of course, the workers would remain vulnerable to dismissal and plant closures, the market's ultimate discipline. At any rate, these new modes of organization are conceived not as new forms of democracy, making the organization more accountable to its workers, or to the community at large, but on the contrary, as means of making the workers more responsive to the economic needs of the organization. These organizations do not satisfy the most basic criteria of democracy, since the 'people' – neither the workers nor the citizen-body as a whole – are not in any sense sovereign, nor is the primary purpose of the organization to enhance the quality of life enjoyed by its members or even to pursue goals which they have set for themselves.

Even outright takeover by workers would not by itself circumvent the alienation of power to the market. Anyone who has listened in on the debates surrounding the buy-out of United Airlines in the US will understand the problem. The most powerful argument the workers were able to muster in defence of their bid was that they would be no less responsive than their capitalist employers had been to market imperatives – including, it must be supposed, the disciplines of closure and dismissal without which the market cannot function as a regulator.

New, more democratic ways of organizing the workplace and workers' takeovers are admirable objectives in themselves and potentially the basis of something more; but, even if all enterprises were taken over in this way, there would remain the problem of detaching them from market imperatives. Certain instruments and institutions now associated with 'the market' would undoubtedly be useful in a truly democratic society, but the moving force of the economy would have to emanate not from the market but from within the self-active association of producers. And if the motivating force of the economy were to be found within the democratic enterprise, in the interests and objectives of the self-active workers themselves, modalities would have to be found for harnessing those interests and objectives to the management of the economy as a whole and to the well being of the larger community; and that means, in the first instance, working out the modalities of interaction among enterprises.

I do not pretend to know the answers; but, as always, the questions need to be clarified first. And, on that score, we have barely made a start, to judge by the state of current debates. For the moment, I simply want to emphasize one point: what we are looking for is not only new forms of ownership but also a new driving mechanism, a new rationality, a new economic logic; and if, as I think is the case, the most promising place to start is in the democratic organization of production, which presupposes the reappropriation of the means of production by the producers, then it also needs to be emphasized that the benefits of replacing the rationality of the market as a driving mechanism would accrue not to workers alone but to everyone who is subject to the consequences of market imperatives, from their effects on the terms and conditions of work and leisure – indeed the very organization of time itself – to their larger implications for the quality of social life, culture, the environment and 'extra-economic' goods in general.

In the meantime, the current logic of the market is having immediate effects for which the left as it is now constituted is politically and theoretically unprepared. The very developments that are supposed to reinvigorate Western capitalism – European integration and North American free trade – seem to be creating conditions for new class confrontations between capital and labour. For example, as NAFTA, transparently designed to depress the conditions of labour in the US to converge with its Mexican neighbours, has been instituted against the resistance of organized labour, European integration is having the effect of weakening the mechanisms – such as deficits and devaluation – by which European national economies have in the past been able to accommodate wage rises and to cushion unemployment.

The effects have already been manifested in a spate of labour unrest in Europe and in an increasing politicization of trade unions – most significantly, and symptomatically, in Germany. At the same time, one of the Asian 'miracles', Korea, is now for the first time experiencing a 'modern' class politics, while Russia and the so-called 'new democracies' have become fertile ground for class conflict as market disciplines take hold. Where are the political and intellectual resources to deal with these developments, when parties of the left have abandoned the terrain of class politics while the new post-left is off in search of 'identity'? What, for example, will fill the political vacuum left by the defection of working class parties, as the restructuration of capitalism increases the strains along the fault lines of class and creates new forms of insecure and vulnerable labour? More right-wing extremism perhaps?

No one can deny that the 'new world order' sets wholly new tasks for the left, as for everyone else. But the collapse of Communism is not the only defining moment of our times, not the only epochal transformation that demands some serious 'rethinking'. In the meantime, something has been happening to capitalism too. So far, the principal solutions on offer have been, in their various ways, contradictory and self-defeating. The 'flexible' market enhances flexibility and competitiveness by undermining its own foundations as it subtracts consumers from the market, while the 'social' market, by submitting itself to capitalist imperatives, sets strict limits on its own capacity to humanize capitalism. The lesson we may be obliged to draw from our current economic and political condition is that a humane, 'social', truly democratic and equitable capitalism is more unrealistically utopian than socialism.

Index